Praise for
The All-or-Nothing M[...]

"After years of debate and inquiry, the key to a great marriage remained shrouded in mystery. Until now. In his *All-or-Nothing Marriage*, Eli Finkel reveals the fascinating ways in which marriage has evolved and the things we can all do to help this all-important relationship flourish. You will definitely want to read this book."

—Carol Dweck, Stanford professor and author of *Mindset: The New Psychology of Success*

"If you've ever wondered what science has to say about how marriage has changed over time and what makes for a great one, this is the book to read. Eli Finkel is one of the world's leading experts on relationships, and his insights are both comprehensive and revealing."

—Adam Grant, author of *Give and Take, Originals,* and *Option B* (coauthored with Sheryl Sandberg)

"This book makes a lot of sense, and it is written by an eminent scholar. It should be an essential part of every therapist's bookshelf."

—John M. Gottman, author of *The Seven Principles for Making Marriage Work*

"Fascinating! Eli Finkel offers us an educated, enlightening perspective on our most important adult relationship; better still, his perspective on marriage is one of hope and inspiration."

—Dr. Sue Johnson, author of *Hold Me Tight* and *Love Sense*

"An engaging, perceptive exploration of a modern paradox. We need marriage less than ever for practical survival and social success, but we demand more satisfaction and meaning from it than ever. The higher we climb in our emotional expectations, Finkel argues, the more oxygen we need to pump into our relationships."

—Stephanie Coontz, author of *Marriage, a History: How Love Conquered Marriage*

"Marriages are like rapids-filled rivers, sweeping us along toward desired destinations, both emotional and practical, while imperiling the journey with unseen rocks of ruin. With an account that is impressive in scholarship and erudition, Eli Finkel has provided a much-needed chart for understanding and navigating the waters."
—Robert B. Cialdini, author of *Influence* and *Pre-Suasion*

"Eli Finkel's *The All-or-Nothing Marriage* is an excellent, accessible guide to today's high-investment, high-reward marriages."
—Andrew Cherlin, professor of sociology and director of the Program in Social Policy at Johns Hopkins University

"No one knows more about the science of relationships than Eli Finkel. This book is bound to spark a conversation. A must-read for anyone interested in building or maintaining a strong marriage."
—Jonah Berger, Wharton professor and author of *Contagious* and *Invisible Influence*

"What a wonderful book by Eli Finkel. He's a natural writer—with an original and scientific view of marriage today and tomorrow. In short, marriage is evolving from a pragmatic survival strategy, to a romantic companionship, to a personal-growth adventure. And our best marriages today are better than anything of the past. It's optimistic, sensible, and engaging. And Finkel adds fascinating historical and cross-cultural facts and some highly useful tips on how to travel the bumpy road to happy coupledom. You'll like it . . . and use it."
—Dr. Helen Fisher, author of *Anatomy of Love* and *Why We Love*

"In his deeply insightful and beautifully written book on the paradox of modern marriage, Eli Finkel shines the bright light of science on the most important, rewarding, and vexing of all human relationships."
—Daniel Gilbert, Edgar Pierce professor of psychology at Harvard University and author of *Stumbling on Happiness*

"What do we actually know about good (and bad) marriages? That simple question is surprisingly difficult to answer, but Eli J. Finkel's *The All-or-Nothing Marriage* is the best place I know to start."

—Tyler Cowen, economics professor at
George Mason University and author of *Average Is Over*

"While pundits debate the ever-evolving institution of marriage, Eli Finkel offers a fresh, nonpartisan analysis of changing trends, and even practical advice for the long-coupled. Anyone in a committed romantic relationship—whether or not they're legally wed—will benefit from the generosity and care he brings to the topic."

—Kate Bolick, author of
Spinster: Making a Life of One's Own

"A thorough analysis of American marriage throughout the ages. In this comprehensive examination, Finkel . . . traces the evolution of this sacred institution from the earliest days of hunter-gatherer societies to modern times. . . . In addition to extensive research, the author bolsters the narrative with charts, diagrams, and numerous quotes from a variety of sources. As the author writes, it is possible to create a loving, lasting union, but it requires work, communication, and commitment on the part of both parties, and the process will change as time progresses."

—*Kirkus Reviews*

"The beauty of [Finkel's] new model is that the potential psychological benefits increase as you climb the hierarchy of needs."

—*Chicago Tribune*

"In his new book, *The All-or-Nothing Marriage*, Finkel argues that twenty-first-century spouses seek partners who bring out their best, most authentic selves."

—*Time*

"An important book . . . full of interesting insights on contemporary marriage."   —David Brooks, *The New York Times*

"Truly . . . an excellent book."   —*Scientific American*

"The good news is that, unlike the fate of competitors in a winner-take-all financial transaction, one person's spectacular marriage doesn't doom anyone else's to failure. Mr. Finkel's book shares research on what happens in the best marriages, with the aim to help everyone else likewise score an 'all' rather than a 'nothing' partnership. . . . Finkel offers tough-love advice."   —*The Wall Street Journal*

"Mr. Finkel [is] one of the leading lights in the realm of relationship psychology."   —*The Economist*

"An impressive work that not only charts the history of marriage from hunter-gatherers onward and explores all the ways marriage has evolved over the years but also boils the wealth of data to simple, attainable advice."   —*The Huffington Post*

"A fantastic new book that looks at our complex history with the institution, exploring how marriage has changed and evolved, and how we can change and evolve along with it."   —*Toronto Star*

"*The All-or-Nothing Marriage* is a fascinating read about our culture's relationship to relationships."   —Books for Better Living

"For Finkel it's fine to look at marriage as a means to personal happiness, but it's a 'two-way street.' It's about giving as much as it is getting, and forgetting that is the surest way to let your marriage fall apart."   —Vox.com

The
All-*or*-Nothing
Marriage

How the Best Marriages Work

ELI J. FINKEL

DUTTON

DUTTON

An imprint of Penguin Random House LLC
375 Hudson Street
New York, New York 10014

First trade paperback printing, November 2018

Photo credits: Page 15, Michelangelo: Jörg Bittner Unna. Page 147,
The Grants: K.T. Grant

THE LIBRARY OF CONGRESS HAS CATALOGUED THE HARDCOVER
EDITION OF THIS BOOK AS FOLLOWS:

Names: Finkel, Eli J., author.
Title: The all-or-nothing marriage : how the best marriages work /
Eli J. Finkel.
Description: New York, NY : Dutton, [2017] | Includes bibliographical
references and index.
Identifiers: LCCN 2017013524| ISBN 9780525955160 (hardcover) |
ISBN 9780698411456 (epub)
Subjects: LCSH: Marriage. | Married people. | Interpersonal relations.
Classification: LCC HQ734 .F466 2017 | DDC 306.81—dc23
LC record available at https://lccn.loc.gov/2017013524

Printed in the United States of America

Charts and Graphs by Daniel Lagin

Set in Sabon LT Std
Designed by Cassandra Garruzzo

Dutton trade paperback ISBN: 9781101984345

To my wife, Alison,
who finds it hilarious that I'm a marriage expert

Contents

PREFACE
Panic in Evanston

I was working hard to look relaxed, as if the two of us were just having a regular research meeting. Professors meet with graduate students all the time to work through the sorts of thorny conceptual issues that arise when writing articles.

Grace Larson had just finished her first year as a doctoral student at Northwestern, and she was looking to me for answers. But what she told me in that meeting had, in under an hour, shattered some of my most central assumptions about marriage.

Meanwhile, a deadline loomed. I had promised to submit a feature article presenting an ambitious new theory of marriage in America. The article, which would eventually clock in at a novella-length thirty thousand words, was due in October of 2013. Three of my students and I had divided up the initial tasks, and Larson was, in that meeting in June of 2013, reporting back to me on what she had learned.

The Invitation

Two months earlier, the psychologist Ronnie Janoff-Bulman had invited me to submit a Target Article for the scholarly journal

Psychological Inquiry. This journal has a distinctive structure: Each issue consists of a Target Article, around a dozen expert Commentaries, and a Response to Commentaries from the authors of the Target Article.

I proposed an article on an idea I'd been playing with: that diverse forces had increasingly freighted marriage in America over time, piling so much expectation and responsibility on this one relationship that it threatened to buckle under the strain. We Americans increasingly look to our spouse to be our best friend and closest confidant, to provide sizzling sex, to help us grow as individuals—the list goes on. At the same time, we spend less time with our friends, parents, and siblings, and we are less engaged in organized civic activities outside the home. Collectively, these forces place tremendous pressure on the marital bond, and few marriages are able to withstand the stress. Janoff-Bulman approved this topic, and my students and I started scouring the research literature for evidence that marriage is in trouble.

As social psychologists, our primary expertise revolves around the thoughts, feelings, and behaviors that enhance or undermine relationship quality. We study topics like commitment, forgiveness, and sexual desire, and we do so by collecting data on people who are involved in serious romantic relationships. Neither historians nor sociologists, we lack primary expertise on how the institution of marriage has changed over time. Larson's first task was to start delving into the history of marriage.

Her findings, as preliminary as they were, revealed that my central thesis was wrong. The idea that Americans have, over time, been asking more and more of our marriage sounds reasonable, but the historical record makes plain that we are, in crucial respects, asking less and less. During the colonial era, people looked to their marriage, and to the broader familial alliances linked to it, for things like food production, shelter, and health care; in a literal sense, they looked to their marriage to help them survive. We're asking a lot of our marriage today, but few of us are asking for life itself.

After the meeting with Larson, I became consumed with the effort to reconcile this stubborn fact with the theory I had proposed for the Target Article. How, exactly, had American marriages changed, and how did these changes influence marital success and failure? I didn't know the answer. I felt like a skydiver who realizes after jumping out of the plane that he isn't sure how to deploy his parachute.

An Unfinished Task

In the ensuing weeks and months, I worked with my collaborators—not only Larson, but also the doctoral students Chin Ming Hui and Kathleen Carswell—to overhaul my theory of marriage. Correcting a theory like this is a scientific duty, but doing so also had a happy, unexpected consequence: The story changed from one of pessimism to one of optimism. It's true that the institution of marriage in America is struggling. But I came to realize that the best marriages today are better than the best marriages of earlier eras; indeed, they are the best marriages that the world has ever known. In addition, although the average marriage is shaky, many floundering or passable marriages can flourish by adopting strategies pioneered by the best marriages.

I was pleased with the *Psychological Inquiry* Target Article—and with our Response to Commentaries—but not entirely. Some of my reservations derived from the sorts of minor imprecisions and omissions that are inevitable in deadline-based scholarship, but others were more troubling. I have written this book, which presents a heavily revised version of my all-or-nothing theory of marriage, to address these reservations. Along the way, I reverse engineer today's best marriages, gleaning insights that the rest of us can use to achieve the sort of marital fulfillment that modern economic and cultural forces have, for the first time, placed within reach.

A Personal Voyage

Every year, shortly before Valentine's Day, I commandeer the official Northwestern University Twitter handle (@NorthwesternU) for an hour to answer questions about relationships. At the university's request, I spend this time engaging with people who tweet questions containing the hashtag #AskFinkel. Once, my wife submitted a tongue-in-cheek question, and I seized the rather public opportunity to get romantic:

Alison Finkel,
Northwestern News replied to your Tweet!

Alison Finkel @AlisonFinkel
@NorthwesternU What is the most important lesson you've learned from your own marriage? #askfinkel - Feb 13

Northwestern News @NorthwesternU   ✔ Follow

.@AlisonFinkel That my wife is perfect. Not to mention brilliant, sexy, and charming. And kind. Love you, baby. #askfinkel

07:14 PM - 13 Feb 15

Even in retrospect, I'm pretty pleased with that response, especially given the Whac-A-Mole pace of those Twitter chats. If marriage were a 140-character undertaking, I'd be crushing it.

But the reality is that marriage is much more complicated than a tweet—much more complicated than almost anything else we do, really. In real life, I mess up a lot.

That's one of the reasons why I study relationships for a living. Yes, I find the topic fascinating in its own right, but I also seek evidence-based solutions to challenges in my own marriage. Like the formerly bald spokesman for Hair Club for Men—who declared in those kitschy 1980s ads that he's not only the company's president, but also a client—I'm not only a scholar who conducts research to understand how marriage works, but also an avid consumer of such research.

Alison and I have enjoyed extended periods of bliss, but we have also endured difficulties severe enough to raise questions about our marriage's long-term viability. Both the blissful and the difficult times inform the scientific questions I investigate, and the data-based answers to those questions inform how I behave in our marriage.

Over the years, I have leveraged this dialectic between the personal and the professional to develop a unique marital tool kit. It isn't the tool kit of a master craftsman, unfortunately, but it does have some unorthodox tools in it, and those are among the most useful. Periodically throughout this book, we'll revisit this tool kit, not only to study the tools themselves, but also to examine the failures that necessitated their development.

Partisanship and Truth

It would be convenient if we could, in this science-based book, side-step the culture wars surrounding marriage in America, but doing so would be cowardly, even if it were possible. Some readers will come to this book armed with ideological convictions forged in partisan trenches. To these readers, I apologize in advance—because I am receptive to arguments from across the political spectrum, you will surely find elements in the book that you dislike.

Liberals are correct that marriage isn't a prerequisite for a fulfilling life, that there are diverse routes to marital success, that poverty makes marital success difficult, and that building a successful marriage would be easier if America had more family-friendly policies like paid parental leave and affordable child care. Conservatives are correct that marriage is a particularly promising avenue for achieving a prosperous and fulfilling life, that the family stability afforded by successful marriages provides a healthy environment for children, that cultural factors and personal responsibility are important determinants of marital success and failure (*till death do us part* has become something closer to *till death do us part or we become unfulfilled*), and that an excessive emphasis on broad economic forces like poverty and inequality strips agency from individual Americans, who, regardless of their economic circumstances, still have some control over their personal decisions. "Between stimulus and response there is a space," observes the psychiatrist Viktor Frankl. "In that space is our power to choose our response. In our response lies our growth and our freedom."

When I published an early version of the all-or-nothing theory of marriage in a 2014 *New York Times* article, some scholars and journalists argued that my analysis was more sophisticated than necessary—that changes in marriage over time result entirely from socioeconomic forces. *Slate* published a response that carried the title "The NYT Congratulates Rich People for Having Better Marriages than Poor People," arguing that "the all-or-nothing nature of marriage does not belong in the discussion with quality time or multitasking or any of the things we readers of the *New York Times* often worry about. It's part of the story about growing and radical inequality in America."

The all-or-nothing theory presented here counters this sort of black-and-white, either/or thinking. Any compelling analysis must explain not only why economic factors are so strongly linked to marital quality, but also why millions of wealthy people have terrible marriages and millions of poor people have excellent marriages. Income and wealth are certainly an important part of the story—it is no accident that the rise in income and wealth inequality is linked to the increasing divergence in the marital well-being of wealthier and poorer Americans (see chapter 7)—but they are far from the whole story.

This is a pro-marriage book, but that doesn't mean it's a book for conservatives. It's a book that recognizes the value of lifestyle flexibility, but that doesn't mean it's a book for liberals. Across the political spectrum, we can all agree, I hope, that figuring out how to increase the proportion of marriages that are stable and fulfilling is a good thing. This book can help.

Part One

Marriage Today

1.

Temperamental but Thrilling

> I wanted to explore the art of pleasure in Italy, the art of
> devotion in India, and, in Indonesia, the art of balancing
> the two. It was only later, after admitting this dream,
> that I noticed the happy coincidence that all these
> countries begin with the letter *I*. A fairly auspicious sign,
> it seemed, on a voyage of self-discovery.
>
> —Elizabeth Gilbert

*E*at Pray Love, the blockbuster memoir from Elizabeth Gilbert, reports on the year she spent traveling in her midthirties as a means of "spiritual and personal exploration" following her divorce and a heartbreaking rebound relationship. The voyage is a success: By the end, she finds herself thinking "about the woman I have become lately, about the life that I am now living, and about how much I always wanted to be this person and live this life, liberated from the farce of pretending to be anyone other than myself." Not incidentally, she falls deeply in love with a Brazilian-Australian man in Indonesia, eventually achieving marital harmony with him (at least for a while).

In *Wild*, Cheryl Strayed offers a higher-stakes, working-class variation of the themes Gilbert explores in *Eat Pray Love*. Strayed's memoir, subtitled *From Lost to Found on the Pacific Crest Trail*, is

3

another voyage of self-discovery that begins with the failure of one marriage and concludes with the promise of another (one that, as of this writing, has stuck).

In their searing narratives of self-discovery, personal growth, and redemptive love, *Eat Pray Love* and *Wild* are archetypes of a distinct literary form. These stories tap into our cultural zeitgeist— the contemporary American hunger for a life that is true to the self rather than beholden to rules and restrictions. Gilbert and Strayed are, at the beginning of the memoirs, married to loving, decent men, and they know it. But they also crave a sort of personal growth that the marriage isn't providing, and settling for love and decency doesn't feel like an option for them. After their divorces and their voyages, they have found themselves, setting the stage for second marriages, ones that afford the authentic expression of their newly discovered selves.

As mainstream as such narratives are today, they certainly aren't standard literary fare. The Western canon is waterlogged with the tears of women enduring failures in love and marriage—Emma Bovary's suicide by arsenic, Anna Karenina's suicide by locomotive, Hester Prynne's disgrace by scarlet letter—but these women tend not to achieve salvation on voyages of self-discovery. It is hard to imagine Karenina responding to the estrangement from her son with a spiritual pilgrimage to India, or Prynne responding to her ignominy by initiating a thousand-mile trek. Such women generally lacked the resources and the freedom to embark on solitary adventures, even if they'd wanted to.

Our cultural zeitgeist is not limited to women. Men, too, are seeking an authentic life and looking for a relationship that elicits their authentic self. Neil Strauss, the infamous author of *The Game*, a 2005 memoir of becoming a pickup artist, provides a hypermasculinized example—his voyage revolves less around solitude than around sexual conquest. In *The Truth*, published a decade later, Strauss now has a serious girlfriend, whom he loves. Even so, he's unwilling to commit to her. After they break up, he searches for a (nonmonogamous) relationship arrangement that allows him to live "my authentic life." As Strauss explores various relationship structures, he reflects: "I feel like these experiences are bringing me closer to something true and honest." Eventually, and to his own amazement, the buried treasure at the end of his quest turns out to be a monogamous marriage to his girlfriend from the beginning of the book. "Life is a test and you pass if you can be true to yourself," he observes. "To get the first question correct, all you have to know is who you are."

Gilbert, Strayed, and Strauss embark from different ports and travel to different destinations. But their shared emphasis on self-discovery and authenticity, especially as these qualities relate to love and marriage, distills a dominant theme in American culture today.

Is this theme leading us to better or to worse marriages?

Yes—both. The pursuit of self-expression through marriage simultaneously makes achieving marital success harder and the value of doing so greater. Consequently, the average marriage has been getting worse over time, even as the best marriages have been getting better.

Culture and History

We all have a sense of what a "traditional marriage" looks like—a matte image, of folks like June and Ward Cleaver, that provides a benchmark against which we can contrast marriage today. The anthropologist George Peter Murdock declared in 1949 that marriage is a cultural universal: a union between a man and a woman characterized by residential cohabitation, economic cooperation, and sexual activity. And, at least until the recent surge in approval of same-sex marriage, few Americans would have quarreled with this definition.

But the reality is that marriage varies drastically across cultural and historical context. In some societies, husbands and wives live apart. In others, they don't share economic resources. Approximately 85 percent of the 1,231 cultures documented in the *Ethnographic Atlas Codebook* practice polygyny (multiple wives for a given husband), which also has deep roots in mainstream Western culture. The Old Testament—the Jewish Torah—which provides foundational religious beliefs for most Americans today, depicts polygyny as a normative marital arrangement, one practiced by respected leaders like Abraham, Moses, and King David.

Perhaps the most significant change in marriage over time has been its conquest by love. "Until the late eighteenth century," observes the historian Stephanie Coontz, "most societies around the world saw marriage as far too vital an economic and political institution to be left entirely to the free choice of the two individuals involved, especially if they were going to base their decision on something as unreasoning and transitory as love." People valued love and preferred to love their spouse, of course, but this emotion was not an important reason to marry, nor was its cultivation or maintenance a primary function of marriage.

Consider the courtly love of medieval Europe, which was almost exclusively adulterous. Its idealization and passion were believed to be incompatible with the marital relationship, which was determined by the sorts of political and pragmatic considerations that formed the foundation of marriage for thousands of years. Such considerations included the prospect of bringing more workers into the household and forging alliances between extended family units. In the preindustrial world, the individual household was the unit of economic production—the place where spouses produced the basic necessities of life, including food, clothing, and health care. The primary functions of the marital relationship revolved around this sort of production.

In short, the institution of marriage did not come prepackaged with a set of universal principles or instructions. Rather, it has existed in countless variations across space and time. That said, all societies construe marriage as a means to the fulfillment of certain goals, and despite some variation from person to person, each society develops a loose consensus about which goals are most important to meet through marriage (economic production or emotional fulfillment, for example).

America's Two Great Marital Transitions

America has witnessed three major eras of marriage: pragmatic, love-based, and self-expressive. The first, which extended from the colonial period until around 1850, had a *pragmatic* emphasis in which marriage was primarily oriented toward helping spouses meet their basic economic and survival needs. The industrialized economy began to emerge during this era, but, for most Americans, the small farm remained the primary economic unit. Wives, husbands, and their children—and, frequently, extended family members— worked in and around the farmhouse to produce enough food to keep everybody fed and to create sufficient shelter and clothing to keep everybody warm.

In the pragmatic era, having a marriage that functioned effectively could be, during summer droughts or winter freezes, a matter of life and death. In an era when wage labor was scarce, governmental welfare programs meager, and civic institutions like police forces weak or nonexistent, people looked to marriage, and the broader familial alliances linked to it, to help them achieve physical and psychological security.

The Sentimentality Transition

During the latter half of the 1800s, industrialization brought massive increases in efficiency and productivity, greatly reducing the prices of consumer goods. Improvements in transportation infrastructure, including steamships and railroads, bolstered the quality and quantity of trade and mitigated the devastation of local crop failures. In 1876, the Transcontinental Express arrived in San Francisco three and a half days after leaving New York, a voyage that, ten years earlier, would have taken months. Such developments dovetailed with improvements in industrial production, including the assembly line and the mass production of steel, to make available a broad range of new products, among them household objects like sewing machines and typewriters.

Meanwhile, agricultural advances, including the invention of high-quality fertilizers and heavy machinery, made food more plentiful and less expensive. Health-related advances, including pasteurization and sanitation enhancements, substantially reduced early mortality rates. In general, the astounding pace of economic development during the second Industrial Revolution eased the everyday struggle to meet basic survival needs, which reduced people's dependence on marriage to achieve basic subsistence.

A sudden surfeit of jobs in industrial cities attracted people from rural areas and other countries. For the first time in history, young people were both geographically and economically independent of their parents. This new freedom ushered in a second era, one in which people sought to achieve personal fulfillment through marriage. During this second era, from around 1850 until around 1965, marriages had a *love-based* emphasis that placed a premium on helping spouses meet their love and intimacy needs.

Husbands increasingly worked as wage laborers. Wives increasingly worked as homemakers and as providers of a secondary source of income, taking on boarders or doing piecework like assembling hats and shoes. These changes yielded a new social structure in which men spent much of their time in the predominantly male world of paid employment and women spent much of their time in the predominantly female world of domestic family life. In conjunction with the elevated standard of living afforded by industrialization, the development of these sex-segregated spheres reinforced the emerging emphasis on sentimental reasons for marriage. As it became easier to meet their most basic economic and safety needs as a single person, Americans increasingly looked to marriage for love and romantic passion. For many, love became a precondition for marriage, a requirement that remains strong today.

The Authenticity Transition

The breadwinner-homemaker ideal from the love-based era had been teetering for decades, especially as more and more women entered the workforce, but it had a major last gasp in the 1950s and early 1960s. Because television shows, including *Leave It to Beaver* and *The Adventures of Ozzie & Harriet*, first rose to prominence during this era, the 1950s marriage has been enshrined in popular consciousness as the "traditional marriage," even though it was, by historical standards, bizarre.

In the 1960s, a series of cultural events set the stage for the countercultural revolution during the second half of the decade. The birth control pill became widely available in 1961, helping to launch the sexual revolution. The journalist Betty Friedan published *The Feminine Mystique* in 1963, triggering the second-wave feminist movement.* Leveraging the Reverend Martin Luther King Jr.'s influence, President Lyndon Johnson signed the Great Society legislation into law in 1964 and 1965, further bolstering the emphasis on individual rights. The erstwhile Harvard psychology professor Timothy Leary released the spoken-word album *Turn On, Tune In, Drop Out* in 1967, exhorting Americans to discover themselves and explore "the meaning of inner life."

Meanwhile, in a growing number of marriages, both spouses were

---

* The first-wave feminist movement had garnered women the right to vote in 1920.

gainfully employed outside the home, and, for broad swaths of the populace, the standard of living was rising rapidly. Over time, the American economy became increasingly postindustrialized, with jobs in the services, information, and research sectors supplanting those in manufacturing. Seeking to develop the intellectual skills that are especially prized in postindustrial economies, more Americans went to college. Entrepreneurship and the generation of novel ideas fueled economic growth.

The trend toward increasingly cerebral lives, especially among the college educated, dovetailed with the countercultural revolution to launch Americans—including Elizabeth Gilbert, Cheryl Strayed, and Neil Strauss—on voyages of self-discovery and personal growth. Consequently, the nature of social connection changed. During the third era, from around 1965 to today, marriage has a *self-expressive* emphasis that places a premium on spouses helping each other meet their authenticity and personal-growth needs. According to the sociologist Robert Bellah, a self-expressive relationship "is created by full sharing of authentic feelings," and love "becomes the mutual exploration of infinitely rich, complex, and exciting selves."

The divorce rate—the number of divorces per year per one thousand married women—had been slowly rising for over a century (with a brief dip during the Great Depression and a brief spike following World War II). But, as illustrated in the chart on the following page, it skyrocketed between 1965 and 1980, largely due to the rise of the self-expressive marriage. As we'll see in chapter 4, however, Americans eventually adjusted to the self-expressive era; divorce rates leveled off and even fell slightly, largely because people stopped marrying so young.*

---

* Despite the clarity of the raw divorce rate in the chart, social scientists disagree about the extent to which—and even *if*—the divorce rate has meaningfully declined since around 1980. For our purposes, the key point is that the surging divorce rate of the 1960s and 1970s ended around 1980.

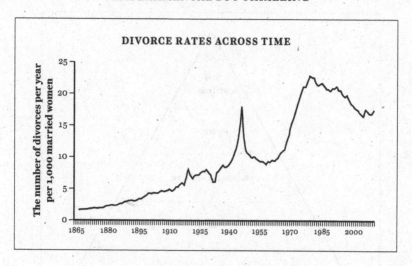

Echoes of Abraham Maslow

The historical changes in American marriage—from the pragmatic to the love-based to the self-expressive eras—exhibit striking parallels to the psychologist Abraham Maslow's famous hierarchy of needs. As illustrated on the following page, this hierarchy is typically represented as a triangle that encompasses, from bottom to top, physiological needs (for air, water, food, etc.), safety needs (for physical protection, psychological safety, economic security, etc.), belonging and love needs (for friendship, intimacy, romantic love, etc.), esteem needs (for self-esteem, self-respect, esteem from others, etc.), and self-actualization needs (to discover one's unique character strengths, to live in accord with those strengths, to live in the moment, etc.). The primary functions of marriage revolved around the fulfilment of lower needs during the pragmatic era, middle needs during the love-based era, and higher needs during the self-expressive era.

When my students and I wrote the *Psychological Inquiry* Target Article, we struggled to find a compelling metaphor for the temporal

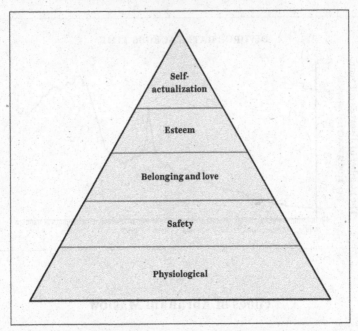

Abraham Maslow's hierarchy of needs

changes in American marriage. The breakthrough came when we reconceptualized Maslow's hierarchy not in the form of a triangle, but in the form of a major mountain, which we dubbed "Mount Maslow."

As with any large mountain, the air gets thinner, and the oxygen sparser, at higher altitudes. As marriage in America has become increasingly oriented toward higher rather than lower altitudes on Mount Maslow, it has required greater *oxygenation*—greater nurturance regarding each other's emotional and psychological needs. If spouses expect their marriage to help them fulfill such needs but are unwilling or unable to invest the time and psychological energy (the "oxygen") required at that altitude, the marriage is at risk for *suffocation*—for lethargy, conflict, and perhaps divorce.

CATEGORY OF NEED	SPECIFIC EXAMPLES	MOUNT MASLOW
Self-actualization	• Self-expression • Personal growth • Autonomy • Spontaneity • Veridical self-assessment	
Esteem	• Self-esteem • Self-respect • Sense of mastery • Prestige • Respect from others	
Belonging and love	• Love others • Be loved by others • Trust others • Sexual intimacy • Belong to a group	
Safety	• Economic safety • A sense of control • Predictability • Psychological safety • Physical safety	
Physiological	• Hunger • Thirst • Warmth • Sleep • Respiration	

Mount Maslow

This Maslow analogy drives home that the major change over time is not an overall *increase* in how much Americans expect from their marriage (more versus less), but rather a dramatic *shift* in the substance of their expectations (from lower to higher altitudes). In contrast to our predecessors, who looked to their marriage to help them survive, we look to our marriage to meet our needs for passion and intimacy and to facilitate our voyages of self-discovery and personal growth. As we'll soon see, success at these higher altitudes requires the investment of significant time and energy in the marriage.

The Michelangelo Effect

Our emphasis on achieving self-discovery and personal growth through our marriage is aspirational. We prize movement of our *actual self* (our current self) toward our *authentic self* (our truest self). The authentic self, sometimes called the "ideal self," encompasses the constellation of traits, skills, and other characteristics that form the core of our identity—and that we hope to cultivate over time.*

My mentor, the psychologist Caryl Rusbult, recognized that our close relationship partners strongly influence how successful we are in our efforts to grow toward our authentic self. In collaboration with Stephen Drigotas, she leveraged comments from the artist Michelangelo Buonarroti to develop a metaphor for this process. Michelangelo didn't view sculpting in terms of *creating* a sculpture, but rather in terms of *revealing* it. In his view, the sculpture was already dwelling in the rock; the sculptor's task was simply to chisel away the excess to reveal the beautiful form slumbering within. In considering Michelangelo's *Unfinished Captive* on the next page, it's easy to see what he meant. Although this man has no head, it certainly feels as if he does. He just needs Michelangelo to reveal it for him.

Across an elegant series of studies, Rusbult and Drigotas found consistent support for the idea that, in like manner, romantic partners (both spouses and dating partners) can sculpt each other toward their authentic selves over time. In this metaphor, the actual self is the raw block of stone, the authentic self is the sculpture buried

---

* "The self" is a surprisingly elusive concept. Centuries of philosophical and scientific debate have failed to settle whether it is spiritual versus corporeal, unitary versus fragmented, stable versus ephemeral, inherent versus socially constructed, conscious versus unconscious—even real versus illusory. Those debates, which are every bit as relevant to "the authentic self," are not our concern here. What matters for our purposes is that most people experience a sense of self, that they believe there is a more authentic version of the self within them, and that they believe movement toward that more authentic version is possible.

Michelangelo's Unfinished Captive

within it, and the partner is the sculptor. The *Michelangelo effect* refers to the process through which partners sculpt each other in ways that elicit each person's authentic self.

The idea that close relationship partners can help us grow toward our authentic self is a major theme in contemporary popular culture. In James Brooks's 1997 romantic comedy *As Good as It Gets*, Melvin (Jack Nicholson) is a misanthropic, obsessive-compulsive novelist, and Carol (Helen Hunt) is a plucky, down-on-her-luck waitress. Melvin pursues a relationship with Carol, but his self-centered insensitivity keeps putting her off. In the pivotal scene, he inadvertently insults her while the two of them are sitting down to dinner. She stands up to leave the restaurant—and the relationship. He begs her to stay. She tells him how much he hurt her feelings and that she'll leave if he doesn't offer her a nice compliment. The compliment, when it finally comes, is pretty great: "You make me want to be a better man." She stays for dinner.

Sometimes, we see the Michelangelo effect in reverse—cases in which relationship partners bring out the worst in each other rather than the best. In Derek Cianfrance's 2010 drama *Blue Valentine*, Dean (Ryan Gosling) is a high school dropout and house painter, and Cindy (Michelle Williams) is a nurse whose plans to become a doctor were derailed when she accidentally got pregnant with a former boyfriend. Dean is happy being married to Cindy, helping to raise his stepdaughter, and working in a blue-collar job without much opportunity for career advancement. Cindy is disappointed in his lack of ambition: "Isn't there something you wanted to do? . . . Doesn't [your career] ever disappoint you? Because you have all this potential." Dean gets defensive: "What does that mean, 'potential'? Potential for what? To turn it into what?" The conversation deteriorates from there. His ideal for himself (to be a family man with a low-pressure job) misaligns with her ideal for him (to be ambitious in a way that capitalizes on his potential). According to research on the Michelangelo effect, misalignment of this sort is linked to relationship problems and unhappiness.

Our Winnowed Social Networks

Okay, some partners bring us closer to our authentic self and others push us further away—but what about our friends? What about our parents and siblings and children? Must it be our romantic partner who plays the Michelangelo role?

The psychologist Bella DePaulo provides a clear and convincing answer: It doesn't have to be our romantic partner. All of us have many sculptors. In her Commentary on our *Psychological Inquiry* Target Article, DePaulo argues that Americans hold an ideology of marriage, one that gives the marital bond extreme priority and, consequently, blinds us to how important other types of relationships are.

She's right, of course, but others' ability to influence us depends on how central they are in our lives. We can readily imagine societies in which our spouse isn't our primary sculptor—societies in which friends or other relatives hammer and chisel each other more than spouses do. But, for the most part, contemporary America is not one of those societies.

Indeed, relative to Americans who are unmarried, those who are married are much less involved with friends and other relatives. The first chart on the next page presents the percentage of never-married, married, and previously married Americans who see their parents and siblings at least weekly. The chart below it quantifies those who socialize with their neighbors and friends multiple times per month. Married people are far less likely than never-married people to see their parents, siblings, neighbors, and friends regularly; previously married people are intermediate.

It wasn't always this way. The chart on the next page depicts changes in how much alone time (time without their spouse) married Americans spend with friends and other relatives on weekends. In 1975, Americans averaged about 2.0 hours per weekend day of alone time with friends or relatives, an estimate that was similar for couples with and without children. In 2003, just one generation later,

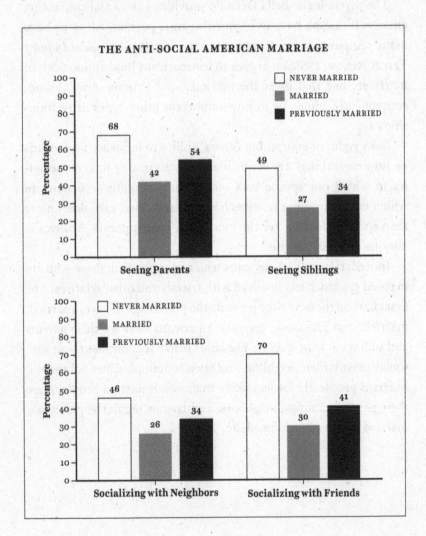

THE ANTI-SOCIAL AMERICAN MARRIAGE

this number had plummeted to about 1.2 hours per weekend day, a decline that was especially stark among couples with children.

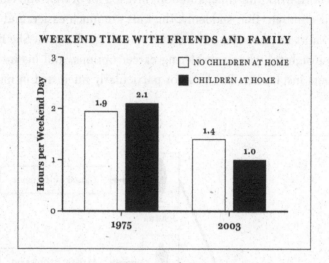

WEEKEND TIME WITH FRIENDS AND FAMILY

Given this social withdrawal, successful pursuit of our authentic-self goals depends on our spouse much more today than in the past. Imagine Jasmine, a twenty-eight-year-old middle-class woman from Atlanta. Jasmine has a college degree and a stable job, but she doesn't find the work fulfilling. Fortunately, she has an active social life. She has a weekly coffee date with Michelle, a friend from college who has become a senior executive at a nonprofit organization. On occasion, she plays open mike gigs with Dylan, a guy she dated a few years back. Jasmine hates exercising, but Beatriz, her friend from work, convinced her six months ago to go to yoga class together on Mondays and Thursdays. Jasmine befriended the yoga instructor, Alice; the two of them love discussing meditation and Eastern philosophy over a bottle of wine. Jasmine goes on an annual camping trip with Kyoko, her childhood friend and something of a party animal.

Let's fast-forward twelve years. Jasmine, now forty, is married to James, with whom she has two daughters, aged nine and seven.

Over the past decade, she has struggled to stay on top of her responsibilities and, consequently, has seen less of her friends. She and James both work full-time, and both invest a lot of time and energy in their children. But, suddenly, the kids are much easier, and Jasmine wants to prioritize other authentic-self goals again. She finds James insightful when considering career options, and his intense workouts inspire her. But he's not particularly interested in music,

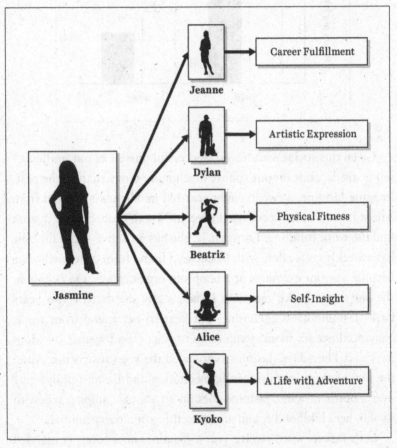

Jasmine at age twenty-eight

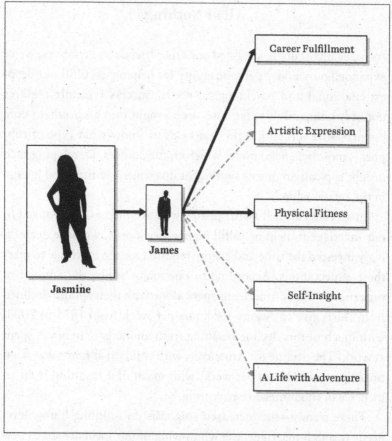

*Jasmine at age forty. James's helpful roles have solid lines;
his unhelpful roles have dashed lines.*

he views philosophical discussions about selfhood as narcissistic navel-gazing, and he's too tame to launch her on adventurous escapades. His limitations here shouldn't surprise us, as few potential spouses are well suited to helping us achieve all of our authentic-self goals. Still, because of Jasmine's intense focus on her nuclear family, he's frequently the only person who's readily available.

All or Nothing

As we've increasingly sidelined our other friends and relatives, we've expanded our spouse's responsibility for helping us fulfill our deepest emotional and psychological needs. Success typically requires not only compatibility, but also deep insight into each other's core essence—the sort of insight that helps us know what type of support is most beneficial under which circumstances. Developing such insight typically requires significant investment of time and energy in the relationship.

In a cruel cultural twist, just as we have increasingly looked to our marriage to help us fulfill higher-level needs, we have decreasingly invested the time and energy required for the marriage to meet these expectations. According to one major study, the amount of time that childless Americans spent alone with their spouse declined from thirty-five to twenty-six hours per week from 1975 to 2003, with much of this decline resulting from an increase in hours spent at work. The decline for Americans with children at home was from thirteen to nine hours per week, with much of it resulting from an increase in time-intensive parenting.*

These trends—the increased emphasis on fulfilling higher-level needs through marriage, the winnowing of our intimate social networks, and the reduced alone time with our spouse—have produced two major consequences, one negative and one positive. The negative consequence is that the proportion of spouses whose marriages fall short of expectations has grown. To be sure, it was no small feat, circa 1750, to produce food during a summer drought or to stay warm during a winter freeze, but doing so didn't require a loving bond or deep insight into each other's psychological essence. Such love and insight—which depend on communication, respon-

---

* A lot of this decline in *spousal time* (time alone with one's spouse) was replaced by an increase in *family time* (time with one's spouse and children). Chapter 6 provides a more detailed discussion.

siveness, and emotional support—are crucial for contemporary spouses seeking to help each other achieve authentic, self-expressive lives. Consequently, a level of investment in the relationship that would have been sufficient in earlier eras is often insufficient today. Indeed, as illustrated in the chart below, the proportion of marriages that are "very happy," rather than "pretty happy" or "not too happy," is in decline.

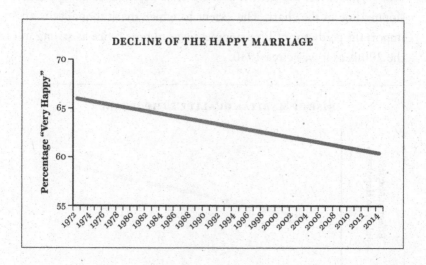

The positive consequence is that the benefits of having a marriage that meets our expectations have grown. As Maslow noted, relative to meeting lower needs, meeting higher needs yields "more profound happiness, serenity, and richness of the inner life." This idea extends to the interpersonal case—relative to having a spouse help us fulfill our lower, more basic needs, having a spouse help us fulfill our higher, more emotional and psychological needs yields more profound marital happiness, serenity in the relationship, and richness of our life together.

As marriage has become both more fragile and more important, its quality—the extent to which we experience it as fulfilling—has become an increasingly important predictor of our overall happiness with life. Consider a meta-analysis from the family scientist Christine Proulx, who scoured all the studies using earlier assessments of marital quality to predict changes over time in happiness with life. As shown in the chart below, these studies revealed positive effects of marital quality on happiness—that is, marital quality was reliably linked to higher rather than lower overall happiness with one's life. That finding isn't surprising.* What's fascinating is that the magnitude of this effect has grown over time, as depicted in the upward-sloping line in the chart. The extent to which marital quality is an important predictor of life happiness was almost twice as strong in the 2000s as it was circa 1980.

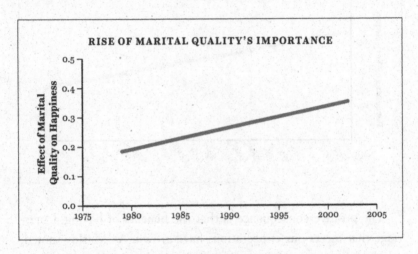

Marriage, in short, has tilted toward an all-or-nothing state. As its primary functions have ascended Maslow's hierarchy, and as we've spent less time with our spouse, it's become more difficult for our marriage to live up to our expectations, which means that more of us wind up feeling disappointed. At the same time, as the nature of our marital expectations has changed, the benefits of fulfilling those

---

* From 2010 to 2014, almost 60 percent of Americans who were "very happy" in their marriage were also very happy with their lives in general, whereas only 10 percent who were less than very happy in their marriage were very happy in their lives in general.

expectations are larger than ever. Consequently, even as the average marriage is getting worse, the best marriages are getting better.

From Cabernet to Pinot

In Alexander Payne's 2004 film *Sideways*, Miles (Paul Giamatti) is a divorced, unsuccessful author, and Maya (Virginia Madsen) is an appealing, easygoing waitress. The two of them bond over their shared love of wine and begin an unlikely romance. In one indelible scene, Maya says, "Why are you so into Pinot? I mean, it's like a thing with you." His answer provides an intriguing metaphor for the changes in American marriage over time:

> It's a hard grape to grow. . . . It's thin-skinned, temperamental, ripens early. . . . It's not a survivor like Cabernet, which can just grow anywhere and thrive even when it's neglected. No, Pinot needs constant care and attention. . . . In fact, it can only grow in these really specific little tucked-away corners of the world. And only the most patient and nurturing of growers can do it, really. Only somebody who really takes the time to understand Pinot's potential can then coax it into its fullest expression. Then, I mean, its flavors, they're just the most haunting and brilliant and thrilling and subtle and ancient on the planet.

Marriage in America has changed from an institution approximating Cabernet to an institution approximating Pinot (at least as Miles characterizes these wine grapes). Relative to marriages in earlier eras, marriages today require much greater dedication and nurturance, a change that has placed an ever-larger proportion of marriages at risk of stagnation and dissolution. But spouses who invest the requisite time and energy in the relationship can achieve a level of conjugal fulfillment that would have been out of reach in earlier eras. To use Miles's words, American marriage today is *temperamental*, but those spouses who nurture it can build something *thrilling*.

Toward a New Marital Paradigm

A recurring theme in the scholarship on marriage is that the massive changes in the institution over the past fifty years or so have left Americans unmoored. In *The Future of Marriage* (1982), the sociologist Jessie Bernard observed that "marriage itself has not yet caught up with our thinking about it." In *Domestic Revolutions* (1988), the historians Steven Mintz and Susan Kellogg observed that "today the United States is a society without a clear unitary set of family ideals and values. Many Americans are groping for a new paradigm of American family life, but in the meantime a profound sense of confusion and ambivalence reigns." In *Marriage, a History* (2005), the historian Stephanie Coontz observed that "today we are entering uncharted territory, and there is still no definitive guide to the new marital landscape."

I think we are, at long last, witnessing the beginning of the end of this turbulent period. A new marital paradigm has emerged, one in which spouses enjoy prolonged periods at the summit and flexibly adapt their expectations when temporary circumstances place the summit out of reach. This new paradigm holds great promise not only for putting the institution of marriage on more solid footing, but also for making it more fulfilling for the spouses involved. As more of us learn how to live successfully within this paradigm, we can potentially usher in the most successful period of marital well-being that the world has ever seen.

Reverse Engineering Today's Best Marriages

In their Commentary on the *Psychological Inquiry* Target Article, the psychologists Arthur and Elaine Aron alerted me to one of Abraham Maslow's lesser-known insights. This one involved chickens. When free to select from diverse foods, some chickens adopt healthier diets than others. But when researchers forced the chickens who had selected unhealthy diets to switch to the diets that the healthier selectors had chosen, the formerly unhealthy chickens became healthier. Maslow argued that people who were struggling to self-actualize can, in parallel fashion, learn from studying the habits of successful self-actualizers.

Can spouses in mediocre marriages learn from those in flourishing marriages? We'll report on those chickens in the final section of the book, where we'll also review the scientific literature on close relationships to consider three sets of strategies for bolstering our own marriage. Before we do that, however, we'll examine the unique opportunities and perils of marriage in America today, especially relative to marriages in the past. To put things in perspective, let's consider the marriage of Thomas and Nancy Lincoln, the parents of the man who emancipated America's slaves.

Part Two

Historical Perspective

2.

The Pragmatic Marriage

In this sad world of ours, sorrow comes to all; and, to the
young, it comes with bitterest agony, because it takes
them unawares. . . . I have had experience enough to
know what I say.

—Abraham Lincoln

When Nancy Lincoln gave birth to Abraham, her second child, in 1809, she and Thomas had been married for almost three years. The growing family lived in a one-room, dirt-floor cabin. A third and final child arrived soon thereafter, but he died in infancy. Nancy died in 1818, and, while Abraham was still a teenager, his sister died while giving birth to a stillborn son. Such experiences served as inspiration for the quotation above, which comes from a letter President Lincoln wrote to a bereaved child in 1862.

Although the Lincolns were perhaps a bit more unfortunate than many of their contemporaries, the sorts of challenges and tragedies they faced were hardly rare. Thomas and Nancy had fewer children than average, and their frontier life differed from that in the more established sections of the Eastern Seaboard, but early mortality and (by today's standards) crushing poverty were pervasive.

A replica of Abraham Lincoln's birthplace

Across the land, life was fragile, and marital functioning could be the difference between life and death. The primary consideration for a successful marriage was running a household that fed its residents and protected them from the elements. People weren't especially concerned with self-expression. Even love was secondary.

The Cultural Animal

As we'll soon see, contrasting marriage in the Lincolns' era with marriage today reveals astonishing differences. Indeed, the pace and magnitude of the changes are sufficiently large that it might be tempting to conclude that marriage, or the human mating system more generally, is arbitrary—that it could have almost any structure imaginable.

Such a conclusion would be wrong. It's true that human mating patterns exhibit wide variation across cultural context and historical epoch, but the variation exists within a set of evolved constraints. Human culture is flexible, but not infinitely so.

As noted by the psychologist Roy Baumeister, we tend to be fascinated by cultural differences, but perhaps the most important thing to understand about human culture is something we all share: Culture is our most distinctive evolved strategy for survival and reproduction. Giraffes have long necks, chameleons change color, and humans have culture. Today, efforts to build autonomous cars require major innovation, but they don't require the invention of the wheel, metal alloys, or electrical circuitry, as such inventions already reside within our cultural repertoire. By scaffolding discoveries across generations rather than limiting them to an individual life span, our ability to function within cultures has placed humans atop the food chain, doubled our life expectancy, and brought comfort to our everyday existence. It allows us to live in temperature-regulated habitats, eat meals in restaurants, and share photos of those meals on Facebook.

Our adaptations for culture achieve these feats by affording a level of cognitive and social flexibility vastly beyond anything else in the animal kingdom. According to the biologist Peter Richerson and the anthropologist Robert Boyd, cultural evolution offers humans express lanes that bypass the bumper-to-bumper pace of Darwin's genetic evolution—albeit within the constraints of what our genes allow. With few exceptions, genetic evolution, such as the emergence of humans' bipedal bodies and large brains, takes eons. Cultural evolution, in contrast, can be extremely rapid, transpiring on the order of millennia, decades, or even weeks. Cultural evolution, which is especially beneficial in rapidly changing environments, affords the flexibility required to produce large behavioral changes in the absence of genetic evolution.

That's a major reason why the mating life of humans—in contrast to that of, say, dogs or gorillas—has witnessed such colossal shifts in recent centuries. Genetic constraints mean that humans can't be pregnant with multiple partners' babies at the same time, reproduce with members of their same sex, or switch sex when their birth sex is overrepresented in the immediate population. But cultural flexibility means that human mating tendencies, including the role of marriage in governing social and reproductive life, can adapt rapidly to changing environmental circumstances, such as those linked to industrialization and urbanization.

According to the psychologists Wendy Wood and Alice Eagly, a central mechanism through which changing environmental circumstances influence human mating tendencies is by altering social roles, including gender roles. As we'll see, the cultural evolution of social roles, along with the psychological and behavioral changes linked to them, is a crucial component in understanding why marriage in America today functions as it does. The first element in this story involves the changing nature of social roles as the advent of agriculture generated previously unimaginable levels of wealth.

From Hunter-Gatherer to Agricultural Societies

Throughout most of human history, all societies procured food through hunting and gathering. Starting around eleven thousand years ago, agricultural societies emerged and slowly conquered the Earth. These societies domesticated wild animals and plants, which allowed them to cultivate livestock and crops. Because humans domesticated only those plants and animals that they were able to digest, they used the land more efficiently—an acre produced ten to one hundred times more edible calories for early agriculturalists than for their hunter-gatherer contemporaries.

Efficient food production profoundly altered human societies, setting in motion developments that would ultimately produce the sort of marital arrangement that Thomas and Nancy Lincoln embodied. As depicted in the diagram below, efficient food production fostered transitions from nomadic to sedentary lifestyles and from low to high population density. In contrast to hunter-gatherer societies, in which people moved around regularly in search of food, people in agricultural societies established long-term residences near the farm they were tending. In addition, the increasing efficiency of food production begat increased population density, a trend that was strengthened by a reduction in how long couples waited between pregnancies once babies could be raised in a long-term residence rather than having to be carried from campsite to campsite.

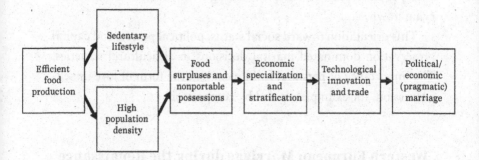

The sedentary lifestyle and increased population density combined with efficient food production to generate robust food surpluses and nonportable possessions, including heavy farming equipment and, eventually, printing presses. These changes radically altered social structures. For the first time, societies could produce sufficient food without the requirement that food production be the primary pursuit of virtually every able-bodied individual. Food produced by peasants could be redistributed to allow others to specialize in full-time roles like soldier, trader, or bureaucrat. With specialization came stratification and hierarchy. The powerful claimed control of food produced by peasants or taxed them in other ways.

Political elites formed a centralized government that coordinated public work projects like irrigation systems and the development of long-distance trading relationships. Over time, more and more elites learned to read and write, which further enhanced the society's ability to produce novel goods and services.

As generations passed, social stratification became increasingly entrenched. Families toward the top sought to retain or expand their wealth rather than redistributing it to those lower down. They refused to allow their children to marry members of less wealthy families—and they treated as illegitimate (and unworthy of inheritance or other economic claims) any children born through pairings they had not sanctioned. Such efforts pervaded the social hierarchy, with people in each stratum forbidding family members from marrying down.

This orientation toward social status, political power, and capital preservation dominated marital decisions in agricultural societies. The importance of personal fulfillment—in the form of love or self-expression, for example—paled by comparison.

Western European Marriage during the Renaissance

As we train our attention on western Europe, we see how the intellectual turbulence of the Renaissance era set the stage for a distinctive marital structure in the New World. Western Europe was already predominantly agricultural as it emerged from the Middle Ages, a deeply religious era in which advances in secular domains like science and philosophy were modest. In the 1300s, the Italian scholar and poet Francesco Petrarch proffered the radical claim that worldly and religious pursuits can coexist peacefully. Indeed, according to Petrarch, God endowed people with intellectual and creative potential, and it was their moral imperative to make the most of that endowment.

This humanistic emphasis converged with economic developments to promote secularism and rationalism, the core values of the Enlightenment. Watermills and other technological innovations strengthened agricultural efficiency, increasing surpluses and launching the Commercial Revolution. This revolution produced a dense trading network, which in turn generated a middle class that garnered property rights. In contrast to agricultural structures that depended on collective irrigation efforts to leverage the power of large rivers—as in Egypt and China—the rainfall agriculture of western Europe during this era led to a system of family farms with market access, a socioeconomic arrangement that afforded greater individual autonomy.

Married couples were expected to be self-sufficient. Young men had to establish some level of financial independence—through farming or working a trade—before getting married, after which the couple was expected to provide for themselves and their children. In contrast to both traditional aristocratic marriages, in which the husband and wife lived largely independent lives, and traditional peasant marriages, in which the lord of the manor or the broader community made the major economic decisions (such as when and how to plant, plow, and harvest), the ability to coordinate effectively with one's spouse was crucial in these northwestern European marriages. "A harmonious, well-functioning marriage," observes Stephanie Coontz, "was a business necessity as well as a personal pleasure."

Meanwhile, the shock waves of the Protestant Reformation were reverberating throughout Christendom. In 1517, the German friar Martin Luther disseminated his Ninety-Five Theses decrying moral failings in the Catholic Church, ultimately influencing American marriage in two major ways. First, Protestantism increased the status of matrimony. In contrast to the Catholic Church, which viewed marriage as a necessary evil—a morally inferior alternative to celibacy—Protestant theology viewed marriage as a sacred, morally righteous institution. Second, the Protestant Reformation spawned Puritanism. A group of Puritans called the Pilgrims, seeking religious freedom, settled the Plymouth Colony, which was less class-stratified and more receptive to religious pluralism than contemporary societies in western Europe.

In short, Luther set in motion a series of theological and religious developments that, a century later, planted in North America colonists who held the institution of marriage in high regard. Contrasting marital practices in America today with those of other Western nations reveals that the legacy of these influences remains strong nearly four hundred years later.

The Colonial Era

The Pilgrims reached the New World on November 11, 1620. Of the 102 passengers who had embarked on the *Mayflower*'s transatlantic journey, about half were dead come springtime. But then, despite some sustained hardships, the colonists' fortunes improved quickly. By the time the survivors celebrated the harvest festival in October 1621—an event now known as the First Thanksgiving—the threat of mass death had declined considerably. Through reproduction and the arrival of additional colonists, the population of the Plymouth Colony had reached three hundred by 1630 and two thousand by 1643.

Along with population growth came a stable social system. Compared to other colonies of that period, including Jamestown in Virginia, the Plymouth Colony was, in the words of the historians Steven Mintz and Susan Kellogg, "a society with roots." Life expectancy and the average duration of marriages increased rapidly.

In Plymouth and other northern colonies, the family was the central social institution, doing much of the work that governments and markets do today. Most of us work for companies or other large institutions, buy food at supermarkets and restaurants, purchase clothing in stores or via the Internet, educate our children in schools, protect ourselves with insurance, and seek medical care in doctors' offices, hospitals, and nursing homes. During the colonial era, in contrast, each family was a largely self-sufficient social and economic system. Family members produced the food and shelter required for their survival. They protected themselves from assault and their property from theft and damage. (At least they tried; Abraham Lincoln's paternal grandfather was killed in an ambush while tending his farm.) They sewed the clothing, built the furniture, and made the soap and candles. They educated their children and tended to their sick and infirm.

Given these responsibilities, it was a great economic and physical challenge to live alone. Nearly all men and women in New England married, with most rapidly remarrying if their spouse died.* Consider the myriad responsibilities of the colonial wife, who was "expected to cook, wash, sew, milk, spin, clean, and garden," note Mintz and Kellogg. "Her activities included brewing beer [which was perceived as healthier than water], churning butter, harvesting fruit, keeping chickens, spinning wool, building fires, baking bread, making cheese, boiling laundry, and stitching shirts, petticoats, and other garments. She participated in trade—exchanging surplus fruit, meat, cheese, or butter for tea, candles, coats, or sheets—and manufacturing—salting, pickling, and preserving vegetables, fruit, and meat and making clothing and soap—in addition to other domestic tasks." She performed these duties despite delivering and raising an average of six children.

The basic societal and political unit was the household, not the individual. When colonists married, they were committing themselves to the family, even when doing so undermined their personal happiness. Although they hoped that love and affection would eventually

---

* Marriage remained a near necessity throughout the preindustrial era. Shortly after Nancy Lincoln died in 1818, Thomas went back to Kentucky from the Indiana frontier to find a new wife. He married Sarah Bush Johnston, a widowed mother of three small children. According to the Pulitzer Prize–winning historian David Herbert Donald, "there was no time for a romantic engagement; he needed a wife and she needed a husband."

blossom, colonists viewed marriage as a pragmatic arrangement revolving around basic economic and political considerations, including those necessary for survival and sustenance.

In the latter half of the 1600s and through much of the 1700s, the colonies became more numerous and robust. Plymouth became part of the Massachusetts Bay Colony in 1692, and with the establishment of Georgia in 1732, all thirteen of the colonies that would declare independence in 1776 had already formed. Collectively, the colonies had strong population growth, surging from a quarter million people in 1700 to 2.4 million in 1775.

Legally, these were colonies of Great Britain, from which they adopted many economic and political systems. However, unlike Great Britain, North America had abundant land—including land acquired through trade and war with the native populations—and no landowning aristocracy, which allowed a relatively large proportion of families (though certainly not all) to claim ownership over parcels of land. Households contributed actively to the political system, with most white men allowed to vote. By the standards of the time, the colonies were prosperous and healthy.

Political and Familial Revolution

In the mid-1700s, the colonies began to function as a collective, if fractious, political entity. Asserting that citizens have "certain unalienable Rights," including "Life, Liberty, and the pursuit of Happiness," they declared independence from Great Britain in 1776. The colonists' grievances, especially their objection to paying taxes despite lacking full representation in the British political system, provided an immediate political context for their revolutionary fervor, but the broader intellectual context was also crucial. Most directly, the Declaration of Independence built on the idea of the *social contract*—the notion that a government exerts its authority by the consent of the governed. The English philosopher John Locke argued that the government has a responsibility to promote the welfare of its citizens.

These Enlightenment-era ideas contributed to a worldview that valued human rights and opposed traditional authority. The Protestant Reformation posed serious challenges to the Catholic Church in the 1500s and 1600s, undermining absolutist beliefs and bolstering the status of personal liberty. In *Discourse on the Method* (1637), René Descartes's skeptical search for any truth that was beyond doubt pointed him not to any external authority, but rather to his own mind: "*Cogito ergo sum*" ("I am thinking, therefore I exist," or, more pithily, "I think, therefore I am"). In *Principia Mathematica* (1687), Isaac Newton ignited the scientific revolution by employing mathematics to explain natural phenomena, like the movement of the planets, that had traditionally been understood in metaphysical terms. Enlightenment-era thinking prized empiricism, scientific rigor, and distrust of established authority—as noted by the philosopher Immanuel Kant, it prized the freedom to use one's own intelligence.

People struggled to reconcile these Enlightenment-era ideas with prevailing views of the family during the early colonial era, which prized hierarchy and obedience. According to these views, each household functioned as a miniature commonwealth, with the husband serving as the all-powerful monarch who ruled over his wife and children. For many colonists and Americans in the 1700s and early 1800s, the logic of the modern social contract—including the Declaration of Independence's emphasis on the government's responsibility to protect the rights of the governed—had clear implications for rights and responsibilities within individual families.

Alexis de Tocqueville, the French nobleman who wrote *Democracy in America* shortly after his study of the United States in 1831 and 1832, coined the term *democratic marriage* to characterize the new American marital ideal that purported to accord equal status to the husband and the wife. The democratic marriage downplayed status differences between the spouses. That said, it did not treat husbands and wives as interchangeable; indeed, the roles of husband and wife became more differentiated than ever.

The central idea underlying the democratic marriage is that men and women have different essences. This idea, which Tocqueville discussed in terms of *separate spheres*, is that biological differences between the sexes (and, in some variations of the idea, divine will) dictate that men and women should occupy different roles. Men should inhabit the public sphere, participating in, and excelling at, domains like politics, commerce, and law. Women should inhabit the private sphere, participating in, and excelling at, domains like child-rearing, domestic work, and religious education.

In certain forms, the separate-spheres idea had been around for millennia. In his *Politics*, for example, Aristotle distinguished between the male sphere of the city-state (*polis*) and the female sphere of the home (*oikos*). But the idea achieved its purest expression in America in the 1800s, during which a "cult of true womanhood" was dominant (in the words of the historian Barbara Welter). The four defining features of the true woman were piety, purity, submissiveness, and domesticity.

According to Tocqueville, "America is the one country where the most consistent care has been taken to trace clearly distant spheres of action for the two sexes and where both are required to walk at an equal pace but along paths that are never the same." The emphasis on *equal pace* warrants close attention. According to the ideology of separate spheres, men and women are such different creatures that it is nonsensical to consider either sex as having higher or lower status. Each has its own sphere in which it is the unquestioned authority. In contrast to the patriarchal view, the separate-spheres view was not that women are inferior to men, but rather that they possess an elevated moral purity that is crucial for promoting societal well-being and child development. The rationale for excluding women from the public sphere was not the assertion of male privilege, but rather that women needed to be protected from the baseness of that sphere. "Americans do not believe that men and women have the duty or the right to perform the same things," observes Tocqueville, "but they show the same regard for the role played by both and they consider them as equal in worth although their lot in life is different."

The ideology of separate spheres performed a remarkable tight-rope walk. It retained the household, rather than the individual, as the central societal and political unit while simultaneously eliminating the sort of explicit hierarchy that had become uncomfortable in an enlightened era of liberalism and democracy. It achieved this feat by cleaving the human psyche into two bodies, placing its rational, assertive side within the husband and its emotional, nurturant side within the wife.

A New Marital Ideal

It was during this period—the 1700s and early 1800s—that love, in its long and ultimately successful battle to conquer the institution of marriage, struck its decisive blow. Now that husband and wife were perceived as equals, with each playing a crucial role that the other was unqualified to play, their marriage focused less on their ability to work well together and more on their sentimental feelings for each other.

This emphasis on love dovetailed with the ideals of the romantic era (late 1700s to mid-1800s), which lionized intense, authentic emotional experiences. Mainstream novels began to depict the lives of ordinary people rather than royalty or knights, and many of these novels focused on romantic love. In Johann Wolfgang von Goethe's *The Sorrows of Young Werther*, the sensitive Werther falls passionately in love with a woman who can't form a relationship with him. He kills himself to escape the agony. In Victor Hugo's *The Hunchback of Notre-Dame*, Quasimodo, a physically deformed man, falls in love with the beautiful gypsy street dancer Esmeralda, who is hanged by the authorities for a crime she didn't commit. Quasimodo remains with her dead body until he dies of starvation. When their intertwined bodies are found eighteen months later, an attempt to separate them makes their skeletons disintegrate into dust. Jane Austen's *Sense and Sensibility* tells the story of the sisters Elinor and Marianne Dashwood. Through a series of romantic encounters and, eventually, a pair of marriages, Austen weighs the relative merits of sense and sensibility—with *sense* referring to prudence or good judgment and *sensibility* referring to sensitivity or emotionality—but she seems unwilling to offer a verdict. In contrast, the Brontë sisters' romanticism, as manifested in Charlotte's *Jane Eyre* and Emily's *Wuthering Heights*, was unrestrained. Eyre, for example, declines an opportunity to pursue a decent man whom she doesn't love in order to pursue a cruel, complicated man whom she does. After losing his hand and going blind in a fire, the latter man leaves cruelty behind. Jane marries him, and he recovers enough vision to see their first child.

An Ideal Ahead of Its Time

In the two centuries preceding the Industrial Revolution, developments in political theory (the social contract), Enlightenment thinking (the freedom to use one's intelligence), gender relations (separate spheres), and romantic beliefs (the primacy of authentic emotional experience) set the stage for a new marital ideal. This ideal "shifted the basis of marriage from sharing tasks to sharing feelings," observes Stephanie Coontz. "The older view that wives and husbands were work mates gave way to [the] idea that they were soul mates."

It's easy to see why many Americans preferred this new ideal to the more impersonal, patriarchal ideal it replaced. But ideals and behaviors are not the same thing, and the transition from the pragmatic ideal to the love-based ideal was slow. As long as American society was predominantly agricultural, with the individual farmhouse serving as the primary unit of economic production, it was virtually impossible to complete the transition; there were too many other, more essential, demands on the relationship.

However, it wouldn't take long for industrialization and urbanization to crush the pragmatic model of marriage. These forces sharply increased the proportion of households that subsisted on wage labor rather than farming and domestic production. In doing so, they created a social and economic context well suited to the ideology of separate spheres. They also reduced restrictions on individual freedoms, and people used these freedoms to marry for love.

3.

From Pragmatism to Love

> When two people are under the influence of the most
> violent, most insane, most delusive, and most transient of
> passions, they are required to swear that they will remain
> in that excited, abnormal, and exhausting condition
> continuously until death do them part.
>
> —George Bernard Shaw

An underappreciated aspect of Shaw's comical remark, which he offered in the preface to his 1908 play *Getting Married*, is that, in the words of Stephanie Coontz, "for thousands of years the joke would have fallen flat." Because people didn't make marriage decisions based on romantic love, they wouldn't have understood what he was talking about. It's hard to imagine Thomas and Nancy Lincoln's contemporaries, a century earlier, finding much amusement here. And yet, more than a century hence, we still laugh—love's conquering of marriage took a long time, but its grip is tight.

Industrialization

Industrialization set the stage for love's triumph—ultimately producing the breadwinner-homemaker, love-based marriage immortalized in 1950s sitcoms—by radically altering America's economy and social structure. "Except in the rural South," observes the economist Robert Gordon, "daily life for every American changed beyond recognition between 1870 and 1940." Horses gave way to cars and trains, outhouses to bathrooms, candles to electric lights.

Starting in the mid-1800s, industrialization in America increasingly revolved around technological developments linked to railroads, steel, the internal-combustion engine, petroleum and chemicals, communication, and, eventually, electricity. Railroads crisscrossed the country, creating a national marketplace, providing a means of transferring raw materials and manufactured goods, and affording new opportunities for commercial farming. The availability of goods soared, and their cost plummeted. As the country became more interconnected, and as productivity outpaced population growth by a large margin, the threat that a local crop failure would cause starvation declined.

Industrialization produced a societal shift from traditional to secular-rational values. According to the political scientists Ronald Inglehart and Christian Welzel, *traditional values* revolve around religious faith and obedience to conventional sources of authority. In preindustrial societies, human survival depends on unpredictable natural forces like sunlight, rain, droughts, floods, and plagues. People have minimal understanding of science and technology, so they experience these forces as arbitrary and inscrutable. They attribute the forces to anthropomorphic gods, praying for rain or relief from insects. *Secular-rational values*, in contrast, revolve around rational science and technological progress. In industrial societies, production takes place in man-made environments like factories. People counter darkness by turning on the lights, coldness by turning on the heat, disease by turning to antibiotics. Fertilizer, irrigation, machinery, and insecticide make farmers (who increasingly work on industrial scales) much less vulnerable to natural forces. People increasingly treat God as expendable.

Industrialization also produced a massive urbanization of American society. As a surge in wage-labor jobs in American cities attracted rural Americans and Europeans, the percentage of Americans living in urban rather than rural settings—as defined in terms of population density—increased from 5 percent in 1830 to 40 percent by 1900, 60 percent by 1950, and 80 percent by 2000.

With industrialization and urbanization came a sharp decline in the average number of children born per woman, which meant that households became less populated. Spouses endured fewer tantrums and less diapering (and for fewer years), which afforded more opportunity for relaxed time together. As illustrated in the chart below, lifetime fertility for married women plunged 60 percent between the 1850s and World War II.

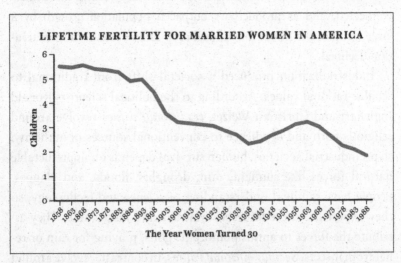

. There are several reasons for this reduction in family size, but perhaps the most important is that the intergenerational wealth flow reversed. On a pragmatic-era family farm, children made significant contributions to the household economy—serving as a courier, collecting eggs, churning butter, plowing, harvesting, and so forth. Even in the industrial era, before laws were passed to protect them from abusive work practices, many children continued to provide net economic value for the household by working in factories or mines. Eventually, however, the expenses linked to raising children exceeded the economic yield that children contributed to the household, sometimes by a large margin. As children became a source of economic burden, rather than economic benefit, parents had fewer of them.

Industrialization also altered family structure in a second way—it created an entirely new family arrangement, the *working-class family*, which emerged in the early 1800s and rose in prominence until the 1970s. If we adopt the sociologist Andrew Cherlin's definition of the working-class family—one in which a working-class married man between twenty and forty-nine years old lives with his wife and at least one child under age eighteen—almost 50 percent of American families fit into this category at its peak.

As noted by Cherlin, the working-class family was strongly gendered. Husbands were expected to work full-time, typically six days per week for ten to twelve hours per day (until labor laws curtailed such long hours). Jobs centered around three sectors: (1) manufacturing, like producing automobiles, meat products, and clothes; (2) transportation and utilities, like driving trucks, serving as railroad porters, and working on power lines; and (3) construction, like carpentry, masonry, and plumbing. Such jobs represented the medium-skilled center of the labor market, between low-skilled service jobs like restaurant and hotel workers and high-skilled professional, technical, and managerial jobs.

Working-class wives were expected to focus on the home, attending to the needs of their husband and children, managing the household budget, and performing housework in an era before washing machines, refrigerators, and dishwashers. Wives supplemented the household income by taking in boarders or doing piecework.

The working-class family, which gained prominence alongside the ideology of separate spheres, "separated the work worlds of husbands and wives." Farm households were gendered, too—husbands typically plowed the fields and wives typically tended to the vegetable garden, for example—but factory work required the husband to leave home, to *go* to work.

Working-class families also experienced time in a new way. In agricultural settings, time revolved around tasks—how long it took to plow a field or sew a shirt. People didn't think of these tasks primarily in terms of the hours or minutes they required, and they didn't plan around doing set tasks at certain times of the day. As the timing of sunrise and sunset changed across the year, so did the time when people started and completed the day's work tasks. Industrial labor, in contrast, was strictly time-regimented, especially as scientific management and assembly-line procedures split large, complex tasks into small, repetitive subtasks. Factory workers arrived at a set time in the morning, left at a set time in the evening, and took a lunch break at a set time in between. Families had to adapt their domestic routines to the factory schedule, which, for some, also demanded disruptive night shifts.

A third distinctive property of working-class families revolved around the source of the husband's familial authority. Traditionally, this authority came from landownership, which was stable and absolute. As the basis shifted from land to wage labor, which was neither stable nor absolute, it became shakier, threatening men's sense of masculinity.

The working-class family had a blend of similarities to and differences from the *middle-class family*, which emerged around the same time and which also deviated from traditional family structures. In middle-class families, as in working-class families, husbands worked outside the home and wives tended to the household. However, middle-class husbands worked white-collar jobs, serving as office managers, merchants, doctors, lawyers, and the like—jobs that were, on average, more intrinsically rewarding than factory work. They tended to earn enough money to afford a comfortable living, which meant that middle-class wives tended not to supplement the family income by taking in boarders or doing piecework.

The Love-Based Marriage

Industrialization served as midwife to the love-based marriage. As the nation became wealthier, Americans (especially those in the middle and upper classes) experienced a sharp decline in concerns about their physiological and safety needs. Fewer and fewer experienced the sorts of life-threatening hardships that were everyday realities for Thomas and Nancy Lincoln and their contemporaries, which allowed the prioritization of higher-altitude needs.

We often take the decline in life-threatening hardships for granted, but their influence on marriage remains strong today. In the absence of modern medicine, for example, my wife's first pregnancy likely would have killed her. She had a severe case of *hyperemesis gravidarum*, a pregnancy-linked condition characterized by extreme nausea and vomiting. In 1855, this condition killed Charlotte Brontë, the author of *Jane Eyre*, by rendering her incapable of tolerating food or water for months on end. Alison met a happier fate in 2009, although it required twenty-one emergency room visits for intravenous rehydration and medication, plus the eventual insertion of a PICC line to allow for additional infusions after the veins in her arms neared collapse. And all that treatment might have been for naught without a cesarean section because our daughter was in the sort of breech position that made childbirth lethal for so many women throughout history.

And yet, because of modern medicine, the needs Alison and I seek to fulfill through our marriage are, most of the time, far removed from those toward the bottom of Mount Maslow. Like most of our contemporaries, we generally don't experience survival as precarious. In Maslow's words, "The physiological needs, along with their partial goals, when chronically gratified cease to exist as active determinants or organizers of behavior." As industrialization led more Americans to experience chronic satisfaction of their lower-altitude needs, the love and belonging needs toward the middle of Mount Maslow rose in motivational priority.

As urbanization afforded young adults control over their conjugal decisions, allowing them to prioritize personal fulfillment, they increasingly married for love. As the social forces that had long served as the foundation for marriage—religious adherence, laws, traditions—lost influence, love-based considerations became more important, and pragmatic considerations less so. As the ability to coordinate daily activities became a less central predictor of marital and financial success, romantic compatibility superseded logistical compatibility. "By the middle of the nineteenth century," notes Stephanie Coontz, "there was near unanimity in the middle and upper classes throughout western Europe and North America that the love-based marriage, in which the wife stayed at home protected and supported by her husband, was a recipe for heaven on earth."

A Haven in a Heartless World

This emphasis on love and separate spheres caused Americans to view the nuclear family less in terms of a little monarchy and more in terms of "a haven in a heartless world" (in the historian Christopher Lasch's famous phrase). Industrialization had dismantled the agrarian and artisanal family structures of the pragmatic era, replacing them with a structure in which husbands and wives were physically separated for most waking hours, except on Sundays.

Working conditions were brutal. Many factory owners prioritized efficiency over worker safety, and serious injuries, including dismemberments, were distressingly common. Meanwhile, the increasingly piecemeal approach to production within factories made the work itself monotonous and unfulfilling. Agricultural life had a host of challenges, but it did involve the pursuit of coherent tasks like plowing, gardening, and harvesting. In contrast, and as hilariously illustrated in Charlie Chaplin's *Modern Times*, the factory worker might do little more than tighten a set of screws all day long, feeling disconnected from the final product.

In this context, the home took on new psychological significance. "Instead of being viewed as an integral component of the network of public institutions," observe Mintz and Kellogg, "the family was beginning to be seen as a private retreat. . . . It was a place for virtues and emotions threatened by the aggressive and competitive spirit of commerce, a place where women and children were secure and where men could escape from the stresses of business and recover their humanity. . . . The values of independence, self-reliance, and ambition were appropriate for the marketplace and government, but within the home, a wholly different set of values reigned supreme: love, mutuality, companionship, selflessness, sacrifice, and self-denial. No longer a microcosm of the larger society, the family was now a counterweight to acquisitive values and a refuge from materialistic corruptions." Masculine virtue began to focus less on honor, courage, and service and more on a parochial tendency to love and protect one's wife and children.

Passion and Sex

Meanwhile, as Americans increasingly saw love as a precondition for marriage, they also increasingly viewed it as an uncontrollable force. This view replaced the more traditional view in which spouses sought to cultivate warm affection over the course of the marriage. In the second half of the 1800s, more and more young people wanted to experience strong romantic passion for their partner before deciding to marry.

In the first few decades of the 1900s, the tight constraints imposed by Victorian-era morality began to loosen. Spouses increasingly acted on their romantic desires, and the quality of the sexual experience gained new prominence. Having shed the corsets of their grandparents' generation, women increasingly recognized that they, too, had sexual desires. Social commentators increasingly argued that high-quality sex was a requirement for a successful marriage. So, yes, spouses needed to cherish each other, but they also needed to pleasure each other. An undersexed marriage became unacceptable in the same way that a loveless marriage had become unacceptable a few decades earlier.

Separate Spheres: From Ideology to Reality

It was during this period that the doctrine of separate spheres transitioned from ideology to everyday reality. Even relative to inflation, wages surged across the socioeconomic spectrum, and a growing number of wives ceased to pursue economic production, devoting themselves almost entirely to child-rearing and homemaking. Such an arrangement, with the husband earning enough money that the wife could focus all her energy on the home, became a marker of social status. Even in working-class families that were barely scraping by, wives frequently stayed home, in part because women's wages were so low. These trends reinforced the separate-spheres views of men as independent, assertive, competitive, and unemotional and of women as dependent, docile, cooperative, and emotional.

This perspective was further bolstered by a strange perceptual trick in which wives' traditional tasks—cooking, making clothes, growing vegetables, and so forth—were no longer viewed as economic production. Whereas such tasks had long been vital to the family's economic survival, they were now viewed more as acts of caregiving and love. According to the historian John Gillis, wives became *homemakers* rather than *housekeepers*—a housekeeper performs taskwork that could be outsourced (by a hired maid, for example), but a homemaker serves as the moral and emotional center of family life. The homemaker's labor came to be viewed in symbolic rather than economic terms.

The New Deal

On October 29, 1929—after decades of robust economic growth—the U.S. stock market crashed. This event, called Black Tuesday, piggybacked onto a string of bad economic developments over the previous two months to silence the Roaring Twenties and trigger the Great Depression. Even with the financial and subprime mortgage crises of 2007–2009—and the prolonged hardship they spawned—fresh in our memory, it's almost impossible to comprehend the scale of human suffering wrought by the Great Depression. It was by far the most significant economic disturbance since industrialization changed economic production from a relatively straightforward family affair to an enormously complex international one. From 1929 to 1932, industrial production declined by 46 percent, foreign trade by 70 percent. Unemployment reached 25 percent.

Earlier economic downturns had been devastating, but the Great Depression was calamitous on an entirely different scale. The urban family couldn't fall back on a vegetable garden or drink milk from their goat, as those were trappings of an agricultural society that was rapidly disappearing. There were fewer opportunities to call on family ties, which industrialization had weakened in any case. Consequently, the line between subsistence and abject poverty was especially thin, the pace of descent into destitution especially rapid. As concerns with basic survival, including harrowing efforts to procure adequate food and shelter, reemerged as top priorities, the emphasis on love and sexual fulfillment in marriage waned.

More and more Americans, including political leaders, came to believe that massive intervention was required. President Franklin D. Roosevelt began implementing his New Deal initiatives upon his inauguration in 1933; the Social Security Act of 1935 was the most ambitious social welfare legislation the world had ever seen. The philosophy underlying such legislation was radical because it implied, for the first time, that the federal government was responsible for the welfare of individual families.

The Female Industrial Laborer

Shortly thereafter, as Europe geared up for, and consummated, war, the American economy shook off its prolonged slumber. Suddenly, there was enormous demand for manufactured goods, which America largely met. By mid-1943, America had achieved full employment. Wages surged. Virtually all segments of the population benefited, but the poor profited the most. Income inequality declined sharply.

The mass exodus of American men—some sixteen million of them—to the European and Pacific theaters following Japan's 1941 attack on Pearl Harbor combined with the huge demand for war matériel to produce new norms about the role of women in the workplace. Had women remained confined within their domestic havens, the country's workforce would have been insufficient to meet the Allies' wartime needs.

Rosie the Riveter, the fictional female industrial worker, became both a cultural icon and a rallying cry, a symbol of the role women needed to play to help their country triumph over its adversaries. Rosie's real-world compatriots labored in factories and shipyards to produce military and other industrial goods. They were lauded as patriots and reasonably compensated for their work—a stark contrast to a decade earlier, when working women had faced resentment for (in the perception of many) taking jobs away from men during the Great Depression. The number of women in the workforce grew by 60 percent between 1940 and 1945.

Rosie the Riveter

The war brought many hardships. Even setting aside the 115,000 American residents of Japanese descent (most of them U.S. citizens) who were forcibly relocated to detention camps, millions of American families lived without their sons, husbands, and fathers, many of whom never made it home. The government sharply rationed consumer goods, and there were major housing shortages as industrial centers drew even more workers than before. Prolonged spousal separations and a new sense of female independence increased soldiers' jealousy, and wives were concerned about their husbands' sexual behavior abroad. When spouses—many of whom had sprinted to the altar before the man went overseas—reunited after the war, they often found that they were no longer compatible. Divorces spiked in 1945 and 1946 (see chart on page 11).

The Apotheosis of the Love-Based Marriage

And then everything fell into place. The 1950s—actually the "long decade" from 1947 to the early 1960s—brought several long-term trends to their logical conclusions. Americans married for love and settled into a breadwinner-homemaker lifestyle. Ninety-five percent of Americans who came of age in the 1950s married. Half of women married by age twenty, to men who weren't much older, and they made babies early and often, producing the only period of sustained rising fertility rates in American history (see chart on page 48). The divorce rate, which had been rising (at a modest pace) for more than a century, flattened out.

Following the Great Depression and World War II—sixteen years of uninterrupted turmoil—traditional family values were ascendant. Seeking stability, men and women doubled down on the ideology of separate spheres, and many women became homemakers with gusto. Americans viewed the love-based, breadwinner-homemaker marriage model in "end of history" terms (to borrow an enduring phrase from the political scientist Francis Fukuyama). They were, at long last, living in accord with ideals that had migrated from the progressive fringe to the conservative mainstream over the previous two hundred years. There was broad consensus—oppressively broad at times—that their approach to marriage was ideal in both practical and moral terms.

The sociologist Talcott Parsons argued that the breadwinner-homemaker marriage was optimally suited to meet the demands of America's mobile, bureaucratic society. Americans in breadwinner-homemaker-children units found it relatively easy to switch residences as the husband secured new employment opportunities. Just as specialization in the economic domain increased productivity, specialization within the family, Parsons argued, helped to ensure that every household had sufficient income (provided by the husband) and sufficient nurturance (provided by the wife)—at least in principle.

Meanwhile, America's unrivaled stature in the postwar world dovetailed with an economic boom to increase both corporate profits and employee wages. Even many working-class families could afford to live in single-family homes, and they increasingly adopted the suburban lifestyle pioneered decades earlier by the middle class. When the United Auto Workers union negotiated with the management of the automobile companies on the major 1950 contract that *Fortune* magazine dubbed the "Treaty of Detroit," it procured remarkable concessions, including cost-of-living increases, generous pensions, and health benefits. Other industries followed suit, and the inflation-adjusted median salary earned by high school graduates almost doubled between 1950 and 1973.

Income inequality across different levels of education, which had declined during the Great Depression and World War II, remained modest in the postwar era, during which "a young man could graduate from high school and be confident of finding a steady job with decent wages and benefits." Large numbers of families were able to make ends meet on the back of a single wage earner, which allowed more women to carve up their little slice of heaven inside the home.

Of course, although many American women were enthusiastic about this dash to domesticity, the reality is that society offered them few alternatives. As servicemen returned from fighting in World War II, many women were happy to relinquish their jobs to returning servicemen, but many others were not. Regardless, women—particularly those with well-compensated, unionized jobs—"were ushered out of the labor force in droves."

Federal policy initiatives further bolstered the dominance of the separate-spheres doctrine. The Servicemen's Readjustment Act of 1944, known as the G.I. Bill, a monumentally successful piece of affirmative action legislation, helped to elevate millions of families to the middle class, but it also made women especially economically dependent on men. The bill offered veterans a range of benefits, including low-cost mortgages, cash payments for tuition and living expenses to attend university, low-interest loans to start a business, and, if needed, up to a year of unemployment compensation. Given that virtually all veterans were men, the only way women could share in this government largess was to marry a veteran. And, as of 1948, the law was updated so that married men could get a substantial tax break only if their wife earned little or no money. Given the conservative cultural zeitgeist and these sorts of policies, it is not surprising that most women sought fulfillment through domestic life, nor that 60 percent of women who enrolled in colleges or universities left without graduating—either to get married (the so-called *M.R.S. degree*) or out of fear that a college degree would hurt their marriage prospects.

The domestic life sought by married couples in the 1950s had a distinctive flavor that *McCall's*, the era's leading women's magazine, called "togetherness." Togetherness represented a "new and warmer way of life" in which women and men pursued fulfillment "not as women *alone* or men *alone*, isolated from one another, but as a *family* sharing a common experience." In a 1954 issue, *McCall's* illustrated this togetherness idea with an essay about Ed and Carol Richtscheidt of suburban New Jersey. Ed was a paper mill executive, and Carol was a full-time homemaker. The two of them "centered their lives almost completely around their children and their home," decorating the house together and eating nightly dinners as a nuclear family unit. As Betty Friedan noted in *The Feminine Mystique*, "family togetherness quickly became a national ideal, seized upon by advertisers, ministers, and newspaper editors."

Carol appreciates a hand with the dishes, as well as a chance to talk things over without interruption. She's proud of the color scheme Ed mapped out for the house, admits she never could have found such handsome draperies

Ed and Carol Richtscheidt

It is no accident that *McCall's* featured a couple that lived in the suburbs, which garnered their highest prestige during this period. From 1948 to 1958, as birth rates were soaring, 85 percent of America's thirteen million new homes were built in the suburbs, frequently in neighborhoods relatively far away from friends and extended family members. Governmental policy, including the cheap mortgages available through the G.I. Bill and the expansion of the nation's highway system, was a major factor in this suburban boom, as was the broad availability of cheap gasoline. But these factors would have been insufficient without huge growth in afford-able houses, which arrived when real estate developers like William J. Levitt adapted Henry Ford's production line system for house construction. Levitt began selling his eight-hundred-square-foot, four-room houses in 1949, and the demand, especially from newly-weds and parents of young children, was enormous.

During the 1950s, more and more houses contained amenities, including washing machines, dishwashers, and vacuum cleaners, that previously were either nonexistent or unaffordable for most Americans. By decade's end, most homes had a refrigerator, hot and cold running water, and a gas or electric stove. Almost two-thirds of American adults owned their own homes, three-quarters owned a car, and almost 90 percent owned a television.

It was during the 1950s that television, something almost nobody had seen in 1940, became the dominant form of entertainment in America. The programs that were popular during that era left a deep imprint on the nation's psyche, with some coming to define what we think of as "traditional marriage." Shows like *Leave It to Beaver*, *Father Knows Best*, and *The Adventures of Ozzie & Harriet* de-picted the lives of middle-class, breadwinner-homemaker families.

In a real sense, though, this family structure was the opposite of traditional—it was instead a highly atypical marriage model that endured for an eyeblink of historical time. Steven Mintz and Susan Kellogg refer to it as "the great exception." Stephanie Coontz re-minds us that "*Leave It to Beaver* was not a documentary."

Five Challenges of the Love-Based Marriage

Once Americans were living in accord with the marital ideals that had been sought for centuries, they settled into a state of relation-ship bliss that has lasted until the present day.

Okay, in reality, the opposite is true: The enormous success of the 1950s in fulfilling these ideals laid bare that the ideals were faulty from the start. Strong adherence to them left many spouses unfulfilled. In fairness, the love-based, breadwinner-homemaker marriage did crucial work in breaking down the most destructive elements of the pragmatic marriage ideal, elements like strict patriarchy and a lack of respect for individual autonomy. But it possessed a handful of inherent problems that hampered the pursuit of the highest levels of marital fulfillment.

Women's Economic Dependence

The most obvious issue is that women's forced economic dependence on their husband made it difficult to achieve a marriage between equals. Although Americans born after the 1960s often find this difficult to comprehend, women were legally prohibited from taking out loans or credit cards in their own name. If they worked outside the home, they were routinely (and legally) paid less money than men for the same work.

Women's economic dependence wasn't unique to the love-based marriage, of course. What was new about the love-based marriage was that this dependence existed in a relationship that was purported to be between equals—and that people widely viewed wives' daily activities as irrelevant to economic production. Their economic dependence made women more circumspect than men about marriage decisions, even while still prizing love, passion, and companionship. Women in the 1950s would have resonated with Jane Austen's observation from more than a century earlier: "Anything is to be preferred or endured rather than marrying without affection," but "single women have a dreadful propensity for being poor—which is one very strong argument in favor of Matrimony."

The Social Isolation of the Nuclear Family

As we've seen, industrialization weakened traditional social ties. City dwellers tended to be much less strongly bonded to their immediate neighbors, who were typically strangers or casual acquaintances, than they would have been, a generation earlier, when their neighbors were extended family members or other residents of their small community.

Suburbanization exacerbated this trend. One of the major reasons so many young families moved to the suburbs in the 1950s is that they wanted more space—a larger home, a front porch, a yard. But such desires are hard to slake over the long run; there's always a bigger house, a bigger porch, a bigger yard. Consequently, moving wasn't a one-time event in which people left the city and then settled into a suburban residence for the long haul. Instead, moving became a chronic feature of suburban life. As the postwar economy boomed, suburban population turnover was high, with families relocating as wages increased and as (many) husbands climbed the corporate ladder. This modern-day nomadism fostered a sense of rootlessness and isolation among many suburban residents. One adult relationship was constant: the marriage.

Mothers were especially vulnerable because they lacked daily social interaction with coworkers. Aggravating the problem, the only family car was typically with the husband, who used it to commute to work, imprisoning many women inside their white picket fences. Traditionally, women employed communal strategies to raise children, with mothers and grandmothers working together—and, crucially, socializing—to look after their collective gaggle of kids. Relatively speaking, child-rearing in the 1950s was isolated and isolating. The love-based marital ideal, and the image of home life that came with it, strengthened the spousal bond at the expense of women's broader social networks.

Lack of True Insight into One's Spouse

At the same time, the breadwinner-homemaker structure of the love-based marriage made it particularly difficult for a husband and a wife to have deep insight into each other's lives and experiences. Spouses' daily lives overlapped less than ever, a trend that made it challenging to achieve true intimacy. This separateness revealed an inherent contradiction of the love-based marriage: Two of its defining features—separate spheres and togetherness—are virtually incompatible. In retrospect, it seems bizarre that people sought to build an institution that separated husbands and wives more than ever before while simultaneously expecting them to serve as each other's primary source of intimacy and emotional support; spouses just didn't have enough insight into each other's daily triumphs and tribulations.

If developing such insight were simple, then it might have been reasonable for spouses to expect each other to bridge the chasm separating the two spheres. But even under the best of circumstances, understanding the contents of another person's heart and mind is challenging. The challenge gets larger when the most relevant content is saddled with the sorts of aspirations and insecurities that one might wish to hide from others out of a fear of failure or rejection.

To some degree, the difficulty of developing true insight into one's spouse is a second-generation problem, one located downstream from the problem of developing true insight into the self. People ranging from the ancient Greeks, who sought information from the Oracle at Delphi, to Neo (played by Keanu Reeves), who sought information from the Oracle in the Wachowski siblings' film *The Matrix*, have sought supernatural intervention to garner self-insight. More commonly, people learn about themselves through introspection. "Unfortunately, looking inward to attain self-knowledge is more difficult than it seems," observe the psychologists Katherine Hansen and Emily Pronin. "The lenses through which we look are far from objective, and they can distort, cloud, and color what we see."

Developing insight into one's spouse is, on balance, even more difficult. There are, of course, some ways in which other people know us better than we know ourselves. However, developing accurate insight into our partner's qualities can be challenging, not least because he or she might deliberately hide some qualities from us, especially shameful qualities or qualities that might upset us. Even when our partner discloses openly, we might still fail to develop accurate insight because we might feel threatened by his or her experiences, especially when those experiences reflect negatively on us or on the relationship. And even when our partner discloses openly *and* we interpret that disclosure without defensiveness, it's difficult for our partner to know how we perceive him or her, and vice versa. All these factors make it difficult to live up to the togetherness ideal of the loved-based marriage.

Stunted Psychological Development

The 1950s pinnacle of the love-based marriage also provoked subtler, more insidious problems. One such problem was *existential stultification*. In conjunction with suburban life and the corporate economy, the broad consensus about what sort of family life was optimal stifled individuality and authenticity. The cookie-cutter structure of suburban neighborhoods provides an apt metaphor for the conformity of 1950s suburban life.

The sociologist David Riesman explored these ideas in *The Lonely Crowd*, a book influential enough to catapult him to the cover of *Time* magazine in 1954. Riesman argued that midcentury Americans had lost their inner compass, seeking popularity rather than respect. This approval motive fostered materialistic tendencies in which Americans prioritized the consumption of prestigious goods

Aerial photograph of Levittown, New York

to impress others. These concerns had roots dating to the 1920s—as satirized in Sinclair Lewis's *Babbitt*, for example—but the 1950s raised them to a different level.

In this conformist and materialist climate, many men—even those who served as managers in major corporations—experienced alienation at work. The sociologist William Whyte reported in *The Organization Man* on a soul-crushing pressure to conform to corporate norms. As jobs shifted from small businesses to large corporations, the nature of work changed—competition intensified, stakes escalated, and the cost of mistakes rose. In *Revolutionary Road*, Richard Yates tells the story of Frank Wheeler, who tries to step off the corporate treadmill. The disastrous consequences of this decision suggest that turning away from conventional norms yields outcomes even bleaker than stoically enduring "the dullest job you could possibly imagine." In *The Man in the Gray Flannel Suit*, Sloan Wilson tells the story of Tom Rath, who also battles the oppressive, dehumanizing venalities of corporate life, albeit with somewhat more success than Frank Wheeler had.

As serious as these problems were, the existential psychological challenges of suburban life in the 1950s were perhaps even starker for women. Historically, "it was not unusual for wives to 'bring home the bacon,'" observes Stephanie Coontz, "or at least to raise and slaughter the pig, then take it to the market to sell." But the advancing economy and strong wages—not to mention the dominance of the separate-spheres ideology—meant that many 1950s wives could simply purchase goods like clothes and processed foods. But as homes got larger and contained more things, and as cleanliness standards rose, wives found themselves doing as much housework as in the past, despite the advent of domestic time-savers like washing machines, vacuum cleaners, and refrigerator-freezers.

The freedom from active pursuit of economic production had upsides for wives, but it also had a sinister quality that crept up on them unannounced. By 1960, CBS television had produced a documentary, *The Trapped Housewife*, *The New York Times* had reported that "many young women—certainly not all—whose education plunged them into a world of ideas feel stifled in their homes," and *Newsweek* asserted that housewives' discontent "is deep, pervasive, and impervious to superficial remedies which are offered at every hand." But it was Betty Friedan's *The Feminine Mystique* (1963), especially its evocative opening paragraph, that scorched these ideas into the public consciousness:

The problem lay buried, unspoken, for many years in the minds of American women. It was a strange stirring, a sense of dissatisfaction, a yearning that women suffered in the middle of the twentieth century in the United States. Each suburban wife struggled with it alone. As she made the beds, shopped for groceries, matched slipcover material, ate peanut butter sandwiches with her children, chauffeured Cub Scouts and Brownies, lay beside her husband at night—she was afraid to ask even of herself the silent question—"Is this all?"

Existential stultification wasn't the only insidious problem of the 1950s marriage. Another problem was *psychological atrophy*. The separate-spheres doctrine cleaved the human psyche in half, with women's assertiveness and men's nurturance shriveling through neglect. Today, it is clear that both assertiveness and nurturance are fundamental needs in both sexes—innate drives that require fulfillment if we are to achieve psychological growth and vitality, a feeling of personal integrity, and mental and physical health.

Through rigid socialization, boys in the 1950s were molded to be assertive but not nurturant—to become the sort of independent, stoic, self-assured, and unemotional man exemplified by the Marlboro Man. Girls were molded to be nurturant but not assertive—to become the sort of warm, cooperative, docile, and unaggressive woman exemplified by ads depicting the ideal housewife. Women were bombarded with the message that their value to society had little to do with their cerebral or economic contributions. *Life* magazine

Archetypes of the assertive man and the nurturing woman in the 1950s

opined in 1956 that women "have minds and should use them . . . so long as their primary interest is in the home."

If it were true that men and women are, at their essence, so profoundly different—from Mars and Venus, perhaps—then there's no reason why strict adherence to the doctrine of separate spheres would inflict psychological damage. As it turns out, though, both men and women are, psychologically speaking, from Earth.

Social scientists debate whether innate biological processes influence *the extent to which* men and women differ in tendencies toward assertiveness and nurturance; we'll make no effort to adjudicate that debate here. But there is a huge difference between asking whether men and women have biologically rooted differences in such qualities and asking whether any such differences are best measured on an interplanetary scale. The scholarly consensus today is that, at their essence, men, too, have strong nurturant needs and women, too, have strong assertiveness needs.

The idea that living in accord with only one of these major needs—only assertiveness or only nurturance—undermines well-being has received systematic scientific attention since the 1970s. The psychologist Sandra Bem conceptualizes assertiveness in terms of *psychological masculinity* and nurturance in terms of *psychological femininity*. We often think of masculinity and femininity as occupying opposite ends of a single dimension, but they are better conceptualized as two separate dimensions. Bem assesses psychological masculinity (assertiveness) with traits like "independent" and "forceful" and psychological femininity (nurturance) with traits like "affectionate" and "compassionate." She refers to people who are high on both dimensions as *psychologically androgynous*, and she presents evidence that such individuals, whether men or women, tend to be especially well adjusted. Regardless of gender, unmitigated forms of assertiveness or nurturance—possessing especially high scores on one dimension and especially low scores on the other—are problematic, with unmitigated assertiveness linked to destructive self-absorption and antisocial tendencies and unmitigated nurturance linked to destructive self-effacement and other-pleasing tendencies.

The Often-Insubordinate Sex Drive

A fifth challenge with the love-based marriage is that although the emphasis on sexual fulfillment can certainly align with the emphasis on emotional intimacy, these two experiences aren't always as compatible as they might seem. Indeed, the idea that the hottest sex happens when emotional intimacy is strongest is predicated on a valid but oversimplified understanding of sexual desire. The person who has done the most to challenge this oversimplified idea is the sex therapist Esther Perel. Perel's central insight, which she offers with some playful exaggeration, is that "most of us will get turned on at night by the very same things that we will demonstrate against during the day." In other words, although it's true that emotional intimacy and intimate communication are crucial ingredients in achieving long-term sexual fulfillment within marriage, it's also true that sexual desire is frequently insubordinate to our moral and sociopolitical preferences for kindness, egalitarianism, and respect.

To experience desire, Perel argues, we must "stop being the good citizen who is taking care of things and being responsible." Sustaining desire in marriage requires the reconciliation of our deep-seated craving for safety and security with our deep-seated craving for mystery and adventure. According to Perel, the former craving promotes the sort of intimacy that fosters emotional nourishment—the "anchoring, grounding experiences of our lives that we call 'home'"—whereas the latter promotes the sort of tantalizing excitement that fosters sexual desire. Perel associates love with the verb phrase *to have*, which represents quiet union or oneness; she associates desire with the verb phrase *to want*, which represents bridging a gap: "Fire needs air; desire needs space."

With this insight in mind, we can see why it's so hard to sustain sexual desire in long-term relationships. On one hand, feeling close to our spouse helps us become comfortable with the extreme physical intimacy that sex requires, and communicating openly about our sexual needs is essential for sexual fulfillment. On the other hand, it's tricky to reconcile the desire for predictability and familiarity with the desire for surprise and novelty—to reconcile the selfless caregiving that's appropriate when our spouse is emotionally vulnerable with the raw craving that's appropriate when our spouse wants to be ravished.

Ozzie, Harriet, and the Hidden Fault Lines

From our twenty-first-century vantage point, we can see that the long decade of the 1950s was an outlier—less "traditional marriage" than "the way we never were." Still, given how strongly marriages in that era fulfilled centuries-old ideals for a breadwinner-homemaker, love-based marriage, contemporary observers can be excused for believing that Americans had reached the end of family history.

In reality, cracks were already spreading across the veneer of the love-based marriage, revealing fault lines under the surface. Just as it pushed spouses into increasingly separate existences, it sought togetherness. Just as it elevated women's moral righteousness and piety as part of the cult of true womanhood, it sought sexual adventure. Just as it catered to our often-insubordinate sex drives, it sought the emotional closeness and vulnerability between spouses. Reconciling these paradoxes wasn't easy, especially given the conservative social and cultural forces at play.

Meanwhile, wives were increasingly entering the workforce, and the broad postwar economic expansion increased demand for workers enough that women began to make a living wage. Commercial advances like TV dinners made bachelor life more tenable. As a declining proportion of American marriages consisted of people who were raised during the Great Depression and then endured World War II, the yearning for stability and security lost some of its intensity, and people became less willing to endure an unfulfilling marriage.

Consequently, just as the love-based, breadwinner-homemaker marriage reached full strength, it shattered. A new system was about to emerge, and the transition yielded the most disruptive upheaval that the institution of marriage has ever seen.

4.

From Love to Self-Expression

> Well, maybe it's time to be clear about who *I* am.
> *I* am someone who is looking for love. Real love.
> Ridiculous, inconvenient, consuming, can't-live-without-
> each-other love.
>
> —Carrie to Aleksandr on *Sex and the City*

In 2004, HBO aired the final episode of *Sex and the City*. Carrie Bradshaw (Sarah Jessica Parker), the self-centered but appealing journalist, has moved to Paris to pursue a relationship with Aleksandr Petrovsky (Mikhail Baryshnikov), the brilliant but distant artist. Aleksandr, preoccupied by a major exhibition of his work, neglects Carrie, who increasingly pines for New York and her friends there. We, as viewers, aren't surprised when she leaves him, and we aren't surprised by the explanation she gives for breaking off their relationship. We cheer her on, especially because we know something she doesn't—that the love of her life, Mr. Big (Chris Noth), has conquered his emotional avoidance and wants to commit to her.

But few of us consider her breakup explanation in historical context. Ending a relationship due to insufficient love would have seemed absurd in the pragmatic era. This idea became increasingly palatable in the love-based era, but there's a self-expressive flavor to Carrie's version that dates it uniquely to the self-expressive era. She's disappointed because her love with Aleksandr is insufficient, but her larger concern is that the relationship fails to afford the expression of a central aspect of her identity—note the emphasis on *I* in "it's time to be clear about who *I* am." She's moving on because she wasn't experiencing a suite of authentic emotions she views as necessary for a successful relationship.

It's easy to criticize Carrie here, but it's also easy to see how her willingness to jettison a flawed relationship in pursuit of a more self-expressive one will increase her chances of achieving profound fulfillment. What her experience with Aleksandr illustrates is that developing such a relationship is extremely difficult if the partners don't prioritize each other. They must understand each other deeply, provide each other with sensitive support during difficult times, and help each other savor the good times. Ideally, they'll also have lots of hot sex.

Intellectual Roots

It wasn't inevitable that marriage would prioritize these particular qualities. These priorities emerged in part from an intellectual foundation that resides at the intersection of philosophy and psychology—one that emphasizes the nature of selfhood, especially the role of the self in helping people build meaningful lives in an era when religion plays a diminished role. As these ideas gained currency, Americans increasingly looked to their marriage not only for love, but also for a sense of authenticity and meaning. In doing so, they made marriage a more fragile institution, but they also placed within reach a whole new level of spousal connection.

Existentialism and the Self-Authentication of Meaning

We've seen that industrialization wrought wholesale changes to America's social fabric and to the everyday lives of individual Americans. In conjunction with the increased automation of work tasks, the replacement of task-time with clock-time—which induces a sense that the world is governed by chance rather than personal control—left many Americans feeling less like autonomous human beings than like components in a complex machine. As such dynamics permeated the Western Hemisphere, *existentialism*—a new philosophical-psychological movement—arose to make sense of them. In the words of the psychologist Rollo May, this movement, which focuses on the lived experience of each individual person, is "centrally concerned with rediscovering the living person amid the compartmentalization and dehumanization of modern culture."

As developed by philosophers like Søren Kierkegaard, Friedrich Nietzsche, and Martin Heidegger, existentialism begins with the assumption that life has no ultimate or objective purpose. Individuals, who are confused and terrified by the awareness of their own smallness in a vast galaxy that lacks coherence, are responsible for generating their own sense of identity and idiosyncratic value system to achieve a sense of meaning. According to Kierkegaard, they must try to answer questions like "Who am I? How did I come into the world? Why was I not consulted?"

Although few people adhere to a strict existentialist worldview, the idea that we must work to develop our own idiosyncratic meaning system became increasingly influential as Western civilization secularized. This trend was facilitated by a psychological (rather than philosophical) version of existentialism, which emerged in the 1920s and grew stronger following World War II. In this version, scholars like Otto Rank, Viktor Frankl, and Rollo May—not to mention philosophically oriented social activists like Jean-Paul Sartre and Simone de Beauvoir—emphasize that people who succeed in both developing their own value system and living in accord with it (that is, people who live *authentically*) can build lives that are deeply fulfilling, even if there is no objective truth undergirding their value system.

The most influential treatise on existential psychology is *Man's Search for Meaning*, which Frankl developed while enduring unspeakable horrors at Auschwitz. Building on Nietzsche's assertion that "he who has a *why* to live can bear almost any *how*," Frankl came to appreciate the immense psychological benefits of finding meaning in one's experiences, no matter how bleak those experiences may be.

"Lives may be experienced as meaningful," observes the psychologist Laura King, "when they are felt to have a significance beyond the trivial or momentary, to have purpose, or to have a coherence that transcends chaos." *Significance* refers to the belief that one's life has value and importance, *purpose* to having goals and direction in life, and *coherence* to a sense of predictability that allows one to make sense of one's own life. People who succeed in developing, and living in accord with, a significant, purposeful, and coherent meaning system are buffered against existential angst. They also tend to live long, healthy lives. And, as we'll soon see, people whose marriage succeeds in helping them achieve a meaningful life tend to experience a profound sense of fulfillment in the relationship.

Humanism and the Expression of Self

Starting in the 1930s, the psychologist Carl Rogers leveraged insights regarding the importance of building a meaningful life to develop *humanistic psychology*, which encompassed both a new theory of psychology and a new method of psychotherapy. Humanistic psychology functioned as a "third force" in psychology, one that repudiated the two dominant approaches of the era. The first of these was the psychodynamic approach developed by the psychiatrist Sigmund Freud, who argued that people's personalities are largely set by the age of five, and that, throughout their lives, they are driven by unconscious and socially unacceptable urges. The second was the behaviorist approach developed by the psychologists John B. Watson and B. F. Skinner, who argued that, by and large, people are like Pavlov's dogs, salivating in response to the bell that precedes the presentation of the meat powder, or like Skinner's pigeons, who learn to peck the metal disk to dispense the kibble. The psychodynamic and behaviorist approaches had little in common, but they converged in support of the view that people are largely buffeted about by psychological forces beyond their control and against the view that people are inherently oriented toward personal growth.

According to Rogers's humanistic perspective, in contrast, people are inherently good, and driven toward personal growth. If they enjoy a supportive social milieu, they will construct creative, productive, meaningful lives filled with love and purpose. They will discover, and live in accord with, their authentic self. This humanistic emphasis on living in accord with the authentic self received additional support in Abraham Maslow's hierarchy of needs, which peaks with the need for self-actualization.

These ideas have roots in existentialism. Nietzsche asks: "What does your conscience say?" And he answers: "You shall become who you are."

Doing so is no small feat. In Nietzsche's view, "one's own self is well hidden from one's own self; of all mines to treasure, one's own is the last to be dug up." Rogers argues that the pursuit of self-discovery and personal growth is not "a life for the faint-hearted. It involves the stretching and growing of becoming more and more of one's potentialities. It involves the courage to be. It means launching oneself fully into the stream of life." In the words of the poet E. E. Cummings: "To be nobody-but-yourself—in a world which is doing its best, night and day, to make you everybody else—means to fight the hardest battle which any human being can fight; and never stop fighting."

Shortly after Rogers and Maslow developed humanistic psychology, the ideas went viral. In 1946, the rabbi Joshua Liebman published *Peace of Mind*, which held the #1 spot on the *New York Times* bestseller list for more than a year. This book presented a new set of "commandments," including "Thou shalt not be afraid of thy hidden impulses" and "Thou shalt love thyself." Humanistic psychological ideas continued to gain prominence in the 1950s, but it was in the mid-1960s that they began to exert wholesale influence on American culture. They have remained a staple of self-help books, including in mega-sellers such as Wayne Dyer's *Your Erroneous Zones*, Scott Peck's *The Road Less Traveled*, and Rick Warren's *The Purpose Driven Life*. And, of course, there's always Oprah: "If you are strong enough and bold enough to follow your dreams [your authentic self], then you will be led in the path that is best for you."

One theme within humanistic psychology is that the successful pursuit of self-actualization, the pyramid's peak, depends on our relationships with significant others. Indeed, the existential psychologist Otto Rank, who inspired a young Carl Rogers, defines a *relationship* as a social connection in which "one individual is helping the other to develop and grow, without infringing too much on the other's personality." Increasingly, Americans view this definition as a crucial component of the marital relationship.

Postindustrialization

Existentialist and humanistic ideas became increasingly influential as Americans began transitioning to a postindustrial economy in the 1960s. Whereas preindustrial economies are built on extraction industries like farming and mining, and industrial economies are built on fabrication industries like manufacturing and construction, postindustrial economies are built on service industries. Economic value predominantly derives from the accumulation of knowledge and the ability to apply that knowledge in innovative ways. Larger proportions of the workforce deal with symbols, information, and people.

Organizations in the postindustrial economy are, in the words of the Nobel Prize–winning psychologist Daniel Kahneman, "factories for making decisions." Successful decision-making requires insightful analysis and sophisticated social skills—the ability to develop and implement good ideas in a complex social environment. Postindustrial jobs are especially likely to require that people think independently, apply or combine standard procedures in unique ways as the situation demands, exercise judgment, and occasionally generate radically new solutions.

The transition from an industrial to a postindustrial economy produces a shift from survival to self-expressive values, including an emphasis on individual autonomy and free choice. Postindustrialization is linked to education, access to information, and diversified human interactions, which makes people more capable of thinking for themselves and setting their own priorities. The political scientists Ronald Inglehart and Christian Welzel observe that the "cultural emphasis shifts from collective discipline to individual liberty, from group conformity to human diversity, and from state authority to individual autonomy."

The Rise of the Expressive Self

Taking the long view, we see that this emancipation from authority is linked to a broad redefinition of the nature of selfhood in the

West. According to the psychologist Roy Baumeister, during the late medieval and early Renaissance periods, the self was largely equated with one's role in society, which itself was largely determined by one's family lineage. Social hierarchies were considered perfectly appropriate, and social mobility was minimal. By and large, people sought fulfillment through traditional forms of Christian salvation.

The literary critic Stephen Greenblatt conveyed this idea in *The Swerve*, his Pulitzer Prize–winning book about the discoveries of the Florentine humanist Poggio Bracciolini in the early 1400s:

> The household, the kinship network, the guild, the corporation—these were the building blocks of personhood. Independence and self-reliance had no cultural purchase; indeed, they could scarcely be conceived, let alone prized. Identity came with a precise, well-understood place in a chain of command and obedience.
>
> To attempt to break the chain was folly. An impertinent gesture—a refusal to bow or kneel or uncover one's head to the appropriate person—could lead to one's nose being slit or one's neck broken. And what, after all, was the point? It was not as if there were any coherent alternatives, certainly not one articulated by the Church or the court or the town oligarchs. The best course was humbly to accept the identity to which destiny assigned you: the ploughman needed only to know how to plough, the weaver to weave, the monk to pray. It was possible, of course, to be better or worse at any of these things. . . . But to prize a person for some ineffable individuality or for many-sidedness or for intense curiosity was virtually unheard of.

The Puritans were among the first to find the nature of selfhood troubling. Because they subscribed to Calvinist doctrine of predestination, they were prone to wonder whether they manifested the inner worthiness of the elect. Given that Christian salvation versus damnation hung in the balance, the stakes were high, and Puritans were aware of the possibility that they, and others, might be biased. The self became something elusive, even unfathomable.

As the philosophical movement known as transcendentalism gained currency in the mid-1800s, Americans defined themselves in increasingly individualistic terms. This particular brand of individualism, known as *rugged individualism* or *utilitarian individualism*, was most famously articulated by Henry David Thoreau in *Walden*: "I went to the woods because I wished to live deliberately, to front only the essential facts of life, and see if I could not learn what it had to teach, and not, when I came to die, discover that I had not lived." As noted by the sociologist Andrew Cherlin, "Horace Greeley [the influential editor of the *New-York Tribune*] told young men to go west to find their fortunes, but no one told them to look inward to find their true selves."

That changed in the mid-1960s, when Americans began to prize a new brand of individualism, *expressive individualism*, that cherishes self-discovery and psychological growth. Expressive individualism is characterized by a strong belief in individual specialness; voyages of self-discovery are viewed as ennobling. "There is in you something that waits and listens for the sound of the genuine in yourself," the philosopher and theologian Howard Thurman declared in a 1980 commencement address capturing the essence of expressive self. "Nobody like you has ever been born, and no one like you will ever be born again—you are the only one. . . . If you cannot hear the sound of the genuine in your life, you will all of your life spend your days on the ends of strings that somebody else pulls." In this self-expressive climate, Americans have to make a broad range of self-defining life choices, including mating and career decisions, without strong defaults.

In their Commentary on our *Psychological Inquiry* Target

Article, the psychologists Roy Baumeister and Michael MacKenzie argue that the self has become a fundamental *value base*, an entity "that is itself accepted as an inherently positive good on its [own], without reference to other, even more fundamental values." Religious people typically view God's will as a value base; they don't feel compelled to ask why it's important to prioritize God's will. As Western societies have secularized, "the self has taken on ever more luster as a powerful value base." The pursuit of self-expression has become a moral good in and of itself.

"The moral thread of self-actualisation is one of *authenticity* . . . based on 'being true to oneself,'" argues the sociologist Anthony Giddens. "Personal growth depends on conquering emotional blocks and tensions that prevent us from understanding ourselves as we really are. . . . The morality of authenticity skirts any universal moral criteria." The moral righteousness of achieving authenticity has powerful implications for marriage. "Not long ago," observes the sociologist Eric Klinenberg, "someone who was dissatisfied with his or her spouse and wanted a divorce had to justify that decision. Today it's the opposite: If you're not fulfilled by your marriage, you have to justify staying in it, because of the tremendous cultural pressure to be good to one's self."

The Self-Expressive Marriage

In contrast to the transition, circa 1850, from the pragmatic to the love-based marriage, during which the new ideals *replaced* many of the ideals from the pragmatic era, the transition, circa 1965, to the self-expressive marriage *added* new ideals on top of those from the love-based era. We continue to view our marriage as a central locus of love and passion, and we continue to view our home as a haven in a heartless world, but, for more and more of us, a marriage that achieves those things without also promoting self-expression is insufficient.

The rise of the self-expressive marriage has overhauled our views about the optimal ways for spouses to interact. Consider changes in the advice offered in women's magazines. According to the communications researcher Virginia Kidd, "putting aside of self was defined as loving behavior" during the long decade of the 1950s, "and conversely thinking of self first was unloving and displayed lack of genuine concern for others." Starting in the mid-1960s, the emphasis shifted to the development of one's authentic self and bringing spontaneity to the marriage. In one study, researchers coded advice in women's magazines from 1900 to 1979 for the presence of *traditional themes* like "love means self-sacrifice and compromise" and *self-expressive themes* like "love means self-expression and individuality." As illustrated in the chart below, this period witnessed a strong long-term trend toward self-expression, an effect that would have been even stronger if not for the brief self-expressive surge during the Roaring Twenties. Whereas 20 to 30 percent of the relevant articles expressed self-expressive themes in the 1930s and 1940s, nearly 70 percent did in the 1970s.

In a 2014 study, when American college students were asked to define what the term *mate value* means to them, they recognized

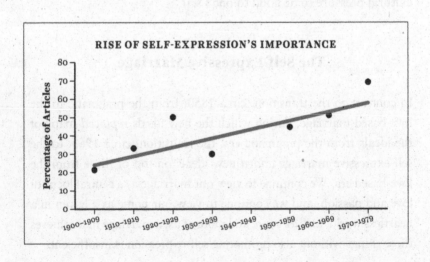

RISE OF SELF-EXPRESSION'S IMPORTANCE

the standard domains like compatibility, commitment, and physical attractiveness, but they also emphasized the importance of having a partner who brings out the best in them. In the words of one student, "I really feel like someone of 'mate value' would be someone who helps me become the best person I can be, the best version of myself." This student's definition, which mimics the definition of the Michelangelo effect, strikes to the heart of the self-expressive era: All of us have many possible selves, but most of them are inferior variations of our authentic or best self; we are looking for a spouse who elicits that version of ourselves.

The Grand Gender Convergence

We saw in chapter 3 that both men and women have assertive ("masculine") and nurturant ("feminine") sides to their personalities—and, consequently, that the separate-spheres doctrine stunted both men's and women's psychological development. To a large extent, the self-expressive era has vanquished both the doctrine and the practice of separate spheres, a process that the economist Claudia Goldin calls the *grand gender convergence.*

America has not, of course, become a place where men and women behave or are treated identically. Major gender-based inequities remain in important domains like income, employment opportunities, housework, and parenting. But the two sexes have much more similar roles, opportunities, and life experiences today than in previous eras. "Of the many advances in society and the economy in the last century," argues Goldin, "the converging roles of men and women are among the grandest. A narrowing has occurred between men and women in labor force participation, paid hours of work, hours of work at home, life-time labor force experience, occupations, college majors, and education." Today, the landscape of paid work, housework, and child care in America is far more shared than ever before. By and large, today's men and women inhabit a single sphere.

The second-wave feminist movement, which launched in the 1960s as a reaction against women's increased domesticity during the "long decade" of the 1950s, hastened the grand gender convergence. This movement sought to address a broad range of issues, including those surrounding family life, the workplace, and de facto inequalities. Among its many legacies are the trend for women to work full-time and have careers (a huge effect) and the trend for men to play active roles in domestic and parenting tasks (a smaller effect, at least thus far).

A second factor facilitating the convergence of gender roles was the emergence of the postindustrial economy. As work depended less on physical strength and more on cognitive and social skills, labor force participation became less masculine. Women today earn about half of professional degrees and PhDs and about 60 percent of undergraduate and master's degrees. The major industries exhibiting job growth are female-dominated—from 1980 to 2002, for example, the middle-class job that grew the most was registered nurse, whereas the one that shrunk the most was machine operator.

These cultural and economic forces have been especially influential in driving married women into the workforce. Whereas a constant 70 percent of *unmarried* women aged twenty-five to twenty-nine have engaged in wage labor from 1920 until today, the percentage of *married* women engaging in wage labor surged from 24 to 62 percent from 1960 to 1990 alone. In general, as illustrated in the chart on the next page, the economic structure of American couples has been radically overhauled over time. The "corporate family," which consists of family farms, artisanships, and the like, was dominant in 1800, but it was no more common than female-breadwinner families by 2000. The male-breadwinner family became increasingly dominant from 1800 to 1950, but the dual-earner family had supplanted it by 2000.

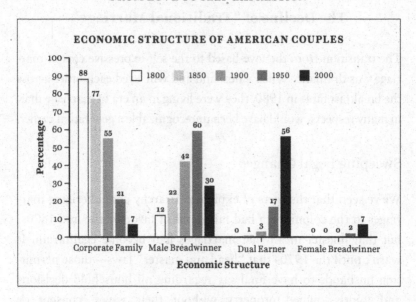

Feminism and postindustrialization also changed societal norms about what makes for a successful marriage. Consider how Americans answered this question in 1977 and 2011: "What kind of marriage do you think is the more satisfying way of life—one where the husband provides for the family and the wife takes care of the house and children [traditional marriage], or one where the husband and wife both have jobs, both do housework, and both take care of the children [egalitarian marriage]?" Both men and women were nearly equally split in terms of their preference for the two types of marriage in 1977, but, by 2011, 72 percent of men and 80 percent of women viewed egalitarian marriages as providing the more satisfying of the two ways of life. And they're correct: In the twenty-first century, marriages characterized by greater gender equality—greater parity in earning, housework, and parenting—are more satisfying, more sexually fulfilling, and at lower risk of divorce.

The Decline of "Traditional Marriage"

The transition from the love-based to the self-expressive eras of marriage was dramatic. When a husband and wife eyed each other across the breakfast table in 1980, they were living in an era of marriage that, in many respects, would have been unrecognizable a generation earlier.

Sweeping Legal Changes

We've seen that the sorts of explicit patriarchy characterizing marriages in the colonial era had fallen out of favor by the mid-1800s, but that doesn't mean that marriages had become egalitarian. It wasn't until the 1970s that "head and master" laws—those permitting husbands to have final say regarding all household decisions and jointly owned property without their wives' consent or knowledge—were fully expunged. Legal structures allowing husbands to force their wives into nonconsensual sex were struck down between the 1970s and the 1990s. Until that time, American law largely aligned with the Renaissance-era English common law that a husband can't be guilty of rape because the wife "hath given up herself in this kind to her husband, which she cannot retract."

No-fault divorce laws swept the nation, both as a response and a contributor to the doubling of the divorce rate, to 50 percent, by 1980. Previously, divorce was illegal unless one spouse could prove *fault* with the other—adultery, cruelty, desertion, and the like. No-fault divorce laws employed new legal terms, like *irreconcilable differences*, that allowed couples to divorce if they simply no longer wanted to be married, even in the absence of fault. The first no-fault divorce statute was signed into law in 1969 by, of all people, the California governor Ronald Reagan. Today, in almost all states, mutual consent is not required for a no-fault divorce; having either spouse plead irreconcilable differences is sufficient.

Even as it became easier to dissolve a marriage, it also became easier to initiate one. Contemporary readers may be surprised to learn that interracial marriage was illegal in many states as recently as 1967, when the U.S. Supreme Court's decision in the aptly named case *Loving v. Virginia*. When Richard Loving, of European descent, traveled to Washington, D.C., in 1958 to marry Mildred Jeter, of African and Native American descent, they violated Virginia's Racial Integrity Act of 1924 and were sentenced to a year in prison. The court eventually found in their favor.

Richard and Mildred Loving

The most vivid illustration of the declining barriers to entry is the tidal wave of approval of same-sex marriage that swept the nation between 2011 and 2015—with most of the action taking place between 2013 and 2015. When Massachusetts became the first state to legalize same-sex marriage in 2003, most of the country disapproved, and the backlash was fierce. In the ensuing years, thirty states—including, in 2008, the liberal bastion of California—passed constitutional amendments outlawing such marriages. Yet by the time the U.S. Supreme Court ruled in 2015 that the constitutional right to marry extends to same-sex couples, the majority of Americans approved of same-sex marriage, which had rapidly become legal in almost three-quarters of the states.

An Institution in Flux

In recent decades, marriage has become decreasingly characterized by obligation and strict rules and increasingly characterized by flexibility and personal choice. Even as divorce rates remain high, marriage rates have declined. Although the proportion of American women married at least once by their early forties remains high, the chart below reveals it has, for the first time in recorded history, dipped below 90 percent in the new millennium, and current trends suggest that it might continue to decline. This decline is driven primarily by people with less education.

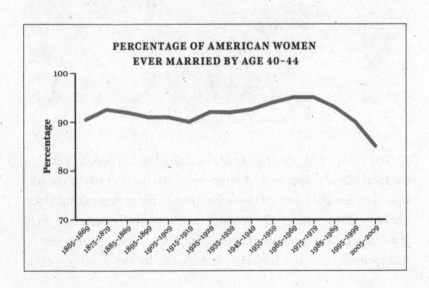

Americans who marry are doing so at older ages. As illustrated in the chart below, Americans married at historically young ages—twenty-two for men and twenty for women on average—in the 1950s, but the age at first marriage has risen sharply since then. By 2013, these average ages had increased to twenty-nine and twenty-eight, respectively.

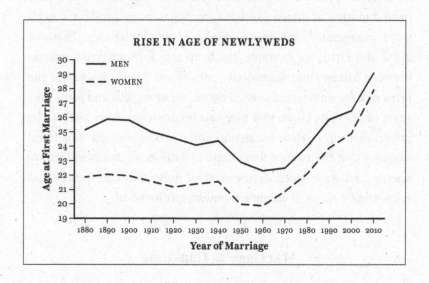

Meanwhile, nonmarital cohabitation rates have skyrocketed. The percentage of American women aged thirty-five to forty-four who had ever cohabited almost doubled (from 33 to 63 percent) from 1988 to 2008. One reason why more Americans are living with partners out of wedlock is that they are delaying marriage, but that's far from the whole story. A second factor is that social sanctions against "living in sin" have subsided. This change is mirrored by enormous increases in approval of premarital sex. For example, among late adolescents during the second half of the 1900s, approval increased from 40 percent to 79 percent among males and from 12 percent to 73 percent among females.

Approval of premarital sex—perhaps more accurately conceptualized as sex between unmarried partners—is one factor contributing to a prolonged surge from the 1960s to the 2000s in the percentage of American babies born to unwed mothers (about 40 percent in the early twenty-first century). But another influential, and underappreciated, factor is the reality that marriage simply isn't an essential precondition for having a baby. The stereotype of the unwed mother as a teenager who got pregnant by accident was always exaggerated, but more so today than previously. Between 2002 and 2012, for example, the birth rate for unmarried women between fifteen and twenty-four years of age dropped, whereas the birth rate for unmarried women between twenty-five and forty-four years of age rose. Given that pregnancies are much more likely to be intentional rather than accidental among older women, this trend suggests that the twenty-first century, with its advances in fertility science and its reduced disapproval of nontraditional lifestyles, is witnessing a surge in voluntary unwed-motherhood.

Marriage as Capstone

Even as Americans retreat from marriage, they maintain high levels of respect for the institution, especially by comparison to western Europeans. Indeed, some of the retreat actually reflects great respect for the institution—people don't want to marry unless they can build a relationship worthy of the label. The percentage of Americans who think it should become more difficult to get divorced increased from 50 to 60 percent from 1974 to 2000, while the percentage who think it should become easier decreased from 30 to 20 percent.

Getting married has shifted from an event signifying that one is entering adulthood to an event signifying that one has achieved all of the hallmarks of adulthood. Growing swaths of the populace view marriage as something that should come after one has already established economic independence, learned from several serious relationships, and experienced a prolonged cohabitation with one's potential spouse. As noted by the journalist Catherine Rampell, "it turns out that a few more life stages need to be spliced into the nursery rhyme 'first comes love, then comes marriage.'"

In short, although it's true that many Americans lost respect for more traditional conceptualizations of marriage, it's not true that they lost respect for the institution more generally. Indeed, although it's too soon to examine long-term divorce trends among the recently married, the chart below offers reason for optimism. Whereas the eight-year divorce rate (the percentage of people divorced by their eighth wedding anniversary) jumped from 13 percent for marriages in the 1960s to over 18 percent for marriages in the 1970s and 1980s, it has declined since then—down to 15 percent for marriages in the 2000s. Proportionally, the eight-year divorce rate was about 20 percent higher in the 1970s and 1980s than it was in the 2000s.

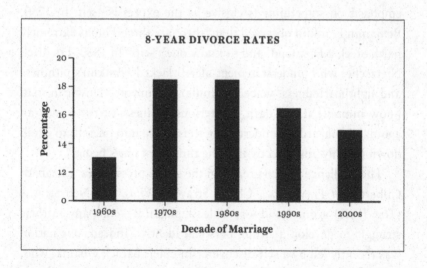

One complexity is that declining divorce rates, and other metrics of marital success, are consolidated at the top of the socioeconomic spectrum. Among Americans with at least a college degree, divorce rates have plunged and marital quality is on the rise. Among those without a high school degree, divorce rates have continued rising, and marital quality (even among the declining percentage who marry at all) is on the decline. We'll delve into the links between social class and marriage in chapter 7.

Five Challenges of the Self-Expressive Marriage

The self-expressive era has mitigated many of the problems of the love-based marriage era. But even as it has done so, it has created a handful of new challenges that make achieving marital fulfillment difficult.

The Elusive Self

A towering challenge of the self-expressive marriage derives from its emphasis on something as elusive as the expressive self. In 1750, Benjamin Franklin observed that "there are three Things extremely hard, Steel, a Diamond, and to know one's self." In 1883, Friedrich Nietzsche, who (understatement alert!) lacked Franklin's pithiness and lightheartedness, voiced a similar sentiment: "How can man know himself? It is a dark, mysterious business. . . . It is also an agonizing, hazardous undertaking thus to dig into oneself, to climb down toughly and directly into the tunnels of one's being."

The challenge is even greater in the self-expressive era. Elizabeth Gilbert (*Eat Pray Love*), Cheryl Strayed (*Wild*), and Neil Strauss (*The Truth*) are in good—or at least plentiful—company in their struggle to develop a strong personal identity. Indeed, our nation was recently led by a self-discoverer-in-chief: Barack Obama, who, in *Dreams from My Father*, provides a travelogue of his arduous voyage of identity formation.

The psychologist Dan McAdams argues it is during young adult-hood that we start working to generate a coherent sense of identity.

Building on concepts from the psychologist William James, McAdams argues that this process, which is essential for building an "adult life with broad purpose and a dynamic sense of temporal continuity," involves the effort to "burnish and synthesize episodic information about the self into a coherent and integrative life story." It consists of generating a coherent identity that articulates "how the self came to be and where it may be headed in the future."

But not everybody succeeds in generating a coherent identity, and not everybody who generates one experiences it as authentic. Very few of us can craft a coherent, meaningful, and authentic identity without considerable effort to engage deeply with our life experiences—to make sense of where we've been, where we're going, and why. And the challenge is even greater than it initially seems because the self changes over time. Because we're not the same person in our forties or our sixties as we were in our twenties, we can't simply perform a grueling self-discovery process in early adulthood and then call it quits.

Of course, our primary emphasis here is on pursuing self-discovery and personal growth *through marriage*. It can be even harder to develop insight into, and promote the personal growth of, our spouse. Relative to the needs lower down Maslow's hierarchy, needs higher up are less tangible and more idiosyncratic; in particular, self-actualization needs "vary greatly from person to person."

As such, our spouse's ability to provide effective support requires precisely tailored actions oriented toward our unique needs and circumstances. Generic forms of support—the cookie-cutter behaviors recommended by self-help books—are unlikely to do the job. Giving us a hug and expressing love will be the ideal form of support in some situations, but exactly the wrong form in others. The same is true of encouragement and practical advice. Our spouse must understand our psychological constitution, recognize the opportunities and pitfalls dictated by the circumstances we're confronting right now, accurately assess his or her support skills and domain-relevant expertise, take account of the current emotional tenor in the marriage, and so forth.

And the skills and proclivities that are helpful when our spouse tries to help us today may be poorly suited to our needs in the future. As we're first launching an ambitious career, for example, we might benefit from assertive, tough-love treatment to push us to excel, but once we've achieved success, we might benefit from laid-back, fun-loving treatment to help us savor our accomplishments. Given the till-death-do-us-part ethos of marriage, those two quite distinct types of treatment must come from the same person.

The same issue can emerge when the change comes from within the marriage. A marriage that successfully facilitates its spouses' personal growth changes the marriage itself, ultimately altering the spouses' ways of relating to each other. In most situations, such changes benefit the marriage, or at least don't harm it. But some changes reduce the spouses' compatibility, perhaps even bringing about the demise of the marriage.

The journalist Robin Rinaldi illustrates this point in an essay for the 2016 feminist anthology *The Bitch Is Back*. As an anxious young woman, she met a man who "offered the calm, stable presence I'd never known in childhood, a counterbalance to my own recurrent panic attacks and my general sense of the world as too big and threatening." Rinaldi continues: "I'd emerge from a good cry feeling I had taken him in, his clothes wet with my tears. . . . It functioned so well that we married." It also functioned so well that his ability to soothe her became irrelevant: "Sometime around age thirty-nine, I started to feel much less afraid." As the fear dissipated, the threads that bound them together began to fray, and he wasn't able to meet her new desires and expectations, including those for a relationship characterized by unbridled passion and kinky sex: "I was growing, but my marriage wasn't. Destruction was the first step to re-creation." In this case, destruction took the form of divorce.

The take-home message is as simple to state as it is hard to implement: To achieve optimal communication in the self-expressive era, and to support each other effectively, we need to develop deep insight into our own and our spouse's psychological experiences—needs, goals, anxieties, frustrations—and to harmonize our behaviors with them. To achieve long-term stability and success, we must remain compatible over time, even as we grow and change.

The Porcupine's Dilemma

The level of mutual insight and interdependence such support requires can be scary. Spouses must navigate the *porcupine's dilemma*—the desire to achieve deep intimacy while remaining invulnerable to pain. This term comes from the philosopher Arthur Schopenhauer's famous parable:

> On a cold winter day, a group of porcupines huddled together closely to save themselves by their mutual warmth from freezing. But soon they felt the mutual quills and drew apart. Whenever the need for warmth brought them closer together again, this second evil was repeated, so that they were tossed back and forth between these two kinds of suffering until they discovered a moderate distance that proved tolerable. . . . To be sure, this only permits imperfect satisfaction of the need for mutual warmth, but it also keeps one from feeling the prick of the quills.

The psychiatrist Sigmund Freud introduced this porcupine idea to psychologists in the 1920s, and a number of twenty-first-century psychologists have investigated it in the context of intimate relationships. These researchers are interested not only in how people achieve a safe, middle-ground solution that leaves both needs (for intimacy and security) partially satisfied, but also in how people can achieve deep intimacy while maintaining a strong sense of security. We want to be truly, deeply known without any concern about rejection or abandonment. We share the desire of the philosopher Howard Thurman: "I want to feel completely vulnerable, completely naked, completely exposed, and absolutely secure."

Navigating this terrain is especially challenging for spouses who are prone to emotional insecurity. Researchers assess such proneness with measures of low self-esteem, high rejection sensitivity, or high attachment anxiety, which tap the extent to which people feel unworthy of love. Such feelings are painful in their own right, but, as demonstrated in an extensive program of research by the psychologists Sandra Murray and John Holmes, they're doubly cruel because they undermine precisely the sorts of emotional intimacy that could otherwise help make people feel worthy of love.

Because they fear rejection, such individuals tend to prioritize self-protection over relationship enhancement. They underestimate how much their partner loves them, which makes them wary of being vulnerable in the relationship—wary of feeling as if they need their partner or as if their partner has the power to hurt them. They are skeptical of genuine compliments and tend to lash out in response to minor or ambiguous transgressions. They also tend to view their partner less favorably and, ultimately, to evaluate the relationship as less fulfilling. Not surprisingly, their partners start to evaluate the relationship less positively over time. Through these self-fulfilling dynamics, fear of rejection places individuals at elevated risk for being rejected, which in turn reinforces the view that they aren't worthy of love.

There's a second type of emotional insecurity relevant to the porcupine's dilemma, this one focused less on fear of rejection than on discomfort with intimacy. People characterized by such tendencies, which are captured by the term *attachment avoidance*, tend to withdraw from others when under distress. They are distant—sometimes brandishing their quills as a signal that others should keep away—precisely in those circumstances when intimacy would otherwise be the most helpful, such as in the immediate aftermath of an injury or a public failure.

I'm not proud to admit that I had considerable leanings toward emotional avoidance in my earliest dating relationships, and that these leanings haven't entirely dissipated. Alison certainly didn't ask for a husband with avoidant tendencies, and she's had to adapt. She's securely attached, so her natural impulse when someone she loves is hurting is to approach and nurture. Over the years, she's learned to do the opposite with me—to give me space and let me heal myself. These days, if I double over in pain because I've slammed my fingers in a door or am unusually quiet following a setback at work, she hangs back. In our early years together, my independence under duress hurt her feelings, but she's learned that my withdrawal has nothing to do with her. One metric of how much she understands and loves me is her willingness to let me recover on my own in those situations, at least for the first stage of the recovery.

Her ability to do so has also made me less avoidant over time. Her willingness to give me space when I need it has made me less protective of my independence. And it looks as if I'm not alone. Research I conducted with the psychologist Ximena Arriaga and others reveals that the ability to trust our spouse—to have faith that he or she will treat us, when we're vulnerable, in a way that's sensitive to our needs—predicts a reduction in avoidant tendencies over time.

The Struggle for Balance

Even when we work through our insecurities to develop deep mutual understanding and resolve the porcupine's dilemma, building a successful marriage also requires that we navigate major logistical hurdles. Americans today struggle to build and sustain a balanced life—one characterized by fulfillment in both professional and personal domains—and the arrival of children makes this struggle even more difficult. At a cultural level, we see consternation about whether it's possible to "have it all" and robust debate about whether individuals, especially women, must make significant sacrifices in one domain to achieve fulfillment in the other. This debate became heated in the 2012 kerfuffle between the Facebook chief operating officer Sheryl Sandberg and the Princeton dean Anne-Marie Slaughter. Sandberg argued that women can achieve full success in both domains only if they "lean in" at work, whereas Slaughter argued that Sandberg's advice can work only for women who are "superhuman, rich, or self-employed."

Proponents on both sides agree that having a supportive and competent spouse is crucial. They argue that it's difficult to have a fully successful career and a fully successful personal life—especially one that includes children—if one is romantically unattached or attached to an unsupportive or incompetent partner. But the existence of a supportive and competent spouse is not sufficient—the two spouses must achieve strong coordination across a complex and extensive range of tasks.

Marital communication and coordination have always been important, of course. Husbands and wives had to reach an understanding about who would perform which tasks, and they had to follow through on that understanding. But doing so was simpler when gender roles were clearly defined. There wasn't much discussion of who would feed the baby or patch the hole in the roof.

Gender-based defaults within marriage are much weaker today. Couples must figure out—sometimes on a daily or hourly basis—the role each spouse will play regarding paid employment, child-rearing, cooking, and other household chores. Rather than adhering to traditional gender roles or making long-term decisions early in the marriage and settling into a routine, the relative lack of role differentiation in today's marriages means that spouses must engage in extensive and frequent communication and coordination.

Much of the communication and coordination in today's marriages comes in the form of negotiation, with spouses seeking courses of action that benefit both of them. Ideally, these courses of action also take account of their other responsibilities and aspirations, including those surrounding children, other people, and professional tasks. All this communicating, coordinating, and negotiating can take a toll on the marriage above and beyond the issues that triggered those processes in the first place. Indeed, marital problems often result from difficulties with those processes rather than from the underlying issues themselves. Americans had traditionally blamed marital problems on the emotional immaturity of one or both of the spouses, but, during the self-expressive era, we increasingly blame such problems on poor communication.

A critical period for communicating, coordinating, and negotiating surrounds the transition to parenthood. Between the cooing and the cuteness, the first baby tends to nestle into its parents' daily schedules like a grenade. The baby's arrival requires a major restructuring of responsibilities, and—with the exception of activities like breastfeeding—today's parents have neither the burden nor the luxury of strong defaults. Which one of us wakes up when the diaper leaks at 2 A.M.? If the source of the leaky diaper is the older of two young children, do both of us get up—perhaps with one soothing the child and the other changing the sheets—to minimize the likelihood that the screaming awakens the baby?

Even if we communicate, coordinate, and negotiate the parental transition effectively—and even setting aside the exhaustion and the irrationality of life with a newborn—babies just gobble up a massive amount of time. According to a 2015 estimate, mothers and fathers in dual-income households spent an average of 33.5 hours parenting the newborn. If you're married without children, it might be difficult to understand how much the arrival of the first baby changes things. Where would the two of you find an additional 33.5 hours per week?

Even today, the time investment is disproportionately borne by the mother (in heterosexual couples), with 21 of the hours coming from her versus 12.5 from the father. Much of the work comes in the form of little, almost invisible tasks that collectively serve as a significant drain on time and cognitive resources. The journalist Judith Shulevitz recalls coming home from the hospital with her first baby and breaking down, terrified by the prospect of ensuring that he'd have enough socks. "New parenthood," Shulevitz observes, "does things to your brain. But I was on to something, in my deranged, postpartum way. I should state for the record that my husband is perfectly handy with socks. Still, the parent more obsessed with the children's hosiery is the one who'll make sure it's in stock. And the shouldering of that one task can cascade into responsibility for the whole assembly line of childhood. She who buys the bootees will surely buy the bottle washer, just as she'll probably find the babysitter and pencil in the class trips. I don't mean to say that she'll be the one to do everything, just that she'll make sure that most everything gets done."

The Inexorable Rise in Demands for Sexual Fulfillment

Meanwhile, the Summer of Love and the Age of Aquarius shredded many of the restraints on sexual expression, both inside and outside of marriage. Americans increasingly viewed sexual fulfillment less as a *perquisite* than as a *prerequisite* of a good marriage. Infrequent or unsatisfying sex was increasingly viewed as an indication that one's marriage is flawed, perhaps even rotten.

The journalist Rachel Hills drives home the novelty and distinctiveness of this emphasis: "Sex is no longer just something we are told not to do, or else risk being judged as dirty and depraved. It is also something we must do, or else be declared pathetic, prudish and undesirable. It's not that the old orthodoxies have disappeared completely: We still live in a world that is rife with slut shaming and homophobia. But these standards are now accompanied by a new, more insidious set of ideals and aspirations around sexual frequency, performance and identity. . . . Sex is a measure of the health of your relationship—an unbiased barometer of how much you desire your partner and how much he or she still desires you."

This unbiased barometer point is crucial. "The reason such physiological reactions [a partner's genital arousal] are emotionally so . . . erotic is that they signal a kind of approval that lies utterly beyond rational manipulation," observes the philosopher Alain de Botton (albeit with some exaggeration). "Erections and lubrication simply cannot be effected by willpower and are therefore particularly true and honest indices of interest."

But there are two sides to this equation. That these genital responses are so hard to fake does indeed make them especially satisfying, but it also makes them . . . well, hard to fake. We might find ourselves begging our body to respond when our spouse starts to seduce us—rifling through the hottest thoughts in the naughtiest recesses of our brain—but it betrays us. There are instances in which, no matter how much we love our spouse and no matter how much we see our lack of arousal hurting him or her, we simply can't make our genitals respond as we want them to.

In the self-expressive era, when we believe that frequent and mutually orgasmic sex is an essential component of a healthy marriage, difficulties becoming physiologically aroused at the right moments accrue great significance. More than ever before, spouses view such difficulties as evidence of profound incompatibility. If the problem persists, it can become sufficient, on its own, to justify a divorce; the prospect of a lifetime devoid of sexual passion and fulfillment is sometimes viewed as too steep a price for maintaining the marriage.

Men's (Continued) Stunted Psychological Development

We've seen that one of the great achievements of the self-expressive era is the increase in psychological androgyny. But the reality is that the grand gender convergence has not been entirely symmetrical.

Women's adoption of assertive qualities has been stronger than men's adoption of nurturant qualities, a gender difference that is especially large among the less educated.

"The list of working-class jobs predicted to grow is heavy on nurturing professions," observes the journalist Hanna Rosin in *The End of Men*. "Theoretically, there is no reason men should not be qualified. But they have proved remarkably unable to adapt. Over the course of the past century, feminism has pushed women to do things once considered against their nature—first enter the workforce as singles, then continue to work while married, then work even with small children at home. Many professions have gone the way of the pharmacist, starting out as the province of men and now filled mostly with women. Yet I'm not aware of any that have gone the opposite way. Nursing schools have tried hard to recruit men in the past few years, with minimal success. Teaching schools, eager to recruit male role models, are having a similarly hard time."

As Rosin intuited, men's relatively slow embrace of nurturant qualities—and, consequently, their struggle to adapt to an economy increasingly oriented toward the caring professions—has many causes, but a major one derives from long-standing definitions of masculinity. Relative to femininity, which typically doesn't require social validation, masculinity is more fragile; it requires repeated demonstration and social proof. Research by the psychologists Jennifer Bosson and Joseph Vandello randomly assigned men to perform a masculinity-threatening task (publicly braiding hair) or a nonthreatening task (publicly braiding rope for structural reinforcement), and then offered them an opportunity to reassert their masculinity. Relative to men in the nonthreatening condition, men in the masculinity-threatening condition were more likely to choose to perform a punching bag task than a brainteaser task. They also punched with greater force, presumably because such behavior helped them reestablish their sense of masculinity. Fragile masculinity of this sort seems to be a major reason why men have been reluctant to enter female-dominated fields like nursing and elementary school teaching.

New Opportunities and the Ascent of Marriage

These challenges of the self-expressive era—the elusiveness of the expressive self, the porcupine's dilemma, the struggle for balance, the increasing demands for sexual fulfillment, and men's sustained stunted psychological development—have made it more difficult than in the past to sustain a happy marriage. As the standards rise for our marriage to help us fulfill our deepest social and psychological needs, more marriages are falling short. And yet, the self-expressive era affords new opportunities that can offer a profound and powerful sense of connection.

Richness of the Inner Life

Maslow conceptualizes the drive to self-actualize in terms of "the desire to become more and more what one is, to become everything that one is capable of becoming." The specific manifestation of self-actualizing needs varies markedly from one person to the next: "In one individual it may take the form of the desire to be an ideal mother, in another it may be expressed athletically, and in still another it may be expressed in painting pictures or in inventions."

Maslow is correct that making progress toward self-actualization yields "profound happiness, serenity, and richness of the inner life," but he underappreciates how essential significant others are in facilitating this process, how relationship partners can sculpt each other toward their authentic selves. As our intimate social networks have winnowed—as we look to our marriage to help us work toward a larger proportion of our self-expressive goals—our spouse plays an even larger role in the success versus failure of our self-actualization efforts. As such, our ability to achieve profound happiness, serenity, and richness of the inner life depends, more than ever before, on the quality of our marriage, and a high-quality marriage today is uniquely fulfilling.

The Fully Functioning Couple

As the grand gender convergence increased women's assertiveness and (to a lesser extent) men's nurturance, it ushered in an era in which more marriages consist of two well-rounded partners. Psychologically androgynous individuals have high emotional intelligence, and they're especially effective at adjusting their behavior to address the demands of a particular situation. They are good relationship partners.

Beyond these benefits of androgyny, the greater mutual insight spouses can achieve as a result of the grand gender convergence affords additional opportunities for them to connect. In the 1950s, it was much easier for spouses to experience compassion for each other than to truly understand what the partner was experiencing. If a wife had never endured the stress of supporting a family solely on her own income, how much insight could she have regarding her husband's shame about being passed over for a promotion as household debts pile up? If a husband had never endured the exhaustion of waking up in the night to soothe a colicky newborn, how much insight could he have regarding his wife's despair at being awakened ten minutes after a feeding following seventy consecutive nights of disjointed sleep?

Today's husbands and wives are not only more psychologically androgynous (both assertive and nurturant), but also much more psychologically similar to each other. Consequently, they have become much more capable of achieving deep mutual understanding, which in turn increases the likelihood that they navigate conflict constructively.

Putting Humpty Dumpty Back Together Again

It took centuries for the love-based, breadwinner-homemaker ideal to become the dominant model of marriage in America. It took only fifteen years to shatter that ideal. The countercultural revolution of the late 1960s and 1970s destroyed it without providing a clear alternative. The institution of marriage appeared to be confronting an existential threat.

Recently, however, a new stability has started to emerge, especially among the college educated: Divorce rates have stabilized or declined, and many of us have settled into a new type of marriage. These new marriages are not easy, but when they work well, they promote spouses' self-discovery and personal growth like never before.

Back on HBO, Carrie's decision to break up with Aleksandr to pursue "ridiculous, inconvenient, consuming, can't-live-without-each-other love" seems prescient when Mr. Big comes to Paris to search for her. As the last episode in the television series concludes, the once-and-future lovers run into each other in the hotel lobby and rekindle their flame. After a romantic walk through the streets of Paris and a flight home, Carrie has found the sort of love she seeks. Four years later, in the *Sex and the City* film, they tie the knot.

Part Three

The All-or-Nothing Marriage

5.

Personal Fulfillment and Marital Commitment: The Détente

TO HELEN
a person in her own right—giving, loving, stalwart;
my companion in our separate but intertwined pathways
of growth;
an enricher of my life;
the woman I love;
and—fortunately for me—
my wife

—Carl Rogers

This is how Carl Rogers, the founder of humanistic psychology, dedicated his book *Becoming Partners* (1972). Much of the content of this dedication is relevant to earlier eras of marriage ("giving, loving, stalwart"; "the woman I love"), but one feature plants it squarely in the self-expressive era: "my companion in our separate but intertwined pathways of growth." Later in his book, when reflecting on what has made their marriage so successful, Rogers underscores this point: "I suppose the most profound statement I could make about our marriage—and I can't explain it adequately—is that each of us has always been willing and eager for the other to *grow*. We have *grown* as individuals and in the process we have grown together."

This humanistic emphasis on personal growth is what infuses the self-expressive marriage with so much power. But it also brings peril. The importance of *the self* has grown in the last half century, and not all variations of this growth are marriage-promoting. Rogers emphasizes that his marriage succeeded in part because he and Helen facilitated each other's voyages of self-discovery and personal growth. But what happens to those of us who adopt a different variation of the emphasis on selfhood—those who focus on self-esteem and pleasure rather than self-expression and meaning? This question has greater relevance today than ever before, but its seeds were planted in the 1700s.

Centuries of Chicken Little

As soon as the idea emerged that a primary function of marriage is to promote the spouses' personal fulfillment (through love, for example), social commentators asserted, sometimes with the melodramatic flair of Chicken Little, that this idea would destroy the institution of marriage. According to the historian Stephanie Coontz, "the history of the love-based marriage from the late eighteenth to the mid-twentieth century is one of successive crises, as people surged past the barriers that prevented them from achieving marital fulfillment and then pulled back, or were pushed back, when the institution of marriage seemed to be in jeopardy."

In the late 1700s, when the ideal of the love-based marriage began gaining currency, Americans worried that it would unleash a pernicious strain of selfishness. If people had the freedom to choose a marriage that they believed would yield personal fulfillment, why would they stay in the marriage if it proved insufficiently fulfilling? In the early 1900s, when urbanization, the automobile, and liberal values began to unleash female sexuality and blur the boundaries separating male and female spheres, Americans worried that these developments were existential threats to the institution of marriage. How could a marriage oriented toward the personal fulfillment of its spouses—love and sexual fulfillment rather than survival and community—withstand the inevitable ravages of time?

The ethicist Felix Adler asserted that "the idea of comradeship is obnoxious and antagonistic to the idea of marriage. . . . Comradeship depends on free choice and free choice can be annulled. . . . You cannot make [happiness] the highest end, without coming to the intolerable position that marriage ceases when happiness ceases." The journalist Anna Rogers opined that "the rock upon which most of the flower-bedecked marriage barges go to pieces is the latter-day cult of individualism; the worship of the brazen calf of Self." Even President Teddy Roosevelt chimed in, expressing alarm at the notion that insufficient love could "excuse the breakup of a home."

These comments speak to a broader anxiety that liberalizing marital norms would undermine the institution in a profound and irreversible manner. There was some validity to these concerns: Divorce rates were rising and traditional norms were weakening. But, by and large, the concerns proved to be more histrionic than prescient— there was no decimation or radical overhaul of the institution of marriage. Despite the change in the central functions of marriage, the institution remained strong.

Partly for this reason, Americans in the 1950s achieved reasonably broad consensus that marriage was doing just fine. The breadwinner-homemaker structure seemed well suited to the postwar economy's employment demands, and Americans seemed to have found a groove in which they married for love but still managed to build stable households.

And Then, Suddenly, the Sky Fell

In retrospect, it looks as if wish fulfillment might have blinded thoughtful observers. Americans had yearned for the love-based, breadwinner-homemaker marriage for generations, so the idea that it might have been poorly designed from the start didn't seem to compute. In addition, people seemed unaware of the ways in which transient economic, military, and cultural forces had converged to produce the 1950s ascendance of this model of marriage. Even as people gained confidence in the current model of marriage, disaster loomed.

A new emphasis on personal rights and liberties trounced the long-standing emphasis on respect for tradition and marital commitment, and a cultural reorientation altered the nature of sexual and family relations. Marriage was demoted from its perch as the defining event of early adulthood and became an increasingly optional life choice. Rather than ordering from "the standard life course menu, as people used to do," notes the demographer Anton Kuijsten, an individual now "composes his or her history *à la carte*." Marriage, "the obligatory entrée" during the 1950s, increasingly became "the optional dessert."

The norms and cultural discourse surrounding marriage changed radically. In 1972, Nena and George O'Neill published *Open Marriage*, which popularized the idea that some couples might benefit from allowing each other to engage in extramarital affairs as part of a respectful, honest relationship. Terms like *swinging* and *wife-swapping* entered the mainstream cultural lexicon.

The emphasis on personal fulfillment in marriage, which had been building for centuries, collided with cultural and economic circumstances to crack the foundation of American marriage. Since the 1700s, alarmed observers had feared what would happen to marriages predicated on personal fulfillment when the fulfillment fizzled. In the 1960s and 1970s, they finally got the answer they'd long anticipated: Marriages failed *en masse*. The sociologist Amitai Etzioni observed in 1977 that if current divorce trends continued, there would be no intact families in America by the 1990s.

Happiness versus Meaning

Now is a good time for a sobriety check: We're well past the 1990s, and we can find plenty of intact families without resorting to carbon dating. Indeed, many millions of Americans are happily married. What happened? Did we pull back from the dream of achieving personal fulfillment through our marriages?

I think not. The more likely explanation is that many Americans in the self-expressive era have adopted a deeper approach to "personal fulfillment" than the one the Chicken Littles had anticipated. The adoption of this new approach, which focuses less on happiness than on meaning, removes much of the adversarial relationship between personal fulfillment and marital commitment.

Philosophical and psychological investigations into happiness and meaning have produced a scholarly literature cluttered with subtle distinctions and contradictory definitions. For present purposes, we'll define *happiness* (or "hedonic well-being") as a psychological state characterized by a high ratio of pleasure to pain—of positive to negative emotional experiences. We'll define *meaning* (or "eudaimonic well-being") as a psychological state characterized by the belief that one's life affords personal growth and self-expression—ample opportunity to discover one's unique strengths and dedicate oneself to excelling at them. Building on ideas from Aristotle's *Nicomachean Ethics*, the psychologist Carol Ryff suggests that a meaningful life results from "the striving for perfection that represents the realization of one's true potential."

Happiness and meaning are linked—people who tend to experience high levels of happiness also tend to experience high levels of meaning. But the two constructs are distinct, and scholars have investigated the correlates of each. In one study, the psychologist Roy Baumeister sought to identify the unique predictors of happiness and meaning.* Research participants indicated their level of agreement with statements designed to measure happiness (e.g., "In general I consider myself happy") and meaning (e.g., "In general I consider my life to be meaningful"). Participants who felt that their lives were easy or pleasurable tended to experience greater happiness, but not more meaning. In contrast, participants who tended to think a lot about the future, or who exhibited strong tendencies to be "a giver," tended to experience greater meaning, but they were actually less happy. A similar pattern emerged for participants who endured high stress levels and a large number of negative life events. In short, whereas the happy life is characterized by ease and pleasure, the meaningful life is characterized by generosity, deep engagement with difficult pursuits, and a coherent sense of how the self develops across time.

The composer Stephen Sondheim captures the essence of meaningful engagement: "I love inventing. The hard part is the execution, obviously. But even that's fun. . . . When I say 'fun,' of course, I'm talking about agonizing fun—I'm not talking about pleasant fun."

Happiness, Meaning, and Marriage

The distinction between happiness and meaning adds clarity to the idea that the pursuit of personal fulfillment through marriage is incompatible with the pursuit of marital commitment. The issue isn't that the incompatibility idea is wrong, but that it's underspecified. The idea is largely correct if personal fulfillment is defined as

---

* This research used a procedure akin to a multiple regression analysis, in which the overlap between happiness and meaning was statistically removed to examine the associations of other variables with both (1) the part of happiness that doesn't overlap with meaning and (2) the part of meaning that doesn't overlap with happiness.

happiness—as a high pleasure-to-pain ratio. Virtually all marriages go through extended periods during which that ratio is low, or where a different relationship seems to offer a more favorable ratio, which places them at risk for divorce if perpetual happiness is required. But the idea is largely incorrect if personal fulfillment is defined as meaning—as a high purpose-to-insignificance ratio, or a process of striving for excellence in domains that are linked to one's authentic self. For many Americans, building a successful, long-lasting marriage is a central means through which we pursue self-expression and a meaningful life.

Throughout this book, we've considered the link between selfhood and marriage in terms of meaning and self-expression. But America also affords the opportunity to pursue happiness and self-esteem through marriage, and its residents have substantial latitude in determining how much we prioritize each approach. To simplify the discussion, we can talk about two variations of "self-based" marriage: a happiness-based model and a meaning-based model. This table distills their essential characteristics.

HAPPINESS-BASED MODEL	MEANING-BASED MODEL
Emphasis on pleasure	Emphasis on meaning
Pursuit of self-esteem	Pursuit of self-expression
Belief that sustaining a happy marriage shouldn't require extensive endurance or forbearance	Belief that sustaining a happy marriage can require extensive endurance or forbearance
Marital and personal fulfillment tend to be incompatible in the long run	Marital and personal fulfillment tend to be compatible in the long run

In the happiness-based model, individuals look to their marriage to promote their hedonic well-being (a high pleasure-to-pain ratio) and to feel good about themselves (high self-esteem). They believe that sustaining a happy marriage shouldn't require extensive endurance or forbearance. Consequently, when spouses undergo periods when their marriage is challenging or painful, divorce feels like a reasonable choice.

In the meaning-based model, in contrast, individuals look to their marriage to promote their eudaimonic well-being (their successful pursuit of meaning by excelling in self-relevant domains) and their personal growth (high self-expression). They believe that sustaining a fulfilling marriage requires extensive endurance or forbearance, just as almost anything meaningful does. Consequently, when spouses undergo difficult periods in the marriage, they perceive opportunities for personal and relationship growth as a consequence of working through the challenges.

The Self-Expressive Marriage's Evil Twin

In their Commentary on our *Psychological Inquiry* Target Article, the psychologists Michelle vanDellen and Keith Campbell argue that the happiness-based model is both prevalent and harmful. By analogy, they discuss two hiking trails that visitors can take to garner a view of North Carolina's beautiful Linville Falls. The Plunge Basin Trail "is challenging but manageable. At the end of the trail, hikers can scramble onto giant boulders mere feet from the falls, ending up with not only a spectacular view but a total sensory experience of the falls." The Upper Falls Overlook is an easier hike that affords a pretty view of the falls from a distance.

In this "tale of two hikes," vanDellen and Campbell argue that the Plunge Basin Trail is like the meaning-based marriage—difficult and a bit hazardous, but highly immersive and fulfilling. The Upper Falls Overlook Trail is like the happiness-based marriage—easy and pleasant, but less immersive and not especially fulfilling. Van-Dellen and Campbell argue that many Americans are choosing the marital analogue of the Upper Falls Overlook Trail instead of the Plunge Basin Trail, and that doing so places their marriage at elevated risk for distress and divorce.

Indeed, America has long taken its pursuit of happiness seriously, especially as the nation became wealthier in the 1900s. In the postwar period, consumerist tendencies surged. The psychoanalyst Martha Wolfenstein argued in 1951 that a new, *fun morality* had emerged, frequently at the expense of a more traditional *goodness morality*: "Instead of feeling guilty for having too much fun, one is inclined to feel ashamed if one does not have enough." Hedonism was king.

The picture below reproduces the cover of a 1959 issue of *The Saturday Evening Post*, illustrating one influential interpretation of the American dream. As noted by the historian Lendol Calder,

when the young lovers in this image look to the sky, they don't see the heavens. They see a cornucopia of consumer goods, along with children happily playing baseball and practicing piano. The magazine tells its readers: "Soon the Good Life will be yours, along with all of the good things of your dreams." Calder identifies a paradox here, with the message being that "the American dream is both fabulously expensive *and* generally affordable." This paradox, which was precariously resolved through a vast new apparatus surrounding consumer credit, simply sidesteps questions surrounding meaning and purpose as psychological states that might be at odds with the surging consumerist ethos.

In the 1960s, a surge in something more psychologically nourishing—the pursuit of a meaningful life—began to complement the empty calories of consumerism. This pursuit is much less visible than its gauche, consumerist cousin, but it's not rare. "There is widespread fear," note the political scientists Ronald Inglehart and Christian Welzel, "that self-expression values are inherently egocentric and tend to destroy the community bonds that democracies need in order to flourish." But, on average, postindustrialization promotes *humanistic* values more than hedonic or egocentric values. Self-expressive values promote a new moral authority in which human autonomy is sacrosanct. "It is not true that everything is tolerated today, in a spirit of postmodern relativism. In fact, many things that were tolerated in earlier times are no longer considered acceptable today, particularly if they violate humanistic norms." Consider, for example, how norms and laws opposing discrimination against racial and sexual minorities have advanced since the 1960s. We see a story not of hedonism run amok, but of a fierce struggle to provide all people with ample opportunity to pursue their own self-expression.

In short, Americans have access to two self-based cultural models of marriage. We've argued that today's self-expressive marriages can be the best marriages ever. But vanDellen and Campbell are right that there's also a happiness-based model, which functions as the self-expressive model's evil twin. At this point, no data exist to tell us what proportions of Americans are pursuing a meaning-based versus a happiness-based marriage—or the extent to which

Americans are prioritizing one over the other. But it seems likely that both models are widespread.

The New Equilibrium

Perhaps the distinction between the meaning-based and the happiness-based model of marriage can help explain not only why the institution of marriage almost shattered in the 1960s and 1970s, but also why it then largely recovered. My tentative hypothesis is that the happiness-based model was more dominant in the early part of the self-expressive era, but that the meaning-based model has since surpassed it.

The marital structure of the 1950s crumbled before a new structure had emerged, which produced a period of familial chaos. According to the sociologists Gøsta Esping-Andersen and Francesco Billari, "a once-stable family equilibrium gave way to a prolonged period of uncertainty and normative confusion as to what constitutes proper gender roles and identities in family life."

The long-simmering battle of the sexes boiled over, and much of the tension pertained to how people should behave in their marriage. Feminist scholars offered compelling arguments that marriage, as it existed at the time, was unfair to women, and activists employed diverse tactics in pursuit of gender equality, including stoking wives' righteous indignation about inequities in their marriage. Husbands, for their part, were caught off guard and often resisted changes to an arrangement that suited them. In many marriages, the personal became the political, and mundane conflicts over housework and child-rearing were infused with cultural significance.

As the political upheaval started dissipating in the later 1970s—in part due to the significant (albeit incomplete) successes of the feminist movement, as manifested in the grand gender convergence—daily marital interaction became less political, releasing some of the pressure. A new, less politically fraught equilibrium began to emerge.

While writing *The End of Men*, Hanna Rosin got to know a young married couple in Pittsburgh: Sarah, a successful lawyer, and Steven, a stay-at-home dad pursuing his education in the evenings. One late afternoon, Rosin was at their house, interviewing Steven, when Sarah—seven and a half months pregnant—came home, attended to their toddler, and prepared dinner while Rosin and Steven chatted in the kitchen. Rosin's reflections are both personal and fascinating:

> Spending a few days with Steven and Sarah made me realize something about my own marriage. My hunch when I got engaged was correct: Over the years my husband and I have in fact split domestic life pretty equally. We both work, we both cook, we both take care of the children. Because of this I assumed that I had shed most of my attachment to traditional gender roles. But now I realized that I am much more deliberate and reactive than I thought. I would never not work, because that decision is loaded with feminist betrayal. I would never let my husband sit back and drink a beer while I was busy in the kitchen. . . . What I realized in Pittsburgh was that even our intimate relationships unfold in a cultural moment, and my moment was still not far enough removed from old feminist rage to divest these tiny domestic decisions of that kind of meaning. . . . Steven and Sarah make decisions on a much cleaner slate. They behave almost like corporate partners at a work retreat, taking stock of trends and proceeding from there.

As the slate gets cleaner, it's easier for spouses to adopt a more instrumental approach to their everyday interactions. Indeed, some evidence suggests that spouses have begun to handle household stressors more constructively as the self-expressive era has matured. For example, having stepchildren living in the home was linked to significantly higher rates of conflict in 1980, but not in 2000. To the extent that Rosin's analysis is correct—and I suspect there's a lot of truth in it—the cleaner slate should help free up emotional and psychological resources for more self-expressive endeavors.

When the Going Gets Tough

We can imagine a mild and a severe variation of the Chicken Littles' concern about the dangers of seeking personal fulfillment through marriage. In the mild variation, people who have worked doggedly, for many years, to turn their marriage into something acceptable eventually give up. In the severe variation, people expect easy fulfillment, and they bolt when the first difficulties arrive.

I don't think we need to be particularly concerned about the mild variation; divorce is probably a reasonable corrective to deeply incompatible matches. But the severe variation, if true, would be alarming; it would pose an existential threat to the institution of marriage.

The idea that people skedaddle when they encounter difficulties lends itself to empirical test, and thousands of studies have investigated how Americans navigate difficulties in their relationship. My mentor Caryl Rusbult, of Michelangelo-effect fame, provides a context for this research: "Sometimes involvement with a close partner is simple. When partners' goals correspond and their preferences are compatible, . . . it is relatively easy for partners to gratify one another's most important needs. The real test of a relationship arises when circumstances are not so congenial—when partners encounter dilemmas involving conflicted interaction, incompatible preferences, extrarelationship temptation, or experience of betrayal. In dilemmas of this sort, the well-being of each person is incompatible with the well-being of the relationship and something must give."

The major conclusion from this body of work is that people generally work hard to sustain their relationship. In collaboration with many students, including me, Rusbult has shown that people regularly engage in a range of *relationship-maintenance mechanisms*. To the extent that they are committed to the relationship, they make sacrifices, forgive their partner's transgressions, and perceive alternative partners as less desirable than they really are. Even individuals who are dispositionally prone to desire sexual activities without an emotional connection tend to resist the temptation to pursue such activities outside the relationship if they're highly committed to it.

Several lines of research suggest that at least some of these effects result from a relationship-promoting form of self-delusion. Consider a study in which Rusbult informed participants, all of whom were involved in an established romantic relationship, that she was developing a new dating service, and she wanted them to evaluate how satisfied they would be if they were to be set up with one of the people in her dating pool—an "alternative partner." By tweaking the photographs and biographical information, she randomly assigned participants to view either a desirable or an undesirable alternative partner. She theorized that participants would not find the undesirable alternative partner especially appealing, and, consequently, that they would not find the idea of meeting him or her threatening to their relationship. In contrast, participants would find the desirable alternative partner attractive and, consequently, they would find the idea of meeting him or her to be relationship-threatening, which might require them to act like the see-no-evil monkey.

The results supported Rusbult's hypotheses. Commitment to the current relationship was largely irrelevant for participants who were slated to meet the undesirable alternative partner, but it strongly predicted the evaluations of participants who were slated to meet the desirable alternative partner. Participants who were not especially committed to their relationship recognized how attractive the desirable alternative partner was, acknowledging that they'd likely be quite happy in a relationship with him or her. Highly committed participants, in contrast, convinced themselves that they wouldn't be any happier with the desirable than the undesirable alternative partner, despite the fact that the profiles were deliberately rigged to be quite different in objective appeal.

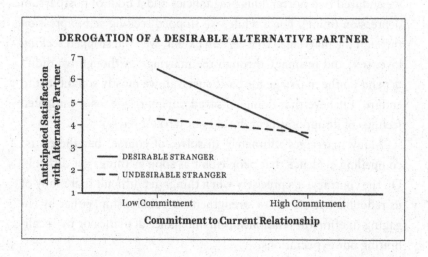

Such results, which have been replicated many times, suggest that people who are highly committed to their relationship exhibit self-delusions that serve to reinforce that commitment. It's hard to reconcile such findings with the view that we tend to cut and run at the first opportunity to bolster our pleasure elsewhere. On the contrary, we tend to perceive our relationship and the world in a way that biases us toward sustaining commitment over time.

Research on social support casts additional doubt on the idea that we tend to approach our relationship with a demanding, service-my-needs mentality. It's true that we want our spouse to meet our needs, but it's also true that we want to meet his or her needs. We're often happy to endure costs in our relationship if doing so benefits our spouse, and some evidence suggests that providing support is even more strongly linked to feeling good than receiving support is.

But perhaps our most powerful strategy for navigating difficult circumstances in our marriage is the ability to descend to a lower altitude on Mount Maslow. As we'll see in chapter 11, Alison and I used this strategy for a few years when our kids were young—when we endured two horrendous pregnancies and a bout of postpartum depression (mine). For a while, we stopped seeking self-expression through the marriage. To a certain extent, we even stopped seeking love, sex, and intimacy through the marriage. Although we didn't depend on the marriage for basic survival, we mostly sought just to endure. I believe that doing so saved our marriage, as it mitigated feelings of disappointment during our darkest days.

Many marriages ultimately dissolve, of course, but there's no compelling evidence that people bolt as soon as things get difficult. On the contrary, it's precisely when things get difficult that many of us redouble our efforts to strengthen our relationship, either by engaging in effortful relationship-maintenance activities or by recalibrating our expectations.

The Fork in the Road

The self has become profoundly important in recent decades, but that doesn't mean America has become a society of narcissists. It's true that some of us have interpreted the rising status of selfhood as a justification for treating pleasure and self-esteem as imperial values—as sacred goals that should not be compromised, even when one's marriage hangs in the balance. But others have interpreted the rising status of selfhood in a very different way—as an opportunity to pursue a meaningful life. Those of us in this latter group experience much less conflict between personal fulfillment and marital commitment. Rather, we work hard to make our marriage strong, in part because doing so helps us become the best version of ourselves.

6.

Marriage at the Summit

We are like two flowers in one pot. It's difficult.
Sometimes we don't get enough nutrients for both of us.
But when everything goes well, we become two beautiful
flowers. So it's either heaven or hell.

—Noriko Shinohara

The 2013 documentary film *Cutie and the Boxer* explores the marriage and careers of the Japanese-American spouses Ushio and Noriko Shinohara. Both are artists in New York, and both seek professional respect. For a long time, Noriko (the wife) served as Ushio's unpaid assistant. She also handled most of the domestic chores and was the primary caregiver when their son was young.

Ultimately, however, she found this support role insufficiently fulfilling, and she sought to develop her own career. The film documents the marital challenges that emerge as both spouses sought to live authentic, self-expressive lives—the difficulties of finding sufficient time and psychological bandwidth for the two of them to support each other while also working on their own art. As they struggle to make ends meet, they endure conflict and disappointment. But they also enjoy synergy and elation, especially when a SoHo gallery presents a joint show of their work.

The "Freighted Marriage" Perspective versus the "All-Or-Nothing Marriage" Perspective

In discussing the all-or-nothing marriage theory of marriage in chapter 1, we introduced the Mount Maslow metaphor. The idea is that Americans have come to ask much more of our marriage vis-à-vis higher-altitude needs linked to self-discovery and personal growth (where providing sufficient "oxygenation" is crucial) while simultaneously asking much less vis-à-vis lower-altitude needs linked to safety and security. We can distinguish this perspective from an alternative, "freighted marriage" perspective, according to which Americans have simply been asking more and more of our marriages over time. The all-or-nothing marriage perspective suggests that the major change has less to do with *how much* we're asking of our marriage than with *what* we're asking of it.

The freighted marriage perspective, which I had accepted as true when I began working on the *Psychological Inquiry* Target Article, is the prevailing one. Consider this analysis from the sex therapist Esther Perel:

> No longer obligated to marry who we must, we set out with a new ideal of what we want, and we want plenty. Our desiderata still include everything the traditional family was meant to provide—security, children, property, respectability—but now we also want our Joe to love us, to desire us, to be interested in us. We should be confidants, best friends, and passionate lovers. Modern marriage promises us that there is one person out there with whom all this is possible if we can just find her.

The freighted marriage perspective and the all-or-nothing marriage perspective align in the view that Americans are asking more of their marriages regarding higher-altitude needs. As we've seen, we are much more likely today than in the past to require that our spouse be our close friend, perhaps even our best friend, and to hold the belief that "having a healthy, exciting sex life [is] virtually a prerequisite for a happy, satisfying marriage." We are much more likely to require that our marriage facilitate our efforts toward self-discovery and personal growth. Meanwhile, as our life expectancy has increased more quickly than our age on our wedding day, marriages have become responsible for helping us meet such needs for longer than ever. Where the freighted marriage perspective and the all-or-nothing marriage perspective diverge is at the lower altitudes.

Consider economic dependence. Life in the American colonies might not have been nasty, brutish, and short, but it was a whole lot nastier, more brutish, and shorter than life is today. Preindustrial Americans endured living conditions that seem torturous by today's standards. Freezing temperatures, viruses, and floods were life-threatening rather than inconvenient. Supermarkets, governmental welfare programs, major insurance companies, and high-quality hospitals didn't exist.

People looked to their immediate kinship networks to help them fulfill the needs that major social institutions help us fulfill today—food production, protection from violence, tending to the sick, and so forth. But much of the dependence on kinship networks boiled down to dependence on one's spouse, especially in the centuries during which the individual farmhouse was the primary unit of economic production. Incompetence or frailty from either spouse could be life-threatening. As technology advanced and the nation became wealthier, spouses' economic dependence on each other declined. Large-scale community organizations and social policies, like the 1889 founding of Jane Addams's Hull House (to serve the urban poor) and the 1935 passage of the Social Security Act, reduced the lethality of poverty, a development that was especially helpful for singles.

Reductions in the extent to which Americans require marriage to achieve economic subsistence are relevant to both sexes, but the effect has been especially strong for women. There is still significant inequality between the earnings of men and women, but the proportion of women who can make ends meet independently has surged since 1900, and especially since the 1960s, significantly reducing women's economic dependence on marriage.

Technological advances that make housework less onerous—dishwashers, washing machines, microwaves, power drills—have also defreighted marriage. Even as homes have gotten larger and standards for cleanliness have soared, Americans do considerably less housework than they used to. Meanwhile, during the same time period, the fertility rate declined by about half—from a recent high of 3.65 children per woman in 1960 to a low of 1.74 in 1976 before stabilizing at around 2.0—and meeting children's basic needs has become easier due to the advent of disposable diapers, prepared baby food, institutional child care centers, and so forth. Parents spend much more time caring for their children today than they did fifty years ago (a trend we'll discuss shortly), but that time investment has very little to do with ensuring children's basic survival.

Marriage has also become defreighted through a surge in socially acceptable alternatives for fulfilling sexual and lifestyle needs. Throughout most of American history, sex between unmarried individuals was socially unacceptable. During the self-expressive era, it lost much of its stigma and became increasingly widespread. And, of course, the rise of Internet commerce since the late 1990s has made almost all varieties of pornography available to most Americans at any hour of the day, much of it for free. Pornography is much more popular among men than among women, but vibrators are quite popular among American women, especially as discreet Internet-based ordering has eliminated the embarrassment of face-to-face purchasing, and technological advances have made them especially effective ("I have never met a person that can vibrate at 120 hertz," observes the psychologist Bryant Paul). By 2008, more than half of American women had used a vibrator at least once. In short, for both men and women, it's much easier to achieve a measure of sexual fulfillment outside of marriage today than it was in the past.

Many changes in the acceptability of alternative, nonmarital lifestyles emerged alongside these changes in sexual mores. From 1970 to 2010, the number of American singles aged thirty-five to forty-four almost tripled, from 12 percent to 35 percent, and the number of cohabiting unmarried couples surged from 500,000 to 7.6 million. Americans who want to have a baby have a much broader range of nonmarital options available, including artificial insemination and egg freezing. As the stigma of divorce has declined, fewer people feel compelled to remain in a dissatisfying marriage just to be a respected member of the community.

Such examples drive home the broader point. Yes, today's Americans are asking more of our marriage regarding higher-altitude need fulfillment, but we're actually asking less regarding lower-altitude need fulfillment.

Not Enough Oxygen

We've seen that Miles, in the movie *Sideways*, characterizes Pinot as "a hard grape to grow" and in need of "constant care and attention." He observes that "only somebody who really takes the time to understand Pinot's potential can then coax it into its fullest expression." But the payoff of such coaxing is immense.

The same is true of the self-expressive marriage. As we look to the top of Mount Maslow, the investment of time and psychological energy in cultivating the relationship becomes increasingly important. Fortunately, the payoff of taking the time to coax the marriage into its fullest expression is immense. Even at the simplest level, we tend to experience greater happiness and meaning, and greater intimacy, when we're with our spouse than when we're not, and couples who regularly spend "time alone with each other, talking, or sharing an activity" are much happier in their marriage than those who don't. But, alas, rather than oxygenating our marriage in this way, many of us are doing just the opposite.

The Assault on Psychological Bandwidth

One issue is that the pace of life has sped up. The journalist Brigid Schulte illustrates the pace of contemporary life by presenting her own experience of what she calls *the overwhelm*: "*If* I could just finish picking all the weeds, chopping the invasive bamboo, cleaning out the crayons and shark teeth and math papers and toys and bits of shells and rocks and too-small clothes in the kids' closets, buy more cat food, fix the coffeepot, complete this story assignment, pay these bills, fill out those forms, make that phone call, send this wedding present five months late—*then* I could sit down and read a book."

Most of us aren't concerned with chopping invasive bamboo, but we can generate a list of our own personal time goblins that send us into our own personal overwhelm. Maybe we're in a dual-income household with young children, or maybe we're taking on extra freelance work to save for retirement. Regardless of the details, life is getting faster, straining our *psychological bandwidth*— the brainpower available to focus on the task at hand.

TIME CRUNCH

The total number of hours that American couples spend at work has increased in recent decades. The percentage of married women who work full-time increased from 43 percent in 1980 to 54 percent in 2000, whereas the percentage who were not employed at all dropped from 42 percent to 25 percent. And, of course, paid employment is far from the only work we do: American women (4.0 hours/day) and men (2.5 hours/day) spend considerable time engaged in unpaid domestic work like cleaning, cooking, and child care.

Speaking of child care, the amount of time parents invest in intensive child-rearing has also surged in recent decades, as we increasingly view children as "economically useless" but "emotionally priceless." Consider the charts below.

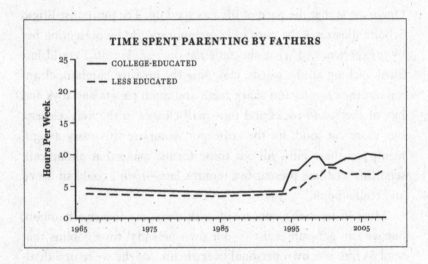

TIME SPENT PARENTING BY FATHERS

— COLLEGE-EDUCATED
-- LESS EDUCATED

Hours Per Week

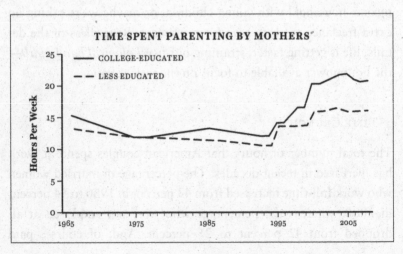

TIME SPENT PARENTING BY MOTHERS

— COLLEGE-EDUCATED
-- LESS EDUCATED

Hours Per Week

The charts on the previous page track the parenting activity of heterosexual fathers and mothers aged twenty-five to thirty-four from 1965 to 2008. (The temporal trends were similar across other age groups.) From 1965 until the early 1990s, fathers spent four to five hours per week, and mothers spent ten to fifteen hours per week engaged in intensive parenting activities. Then, suddenly, both fathers and mothers sharply increased the time they spent in such activities; by 2008, fathers were up to eight to ten hours per week, and mothers up to fifteen to twenty hours per week. These effects were stronger among more-educated than among less-educated Americans, which dovetails with the sociologist Annette Lareau's suggestion that highly educated Americans are especially likely to adopted a *concerted cultivation* approach to childhood, in which parents facilitate their children's development via organized activities, language training, and active school involvement.

We saw in chapter 4 that the total amount of work new parents do (paid work + housework + child care) increases by an estimated 33.5 hours per week when the first baby arrives, with 63 percent of this increase absorbed by mothers. But even spouses without children are time-starved, in part because we work so much. For example, American workers generally get fewer vacation days than people in other Western nations, and yet we reliably forfeit some of our meager allotment because we feel like we have so much work to do.

In light of these recent parenting and work trends, is it any surprise that spouses are spending less time alone together than they did in the past? The charts on the following page illustrate how much *spousal time*—time that two spouses spend alone together—married Americans without children at home (top chart) and with children at home (bottom chart) had on the average weekday and weekend day in 1975 and in 2003. The top panel reveals that, between 1975 and 2003, spouses without children at home endured a 30 percent decline in spousal time on weekdays and a 17 percent

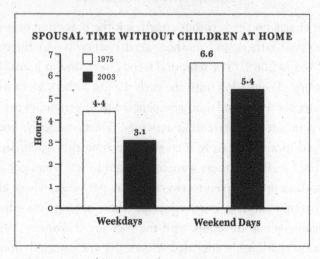

SPOUSAL TIME WITHOUT CHILDREN AT HOME

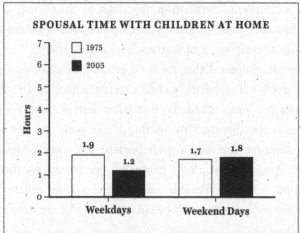

SPOUSAL TIME WITH CHILDREN AT HOME

decline on weekend days. The bottom panel reveals that spouses with children at home endured a 40 percent decline on weekdays—although, surprisingly, they experience almost no change (and perhaps even a small increase) on weekend days. Despite that one anomalous finding, the overarching trend is clear: Spouses spent much less time alone together in 2003 than in 1975.

A more systematic analysis of shared time use—this time including both alone time and time with other people—offers some intriguing insights. As illustrated in the charts below, both nonparents and parents in 2012 were spending comparable amounts of time in shared leisure activities today as in previous decades, and

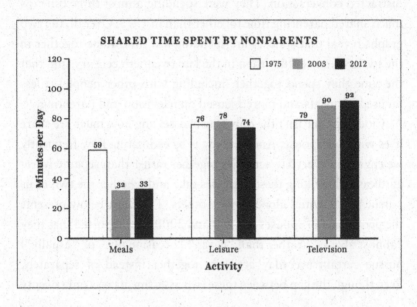

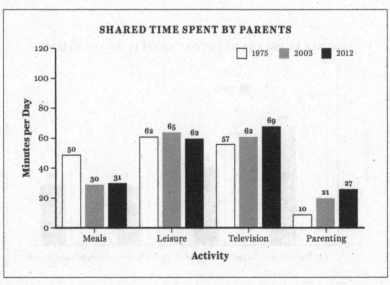

they were actually spending more time watching television together. But, relative to the 1970s, they were spending substantially less time eating meals together—one of the most important activities for undistracted conversation. They were spending almost three times as much shared parenting time together than in 1975. Overall, the two graphs reveal that spouses are spending less time alone together in the twenty-first century than in the late twentieth century, and that the time they spend together (including with other people) is less focused on meals and more focused on television and parenting.

Clocking time isn't the only way of assessing how much we share lives with our spouse. Another way is by estimating how frequently we engage in everyday activities together rather than separately, regardless of how long these activities take and whether the two of us pursue the activities alone or with others. The chart below presents the percentage of spouses in 1980 and 2000 who reported that they "almost always" (rather than "never," "occasionally," or "usually") pursue certain everyday activities together instead of separately. Even though the gap between these two assessments was only twenty

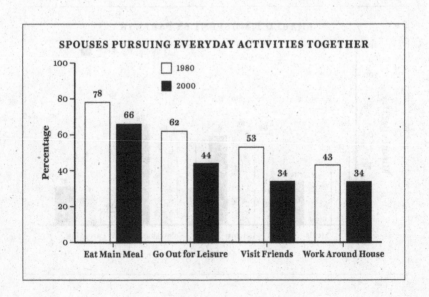

years, spouses were markedly less likely to report almost always eating their main meal of the day together, going out for leisure together, visiting friends together, and working around the house together. Thus, spouses in the early twenty-first century not only spent significantly less time alone together than did their parents' generation, but they also were significantly less likely to reliably pursue their daily activities together.

STRESS

It's possible, in principle, that Americans in the self-expressive era could have highly fulfilling marriages without investing much time in them. If we pursue spousal time in an undistracted, fully present mind-set, perhaps we can still help to facilitate each other's love and self-expressive needs. However, there's a circumstantial case that spousal time in the average marriage is, if anything, of lower quality than it was in the past.

Stress is linked to more selfish, less constructive behavior in our romantic relationship—and, unfortunately, Americans have become increasingly stressed in recent decades. The chart on the following page illustrates how stressed American men and women felt in 1983, 2006, and 2009. Stress was assessed with a set of self-report items like "In the last month, how often have you felt that difficulties were piling up so high that you could not overcome them?" and ". . . how often have you felt that you could not cope with all the things that you had to?" Given how much more stressed Americans felt in the 2000s than in the 1980s, and given how difficult it is to be a sensitive and attentive partner when we're stressed, it's unlikely that we're able to compensate for the reduction in our time together by using that diminished time to help each other feel optimally loved and to promote each other's self-expression.

Americans' elevated stress levels result in part from the increasing difficulty of achieving work-life balance. Whereas 24 percent of

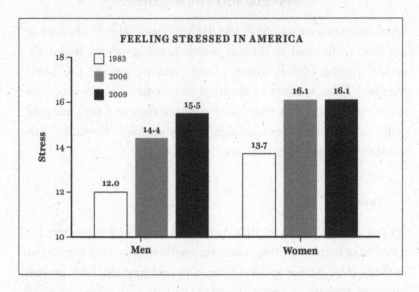

FEELING STRESSED IN AMERICA

husbands and 23 percent of wives endured strong work-life conflict in 1980, the respective estimates had surged to 44 and 33 percent by 2000.

MENTAL FRAGMENTATION

Meanwhile, we're living in the information age, processing massively more information than during any previous period of human history. The Nobel Prize–winning cognitive scientist Herbert Simon's observation in 1971 that "a wealth of information creates a poverty of attention" has never been more relevant. The psychologist Daniel Levitin, in describing "the age of information overload" in *The Organized Mind*, reports that five exabytes (a billion gigabytes) of new data—both storage media (print, film, magnetic, and optical) and information flows (telephone, radio, television, and Internet)—were created in 2002 alone. That is a rate of about two Libraries of Congress per day for the month. A more recent estimate from IBM is that humanity creates 2.5 quintillion (2,500,000,000,000,000,000) bytes of data per day, with 90 percent of the world's data created in the last two years alone. And things are only speeding up. The comedian

Tina Fey summarizes her sense of overwhelm in her autobiography *Bossypants*: "'Blorft' is an adjective I just made up that means 'Completely overwhelmed but proceeding as if everything is fine and reacting to the stress with the torpor of a possum.' I have been blorft every day for the past seven years."

We find ourselves chronically interrupted, multitasking, or both, which makes us feel scattered and fragmented, especially as we increasingly mainline technology into every aspect of our lives. "All those stolen glances at the smartphone, the bursts of addictive texting and e-mail checking at all hours, . . . the constant connection . . . don't show up in time diaries," observes Brigid Schulte. "Yet that activity splinters the experience of time into thousands of little pieces." She calls those little pieces *time confetti*.

Scientific investigations confirm that little disruptions impair our ability to sustain attention. One study demonstrated that a four-second interruption triples error rates on an ongoing cognitive task. In another study, participants were randomly assigned to one of three interruption conditions as they performed an attention-demanding computer task: phone call, text message, or no interruption. In all conditions, participants performed the task without looking at their smartphone, even if they received a notification. Still, both types of notification impaired performance relative to the no-interruption condition.

Mental fragmentation afflicts women (especially mothers) more than men. Even as women have increasingly pursued careers over the past two generations, they haven't been able to relinquish enough responsibility at home to offset the time and energy those careers require. They are more prone to feeling overwhelmed—to having endless to-do lists with items like child care arrangements, nutritious food, dealing with the flooded basement, and getting the report submitted on time.

Women and men alike are at risk for living in a state that the philosopher Martin Heidegger calls *forfeiture*—a lack of self-insight resulting from living busy, distracted lives. The leisure scientist

Benjamin Hunnicutt observes that such lives don't afford much ability to reflect, live in the present, or experience transcendence— and, consequently, "we starve the capacity we have to love." More prosaically, such lives deprive spouses of time together. One spouse poignantly observes that her marriage has fallen to the "bottom of the family food chain."

Bandwidth for Two?

The imbalance created by our tendency to ask our marriage to ful- fill our highest-altitude needs despite our limited investment in the marriage is exacerbated by the fact that marriage is a symmetrical arrangement in which each spouse is responsible for the other. As with the artists Ushio and Noriko Shinohara, each of us is not only a support-seeker, but also a support-provider. The symmetrical na- ture of marriage can help promote the fulfillment of both our own and our spouse's needs, such as when having a deep conversation makes the two of us feel loved and loving, understood and under- standing. But to the extent that our partner's needs make us feel pressured to relinquish the pursuit of our own goals, we may expe- rience frustration and dissatisfaction.

This issue can become especially problematic when both part- ners are stressed or when there isn't enough time to prioritize both partners' needs, a situation that is especially likely in dual-career couples. "I think a big issue," says an anonymous wife, "is that we both want to be taken care of at the end of the day, and neither of us has any energy to take care of the other."

The Suffocated Marriage and the Spouse's Dilemma

In an influential TED Talk, Esther Perel addressed the disconnect between what we're asking of our marriage and what we're investing in it. "So we come to one person, and we basically are asking them to give us what once an entire village used to provide. Give me belonging, give me identity, give me continuity, but give me transcendence and mystery and awe all in one. . . . And we think it's a given, and toys and lingerie are going to save us with that."

That we're looking to our marriage to fulfill all these high-altitude needs while investing less time and energy in our relationship has produced an oxygenation deficit—our marriage lacks the resources to give us everything that we're asking of it. As we've seen, the challenge is especially acute for parents of young children. "In the early childrearing years," observes the sociologist and psychotherapist Francesca Cancian, "the burdens of marriage and parenting are so great that most couples probably have little energy to focus on developing their selves or their relationship." Perhaps we shouldn't be surprised that only 38 percent of mothers of young infants are highly satisfied in their marriage (in contrast to 62 percent of childless women)—or that the link between parenting and marital dissatisfaction has gotten stronger in recent decades. A recent study of twenty-two capitalist democracies, such as Great Britain and Australia, revealed that this "happiness penalty" of parenthood is largest in America, apparently because of our lack of family-friendly employment policies.

We saw in chapter 1 that the quality of the average marriage in America is in decline. We've already considered one major reason for this trend—that more of us are experiencing a disconnect between (1) the higher-altitude needs we seek to fulfill through our marriage and (2) our marriage's ability to fulfill those needs. A second, and related, reason is that the pursuit of personal growth and self-expression can be arduous. If our spouse is to facilitate this pursuit, he or she might have to push us hard, challenging us to be the best versions of ourselves. Pushing and challenging of this sort can be priceless, but it's less likely to promote smooth marital dynamics than adopting a more easygoing interaction style would be.

As noted by the psychologist Carl Rogers, a life characterized by the pursuit of self-discovery and self-expression is the opposite of one characterized by complacency. It involves giving oneself over to insatiable hunger and yearning rather than allowing oneself to feel fulfilled and contented. "Nietzsche had realized that difficulties of every sort were to be welcomed by those seeking fulfillment," writes the philosopher Alain de Botton.

> The most fulfilling human projects appeared inseparable from a degree of torment, the sources of our greatest joys lying awkwardly close to those of our greatest pains. . . . Why? Because no one is able to produce a great work of art without experience, nor achieve a worldly position immediately, nor be a great lover at the first attempt; and in the interval between initial failure and subsequent success, in the gap between who we wish one day to be and who we are at present, must come pain, anxiety, envy and humiliation. We suffer because we cannot spontaneously master the ingredients of fulfillment. . . . Fulfillment was to be reached not by avoiding pain, but by recognizing its role as a natural, inevitable step on the way to reaching anything good.

Assuming that Rogers and Nietzsche are correct about the necessity of tribulation en route to triumph, our spouse in the self-expressive era will periodically confront a dilemma: to comfort us at the risk of inducing complacency and indolence or to challenge us at the risk of inducing conflict and insecurity. Consider the role that Katinka Hosszu's husband and coach, Shane Tusup, played in her training for the 2016 Olympics. Hosszu, a Hungarian swimmer, had underperformed in 2012, going home without a medal. Immediately thereafter, she asked Tusup, her then-boyfriend, to become her coach. The results were golden—she won four medals, three of them gold, in individual events in 2016—even if the process was not.

Shortly before the 2016 Games, *The New York Times* ran an article titled "Katinka Hosszu and Her Husband Raise Eyebrows at the Pool," which cast an alarmed look at how Tusup treated her. "I've seen a lot of inappropriate and not-O.K. behavior in Shane," commented Jessica Hardy, an Olympian who had previously trained with Hosszu. He throws objects to the ground, kicks the wall, and publicly upbraids her for lesser performances. But, Hardy acknowledges, Hosszu is a far better swimmer with Tusup as her coach: "Less than three weeks after the [2012] Olympics, she came back, and she had been training with Shane already, and I saw a different Katinka. More fit and more in shape. She worked hard before, but she wasn't as motivated as she is now." In Hosszu's words, Tusup "expects me to get it perfect right away; that's why I've improved so much."

Hosszu and Tusup are an extreme example, to be sure. Most of us aren't seeking to break world records in high-profile athletic competitions. But their dynamic illustrates the point that achieving ambitious goals is hard work, and helping a loved one do so can sometimes require criticism rather than warmth, challenge rather than comfort. It's hard to reconcile such treatment with the "haven in a heartless world" ethos.

Therein resides the spouse's dilemma: As we seek to help our partner become the best version of him- or herself, to what extent do we employ critical feedback in order to motivate versus supportive feedback in order to nurture? It's difficult to give complacency-shattering feedback while simultaneously making our partner feel competent, loved, and sexy.

The Enriched Marriage and Flourishing at the Summit

In either case, working hard at our marriage has become the new normal. For many couples, the efforts are successful, and the payoff is huge. Recall Maslow's observation that, relative to meeting lower-altitude needs, meeting higher-altitude needs yields "more profound happiness, serenity, and richness of the inner life." Meeting these needs through marriage yields more profound happiness, serenity, and richness within the marriage.

Here we are a bit beyond the available data. There are no studies that have tracked the very best marriages across time, so our case is circumstantial. But we do know that Americans generally didn't look to their marriages to fulfill their higher-altitude needs, especially their self-expressive needs, in the past as they do today. And Maslow is almost certainly correct that fulfilling higher-altitude needs produces a more deeply meaningful life than fulfilling lower-altitude needs does. If we assume that Maslow's logic also applies to the marital case, then fulfillment in a marriage oriented toward higher altitudes will be more profoundly satisfying than one oriented toward lower altitudes.

The psychologists Bianca Acevedo and Arthur Aron have shown that a substantial minority of married Americans today are sustaining deep romantic love—characterized by intensity, engagement, and sexual interest—for the long haul. In one study, a random sample of Americans who had been married for at least ten years reported their love for their spouse on a scale from 1 (*not at all in love*) to 7 (*very intensely in love*). A full 40 percent responded with a 7, even though other options included *very in love* and *intensely in love*.

The participants in this study were people whose marriages had survived, of course; the percentage of people who love their spouse at least ten years after the wedding would be lower if the study had included those who were divorced from that partner. And the intensity of love was higher, on average, among people married less than ten years than among people married longer. That said, the finding shows that a substantial minority of people who remain married continue to feel very intense love for their partner, even a decade or more into the marriage.

Of course, a self-expressive marriage requires more than just the maintenance of romantic love. Given the paucity of empirical research on these marriages, it's useful to examine case studies. Consider Peter and Rosemary Grant, who, walking in Darwin's footsteps, studied finches on the uninhabited Galapagan island of Daphne Major for more than four decades starting in 1973. As the Grants returned, year after year, they were among the first scientists to witness evolution in real time—at a pace Darwin would not have deemed possible. Their discoveries, which burst into public consciousness in Jonathan Weiner's Pulitzer Prize–winning *The Beak of the Finch* and in their own *40 Years of Evolution*, are among the most significant in evolutionary biology in recent decades. Especially remarkable is the Grants' real-time discovery in 1981 of the emergence of an entirely new species of finch. As of 2014, this finch's lineage had lasted seven generations.

Peter and Rosemary Grant

For our purposes, the Grants' marital dynamics are every bit as interesting as their achievements in biology. "They never seemed to age," observed Weiner in 2014, "although Peter's beard grew almost as long and white as the celebrated beard of Darwin, whom he resembles somewhat. When they weren't camped on Daphne, they analyzed their data at Princeton in adjoining offices with the door open between them. They write books and papers together, give lectures together, finish each other's sentences." The Grants were two individuals with an ambitious dream to change the landscape of evolutionary biology, and, working together, they lived their dream.

Consider, too, John Lennon. Lennon was an American by choice rather than birth, having moved to the United States in 1971. Previously, Lennon and Cynthia Powell had a shotgun wedding when they were both in their early twenties. Their typical love-based marriage may have lasted in an earlier era (and if Lennon hadn't been such a star), but he increasingly found himself on a voyage of self-discovery and personal growth that Powell couldn't support. In contrast, his union with Yoko Ono, an avant-garde artist, was typical of the self-expressive marriage. He enjoyed intense self-expression with her—she inspired him intellectually, musically, and politically, helping him grow into a deeper, more authentic version of himself.

Similar dynamics may have been at play when Brad Pitt became involved with Angelina Jolie and when George Clooney became involved with Amal Alamuddin. At the time of these courtships, Jolie was the Goodwill Ambassador for the United Nations High Commissioner for Refugees, and Alamuddin was an internationally renowned human rights lawyer. It is plausible that Pitt and Clooney married these particular women not only because they are brilliant, beautiful, and successful but also because doing so facilitated their own social activism, thereby helping them grow toward their authentic selves.

These examples are obviously atypical. Few of us are world-famous scientists, rock stars, or film icons, and few of us can, at our own discretion, seamlessly merge our professional and intellectual pursuits with those of our spouse. But the themes underlying these marriages generalize to the best marriages of the self-expressive era. As far as we can tell, these marriages were (and, in some cases, still are) built on love and respect. But, more important, the spouses helped each other flourish in ways that might have remained out of reach if they weren't together. They climbed to the top of Mount Maslow and, at least some of the time, invested the resources required for the marriage to flourish at the summit.

As we've seen, however, the very features than can make the self-expressive marriage so fulfilling also make it fragile. Pursuing a marriage at the summit requires that we supply the requisite oxygen. We may have witnessed the consequences of insufficient oxygenation in 2016 when Pitt and Jolie split. According to an insider, here's how things fell apart: "Angelina is very dedicated to her work with the United Nations and working on other charitable endeavors while Brad is consumed with his film projects. Both of their interests have taken them across the world but not together [and] in different directions."

One tool that the best marriages keep in their tool kit is the temporary descent of Mount Maslow. Few of us can live at the summit full-time, so the ability to let go of summit aspirations—at least for a while—is a hallmark of most of today's best marriages. When our children are small, when we have a slow-burning work crisis, when we're entering our third year of infertility treatments, spouses in the best marriages are able to keep marital disappointment at bay by modulating their expectations to align with what the marriage can realistically provide. A great danger of the self-expressive era is that an inflexible, myopic focus on the top of Mount Maslow produces painful disappointment during periods when the marriage falls short of those expectations. The best marriages are able to enjoy exquisite connection at the highest altitudes, but also to lower their expectations as the circumstances dictate.

Suffocated or Enriched?

Marriage's ascent of Mount Maslow has put within reach previously unattainable levels of meaningful connection. If we're compatible with our spouse, and if we exert ourselves to help each other achieve higher-altitude needs, we can enjoy prolonged, frequent enchantment at the summit. If not, our marriage is likely to stagnate, falling short of the lofty expectations we're bringing to them. A marriage that might have been more than adequate in an era with more modest expectations for psychological fulfillment may be a disappointment today.

It turns out, however, that this risk isn't equally distributed across social groups. In particular, relative to wealthier Americans, poorer Americans are at elevated risk for marital failure. Let's consider why that is.

7.

For Richer or Poorer

Postindustrialization brings increasing individual
freedom and growing opportunities for self-actualization
for large parts of society, but substantial minorities—
particularly the less educated and the unemployed—still
feel existential threats.

—Ronald Inglehart and Christian Welzel

We are more than half a century into the self-expressive era, but not all Americans are equally dedicated to the self-expressive ideal, nor do all of us have equal opportunity to pursue it. Before launching into the final section of the book, which addresses how we can leverage insights from the all-or-nothing marriage perspective to bolster our own marriage, we'll take a brief detour to consider how the transition of marriage to an all-or-nothing state influences wealthier versus poorer Americans.

Common Ground

As we do that, it's useful to bear in mind two major sources of shared experience. First, America has witnessed staggering wealth increases since the first colonists arrived, especially since the Industrial Revolution—and, despite today's stark inequality, these increases have touched virtually everybody. The social status of Abraham Lincoln's parents two hundred years ago was somewhere between middle and lower class, and it's informative to compare their circumstances to those of Americans with comparable social status today. On virtually all relevant dimensions—life expectancy, physical safety, running water, medical care, waste disposal—today's Americans are far better off than their status-matched peers from the past.

The efficiencies of scale afforded by economic advancement created vast new wealth, and political developments—the New Deal legislation, Medicare, Medicaid, and so forth—have helped ensure that some of this wealth keeps most poor people from the sort of destitution that was common during the preindustrial era and much of the industrial era. "Throughout history, survival has been precarious," observe the political scientists Ronald Inglehart and Christian Welzel. "In recent decades, the publics of postindustrial societies have experienced unprecedented levels of existential security. . . . Today, most people in rich countries have grown up taking it for granted that they will not starve."

A second major source of shared experience is that, despite robust subcultural differences within America, we do possess broad cultural elements that are uniquely American. Indeed, as noted by Inglehart and Welzel, "the nation remains a key unit of shared experience, with its educational and cultural institutions shaping the values of almost everyone in that society." It's easy to focus on the differences, but, to a large extent, Americans share a cultural ethos, language, political system, media culture, and educational infrastructure. That we lack consensus or universality along these lines should not distract us from the reality that, on average, Americans share these qualities with our fellow citizens to a much greater extent than we share them with citizens of other nations. For example, because Americans are unique among Westerners in how strongly we value *both* marital commitment and self-expression, we tend to both marry and divorce at elevated rates, creating what the sociologist Andrew Cherlin calls "the marriage-go-round."

Cherlin argues that academics sometimes place too much emphasis on "the holy trinity of social science"—class, race, and gender—and "exaggerate the differences in American family life across educational, racial, and ethnic lines. Americans have much in common. . . . From the poorest to the most affluent, young adults seek companionship, emotional satisfaction, and self-development through marriage." In reality, there is deep veracity in America's official motto, *E pluribus unum*: "Out of many, one."*

Social Class

And yet, if we think about "American marriage" as representing some sort of central tendency (remember the mean, median, and mode?), we can also consider variation around that central tendency. For example, the long-term societal increase in existential security masks shorter-term fluctuations. Americans vary in how vulnerable we are to booms and busts in the economic cycle.

We can't discuss all forms of variation in American marriage in this book, as a comprehensive effort along those lines would fill a library. We'll focus on *social class* (also called "socioeconomic status")—an individual's position, relative to others, on variables like income, education, and occupation. Social class is linked to other sociodemographic characteristics, including race, religion, geography, and political orientation.

---

* With the rise of social media and on-demand entertainment options, Americans' cultural experience is less shared than in the past. The extent to which such trends will undermine a shared American identity, including a shared understanding of the functions of marriage, in the coming decades is unknown.

Inequality rates in America started rising in the 1970s and, by the 2010s, had reached levels rivaling those from the Roaring Twenties. In 2013, President Barack Obama declared that "a dangerous and growing inequality . . . is the defining challenge of our time." As noted previously, a central cause of this rising inequality is the decline in working-class jobs—especially manufacturing jobs—that pay a decent wage, largely due to a combination of automation and outsourcing/offshoring. Governmental factors, including the rising influence of trickle-down economics on public policy after 1980 and the decline in public sector jobs in the 2010s, also contributed. Collectively, these forces have hollowed out the middle of the American labor market, creating an "hourglass economy" in which Americans with college and postgraduate degrees are getting wealthier, while those without a college education are getting poorer. In today's service economy, more Americans work in low-skill service jobs that can't be outsourced to other countries or readily automated, such as food and hotel service.

With the disappearance of working-class jobs came the decline of the working-class family. From 1880, when data collection began, until the 1970s, the proportion of men aged twenty to forty-nine and with intact families who worked in manufacturing, construction, transit, or utilities surged from 20 to 40 percent for whites and from 10 to 50 percent for blacks. Then, rather abruptly, labor unions started hemorrhaging power, and high-quality manufacturing jobs evaporated.

Less obviously, marital trends are exacerbating inequality. Wealthier Americans are more likely to marry than poorer Americans are— further concentrating the salutary outcomes linked to marriage among the wealthier—and people who do marry are increasingly doing so within their own socioeconomic stratum. "Fifty years ago, during the *Mad Men* era, an executive might marry his secretary," observe the legal scholars June Carbone and Naomi Cahn. "Today he is much more likely to marry another executive or a doctor or an accountant."

As we consider the links between social class and marriage, it's important to bear in mind that humans, as social creatures, are influenced not only by absolute levels of income, but also by relative levels. For example, regardless of how wealthy we are, we tend to be less happy when our neighbors are wealthier than we are, an effect that gets bigger as inequality gets larger.

Where American Marriage Is in Crisis

The link between social class and marital outcomes is strong. The chart on the next page leverages census data to illustrate the percentage of first marriages disrupted—defined in terms of divorce, separation, or desertion—across the first fifteen years as a function of social class. This study employed neighborhood-level income data to classify women as low-income (bottom 25 percent), middle-income (middle 50 percent), or high-income (top 25 percent). The findings reveal greater disruption rates among lower-income than among higher-income Americans, a difference that emerges in the first year of marriage and gets stronger over time. Longer-term data from the 1990s suggest that 60 percent of women without a high school degree will eventually divorce, whereas 36 percent of women with a college degree will divorce. And data from 2006 to 2010 present a similarly bleak story for women with a high school degree or less (60 percent divorced with the first twenty years), but an even more promising one for college-educated women (only 22 percent divorced); women with some college experience but no degree looked more like the less-educated group in this newer study (51 percent divorced).

As alarming as these findings are, they actually understate the magnitude of the inequality because lower-class Americans are less likely to marry in the first place. And marriages that remain intact tend to be less fulfilling among the lower class than the middle or upper class. Furthermore, the link between low social class and poor marital outcomes has been getting stronger in recent decades:

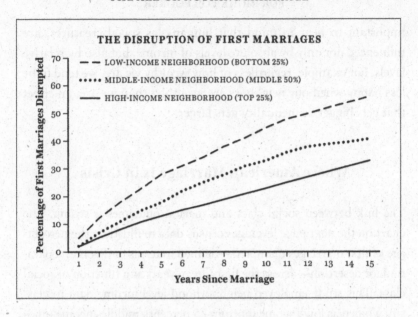

Although the percentage of Americans who report being "very satisfied" in their marriage has declined across the class spectrum, the decline is steepest among the less educated.

An even starker temporal pattern emerges for divorce rates. Consider the chart on the next page, which illustrates the percentage of marriages beginning between 1960 and 1994 that ended in divorce within ten years, separately for Americans without a high school diploma, with high school diploma or some college, or with a college degree or more. This chart corroborates not only that divorce risk is much greater for lower-class than for higher-class Americans, but also that this disparity has swelled since around 1980.

On the left, we see that the surging divorce rates of the 1960s and 1970s were comparable across the three groups—the three lines rose at similar rates. But starting around 1980, the three lines diverged sharply. Whereas the divorce rate continued to surge among lower-class Americans married in the 1980s and 1990s, it flattened out among middle-class Americans and actually declined among higher-class Americans. Indeed, among the higher class,

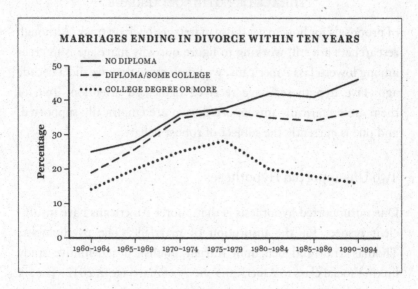

MARRIAGES ENDING IN DIVORCE WITHIN TEN YEARS

divorce rates for marriages that began in the early 1990s was about the same as for marriages that began in the early 1960s.

The most striking comparison involves the high-social-class and low-social-class groups that married in the late 1970s versus the early 1990s. The ten-year divorce rate for these groups was 28 percent versus 38 percent in the late 1970s and 16 percent and 46 percent in the early 1990s. Some quick arithmetic reveals that the difference between the two groups tripled, from 10 percent to 30 percent, during that fifteen-year window, a staggering change. In short, although it is an exaggeration to claim that marriage in America is in crisis, it is no exaggeration to say that it is in crisis among the lower class.

What's Driving This Crisis?

Researchers, policymakers, and social commentators have expressed alarm about the declining satisfaction and surging divorce rates among lower-class Americans, and there has been no shortage of proposals for how to get those marriages back on track. Although researchers are still working to figure out why marriage is in crisis among lower-class Americans, we know more than we did a decade ago. Five hypotheses have received dedicated attention. Two of them are empirically unsupported, two are empirically supported, and one is currently the subject of robust debate.

Two Unsupported Hypotheses

One unsupported hypothesis is that poorer Americans have insufficient respect for the institution of marriage. The psychologists Thomas Trail and Benjamin Karney published a definitive study linking social class to Americans' views of marriage in 2012. The six thousand participants fit into one of four social-class categories: welfare, low income, moderate income, and high income. When Trail and Karney asked them how much they agreed that "divorce can be a reasonable solution to an unhappy marriage," the high-income group—not the lower-income groups—agreed the most. The high-income group also agreed the most that "it is okay for couples who are not married to live together." The four income groups agreed about equally (and strongly) that "a happy, healthy marriage is one of the most important things in life." Findings like these suggest that lower-class Americans attach great value to the institution of marriage, perhaps even more than higher-class Americans do.

The second unsupported hypothesis is that poorer Americans have faulty intuitions about what makes a marriage successful. Here, too, Trail and Karney's study provides a definitive test. Participants reported on the degree to which they viewed each of eleven marital characteristics as important to achieve a successful marriage (0 = *not important*; 1 = *somewhat important*; 2 = *very important*). The chart on the following page illustrates the importance ratings for the characteristics as a function of social class. The lines representing the four social-class groups are virtually on top of one

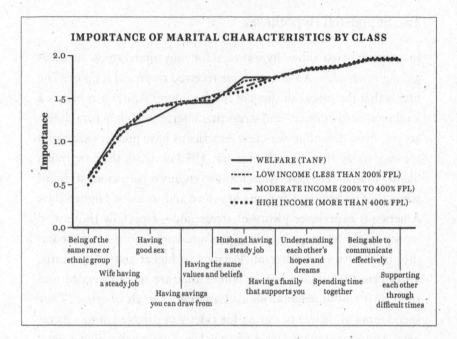

IMPORTANCE OF MARITAL CHARACTERISTICS BY CLASS

another, which provides strong evidence that social class does not meaningfully influence which characteristics people think are important for a successful marriage.

The chart also demonstrates the importance of the key variables in the all-or-nothing theory of marriage. Americans across the income spectrum view the items measuring Mount Maslow's middle altitudes ("Being able to communicate effectively," "Supporting each other through difficult times") and the higher altitudes ("Understanding each other's hopes and dreams") as extremely important for a successful marriage. They also view the item measuring oxygenation ("Spending time together") as indispensible. Indeed, of the eleven characteristics assessed, these are the four that Americans view as most important for a successful marriage.

In short, poorer Americans have every bit as much respect for the institution of marriage as wealthier Americans, and they have virtually identical intuitions about what makes a marriage successful.

Two Supported Hypotheses

In contrast, two other hypotheses for why marriage is in crisis among lower-class Americans have received empirical support. The first is that the precariousness of life for poorer Americans brings a level of unpredictability and stress that interferes with marital interaction. Even though lower-class Americans have greater existential security today than they did in, say, 1930 or 1730, they are much likelier than higher-class Americans to endure a pernicious strain of stress that undermines feelings of safety and security. Higher-class Americans experience plenty of stress, too—especially those who work seventy hours per week in pressure-cooker jobs—but the nature of the stress is different. Relative to higher-class Americans, lower-class Americans live in homes that are more crowded and run-down and in neighborhoods with higher levels of crime. They spend more of their time caring for elderly or disabled family members. And because they lack a financial cushion, challenging events, such as a car breakdown or a torn ligament, wreak particular havoc—unemployment, eviction, even destitution. Such threats have grown since the 1970s, becoming acute during and immediately following the Great Recession of 2007–2009, when the economy hemorrhaged nine million jobs and both poverty and foreclosure rates soared.

As the aftershocks of the Great Recession pummeled lower-class families, sociologists sounded the alarm in books like Jennifer Silva's *Coming Up Short: Working-Class Adulthood in an Age of Uncertainty*, Marianne Cooper's *Cut Adrift: Families in Insecure Times*, and Allison Pugh's *The Tumbleweed Society: Working and Caring in an Age of Insecurity*. "Over the past forty years, large-scale economic, employment, and political changes have come together to alter the means and manner by which many Americans build security," observes Cooper. "Since the 1970s the responsibility for managing risk has shifted from the government and employers onto individuals and their families (think of the change from pensions to individual retirement accounts)." This shift in risk affects people across the social-class spectrum, but it is especially harrowing for the poor, who are the most vulnerable to forces outside of their control.

A 2014 *New York Times* article provides a vivid portrait of daily life for poor Americans. The article features Jannette Navarro, who, at the time of the article, worked a near-minimum-wage job as a barista. She had a boyfriend and a four-year-old son. "But Ms. Navarro's fluctuating hours, combined with her limited resources," the *Times* reported, had "turned their lives into a chronic crisis over the clock. She rarely learned her schedule more than three days before the start of a workweek, plunging her into urgent logistical puzzles over who would watch the boy." In 2014, "she was scheduled to work until 11 P.M. on Friday, July 4; report again just hours later, at 4 A.M. on Saturday; and start again at 5 A.M. on Sunday."

On that occasion, she was able to impose, yet again, on her overburdened aunt to watch her son. But on July 8, she had to wake her son before 5 A.M. "Ms. Navarro hated waking Gavin so early, but the trip from home to [government-funded] day care to work took a mile-long walk, two trolleys, a bus ride and over three hours." Soon, her boyfriend broke up with her, and she and her son were sleeping on an air mattress on the floor of a former coworker.

The breakup of Navarro's relationship was surely multiply determined. But it seems fair to suggest that many of us would have a hard time sustaining a healthy relationship under such precarious economic circumstances.

The second supported hypothesis for why marriage is in crisis among lower-class Americans is linked to the first—poorer Americans have insufficient time and psychological bandwidth for cultivating their relationship. Unpredictable schedules, working evenings and weekends, and having little or no paid vacation time or sick leave not only make life chaotic, but also leave limited opportunity for engaging in loving or self-expanding interaction with one's partner. In their limited time together, it's likely that the partners will have challenging topics to discuss, including fights over money. It's little wonder that marriages in which at least one spouse works nights are at elevated risk for divorce.

The idea that lower-class individuals struggle to prioritize their relationship in part because they are depleted by the demands of everyday life is one that the psychologist Lydia Emery and I have begun investigating empirically. First, we replicated the Trail and Karney effect that social class is negligibly correlated with how much people believe their relationship is important. Next, we tested the model depicted in the diagram below. We asked participants to report how much they are able to prioritize their relationship. Although lower-class individuals rated their marriage as just as important as higher-class individuals did, they were significantly less able to prioritize it, an effect that was driven by their diminished mental bandwidth (relative to their higher-class counterparts). That is, they were less able to prioritize their relationship in part because they felt mentally worn out, a cascade of effects that ultimately predicted diminished relationship quality.

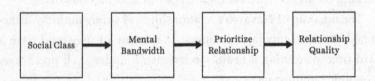

A Fifth Hypothesis

A fifth hypothesis—that poorer Americans struggle to build successful marriages because they lack the requisite cognitive or motivational attributes—serves as something of a third rail in academic circles because many scholars view it as unjustified victim-blaming. I confess that I, too, feel squeamish about it, but, as a scientist, my squeamishness doesn't allow me to dismiss it out of hand.

This hypothesis is most strongly linked to the political scientist Charles Murray, author of the controversial 1994 bestseller *The Bell Curve*. In 2012, he published *Coming Apart: The State of White America, 1960–2010*, in which he attributes the marital struggles of poorer Americans to dispositional qualities like low intelligence, inadequate self-control, and a poor work ethic—and to a general fraying of civic culture since the 1960s. He argues that the "new lower class" emerged in the 1960s and 1970s because these individuals lacked the intelligence and education to compete as the economy transitioned from physical to cerebral—from industrial to postindustrial. The new lower class became entrenched, he argues, as people increasingly married partners within their own social class—or had children out of wedlock—and lived in increasingly class-segregated communities.

Given that dispositional qualities like low self-control are indeed significant risk factors for both low income and relationship difficulties, and that variables like cognitive ability have a substantial genetic component, the prima facie case for Murray's argument is reasonable. That said, social scientists and other thought leaders have offered forceful repudiations of his analysis. High-profile critiques, including from public intellectuals like the neoconservative political analyst David Frum and the liberal opinion columnist (and Nobel Prize–winning economist) Paul Krugman, have excoriated Murray for his insufficient attention to the role of macroeconomic forces—forces outside the control of any individual—in gutting the middle class. Krugman, for example, contends that "the real winner in this controversy is the distinguished sociologist William Julius Wilson." Wilson had argued in *When Work Disappears* (1996) that the family decline in urban black neighborhoods was a result of the decline in working-class jobs, not some sort of cognitive or psychological defect in urban blacks. In Krugman's reading, Murray's *Coming Apart* simply provides another test of Wilson's when-work-disappears hypothesis—this time with white participants—and produces the exact same conclusion.

This conclusion aligns with that from new research by the economist Raj Chetty investigating what happened when poor families were randomly assigned to receive a housing voucher that allowed them to move to a lower-poverty neighborhood. Relative to poor families who did not receive a voucher, the children in the voucher families—especially the girls—grew up to be significantly more likely to marry in young adulthood. They were also more likely to go to college and less likely to become single parents, and they enjoyed greater earnings. Such effects, which only emerged if the residential move happened when the child was young (under age thirteen), suggests that poverty influences marital and other outcomes independent of any effects of inherent genetic or cognitive attributes.

At this point, the debate remains raw, and nothing approximating a consensus has emerged. As such, although both sides bring intriguing data to bear, it is too early to declare Murray's hypothesis either supported or unsupported. Even if the preponderance of the evidence eventually supports the conclusion that cognitive or psychological attributes play a significant role in explaining why the marriages of lower-class Americans are in crisis, however, any compelling explanation would also have to address the corrosive decline in working-class employment opportunities.

Higher-Class Marriages

What about the other end of the income spectrum? To some extent, the experiences of higher-class Americans are simply the mirror image of those of lower-class Americans—better marriages due to more stable lives and more quality time together. But two character-istics of higher-class marriages warrant deeper consideration. First, many higher-class couples are working exceptionally long hours these days, which leaves less time and emotional energy available for the marriage. Second, higher-class individuals are especially likely to have the opportunity to achieve meaning and self-expression through their work, which may relieve some of the pressure to max-imize the achievement of these qualities through the marriage.

These characteristics are part of a broader cultural imperative to "have it all" that frequently involves both spouses pursuing mean-ingful full-time work. Brady Stewart, who serves as vice president of global e-commerce operations at Levi Strauss & Co., provides a case in point. Consider a fairly typical day: Her husband, she tells *The New York Times*, "'has a breakfast meeting, I have a call with Eu-rope, my daughter wants to play baby mermaids, my son is starving, our dogs are barking, I need to get out the door for a work meeting and there's a dinner at night. . . . It's the time squeeze to be a great partner, professional, be in shape and have a great marriage. . . . On the days when it all works out, you've been a baby mermaid, read four books, crushed it at work and had a nice dinner with your hus-band,' she said. 'It's so rewarding. On other days, it's tough.'" Some-where along the way, living a packed life like Stewart's became prestigious, even glamorous. So much for the "leisure class."

Work is an important component of Americans' identities across the social-class spectrum, but the nature of the work-identity link varies as a function of the work itself. "For the male industrial worker," observes the sociologist Andrew Cherlin, "the task was to somehow take pride in the performance of alienating, monotonous work, such as toiling on an assembly line, and to conceive of him-self as successfully meeting the masculinity imperative of working-class life. The solution among white workers was to construct an identity that the sociologist Michèle Lamont calls 'the disciplined self.'" But "this morally based sense of dignity was a reactive identity: It was not constructed by people who had the option of taking high-paying managerial or professional jobs or who could easily find meaningful work."

Higher-class Americans are less likely to depend on reactive identities of this sort because they tend to find more intrinsic fulfillment through work. Higher-class Americans also have greater access to book clubs, art classes, public lectures, travel—countless avenues for the pursuit of self-discovery and personal growth.

Given this abundance, the achievement of self-expression through marriage might actually be less crucial for higher-class than for lower-class Americans. If lower-class Americans are going to achieve self-expression, family life may be among the best options available to them. In contrast, if higher-class Americans don't achieve self-expression through their marriage, plenty of alternative pathways are available.

Variation in American Marriage

We'll have to leave for other books how political orientation and geography influence marriage; how immigrants and their children are buffeted by crosscutting cultural currents; how slavery, Jim Crow, and mass incarceration have influenced African-American marriage; how many social welfare policies, including the Social Security Act and the G.I. Bill, benefited white families more than racial minority families; and countless other aspects of variation across social groups in America. For present purposes, it's worth noting that although social groups vary in how strongly they prioritize higher- versus lower-altitude need fulfillment through their marriage, virtually all groups are higher on Mount Maslow today than they were (or would have been) a century or two ago. And with that ascent, fulfillment in virtually all groups depends more than in the past on investment in the relationship itself—time, mental bandwidth, effective emotional communication, and so forth.

In their analysis of thriving through relationships, the psychologists Brooke Feeney and Nancy Collins ask whether it is only the privileged who can hope to self-actualize through marriage. They conclude that thriving "is not limited in this way—just as Maslow argued that all people, rich or poor, educated or not, can achieve self-actualization. . . . Self-realization is not exclusive to privileged segments of society." The same logic applies to the all-or-nothing marriage analysis: Achieving self-expression through marriage is possible across the social-class spectrum, even if it's significantly harder for poorer than for wealthier Americans.

Part Four

Toward Stronger Marriages

8.

For Better or Worse

I am separating from the man whom many of you know as "Felipe."

—Elizabeth Gilbert

On July 1, 2016, Elizabeth Gilbert posted this note on Facebook to alert her followers that she was breaking up with José Nunes, the Brazilian-Australian importer she fell in love with (and named "Felipe") at the end of *Eat Pray Love*. Shortly after her best friend, Rayya Elias, was diagnosed with cancer, Gilbert realized that Elias was "my PERSON," and she left Nunes to be with her. "Here is the thing about truth," Gilbert wrote in a follow-up note two months later. "Once you see it, you cannot un-see it. So that truth, once it came to my heart's attention, could not be ignored. . . . If I can't be my true self . . . then things will very quickly get messy and weird and stupid in my life."

Gilbert had married Nunes at the end of *Committed: A Skeptic Makes Peace with Marriage*, a sequel of sorts to *Eat Pray Love*. According to the *New York Times* review, *Committed* allowed fans and skeptics alike to "appreciate the closure of knowing that Gilbert and Felipe live happily ever after." Awkward.

The Gilbert-Nunes marriage illustrates both the power and the perils of the self-expressive marriage. Gilbert's initial Facebook announcement included a positive assessment of their relationship— "He has been my dear companion for over 12 years, and they have been wonderful years"—and a link to the poem "Failing and Flying" by Jack Gilbert (no relation). This poem uses the mythological Icarus as a metaphor for the end of a good marriage: "I believe Icarus was not failing as he fell, but just coming to the end of his triumph." The marriage with Nunes, Gilbert suggests, was not a failure because it ended, but rather a feat of ambition and courage because of the joyous years they had together.

As far as we know, this is the second time Gilbert has divorced an impressive and appealing partner who generally treated their relationship with respect and dignity (at least until she announced her divorce intentions). We see in *Eat Pray Love* that she had begun to feel stagnant in her first marriage, shackled to a set of expectations that felt no less confining because she had been instrumental in erecting them. She has not (yet) written a memoir of the decline of her second marriage, but if we take her Facebook announcement at face value, the marriage was excellent—at least until it wasn't.

As was the case with Carrie Bradshaw on HBO, I see no reason for harsh judgment here. Building a successful long-term marriage is hard. Fairy tales and romantic comedies often depict getting married as the end of the story—the beginning of the happily-ever-after. From the perspective of a relationship scientist, such stories are more farce than romance. Building a happy marriage requires that spouses successfully navigate a dense thicket of challenges and opportunities, frequently without a good map of the route ahead.

Part 4 of this book is for those of us who are struggling with or feeling stagnant in our marriage but don't want to throw in the towel. We want to improve the relationship, and we're willing to do something about it. Maybe we're hoping for a quick fix (chapter 9). Maybe we're hoping to double down in pursuit of the sort of stellar marriage that has become possible in the self-expressive era (chapter 10). Maybe we're looking for opportunities to relieve some of the pressure for a while so we can get back into a good groove together (chapter 11). Maybe we're looking for a blend of these strategies (chapter 12). As a backdrop for considering these options, we'll first explore a few crosscutting topics.

The Sooner, the Better

Being deliberate about improving our relationship can help most of us, especially because, left to their own devices, most relationships become less fulfilling over time. Researchers used to think that this downward trend reversed when the children left home, but, as shown in the following two charts, results from two major studies suggest that that's not the case.

On viewing these charts, we might be tempted to pity those poor saps whose marriages are becoming inexorably worse, counting our blessings that we are not among them. But before we get cocky

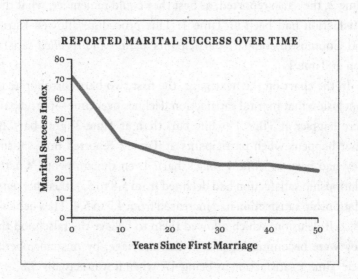

173

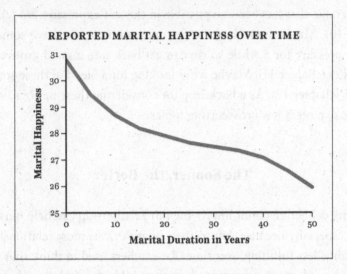

about our own marriage, let's consider sobering evidence that many of us have distorted memories of our own marital trajectory, believing that our marriage is getting better when it's actually getting worse.

In a study by the psychologists Benjamin Karney and Robert Coombs, participants reported on their marital satisfaction twice: at study intake (Time 1) and then again ten years later (Time 2). At Time 2, they also reported, as best they could remember, what their satisfaction had been at Time 1. This procedure allowed Karney and Coombs to compare participants' *actual* and *recalled* satisfaction at Time 1.

In the chart on the next page, the first two bars corroborate the conclusion that marital satisfaction declines over time—participants were happier at Time 1 (white bar) than at Time 2 (gray bar). But what happens when participants at Time 2 reported how satisfied they had been at Time 1 (black bar)? Even though people's *actual* relationship satisfaction had declined from 5.8 to 5.4, their *perceived* relationship satisfaction had increased from 4.7 to 5.4. They achieved this self-delusion, which allowed them to believe the falsehood that they were becoming happier in the marriage, by misremembering their Time 1 satisfaction as being 4.7 when it was actually 5.8.

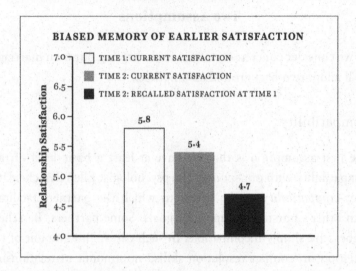

BIASED MEMORY OF EARLIER SATISFACTION

☐ TIME 1: CURRENT SATISFACTION
▨ TIME 2: CURRENT SATISFACTION
■ TIME 2: RECALLED SATISFACTION AT TIME 1

In general, just because we *perceive* that our own marriage is an exception to the depressing longitudinal trends in marital quality doesn't mean that it's truly an exception. There's a good chance we're deluding ourselves, which provides an additional reason to consider strategies for improving our marriage.

Of course, those trends characterize the average marriage; some marriages show even steeper declines, whereas others don't show any decline at all. For most of us, though, it'll be a challenge to sustain the satisfaction of the newlywed years, especially if children arrive to spit up all over our sex lives. But we are not powerless regarding the trajectory of our marriage. If we're proactive about sustaining a high-quality marriage, we can mitigate (and perhaps even reverse) the downward trend.

As we consider whether and how to be proactive, we should also consider *when*. Should we start now, or get to it at some other time? The trajectories in the graphs above and on the previous two pages suggest that we should apply to our marriage the logic of President John F. Kennedy's 1962 argument regarding the economy: "The time to repair the roof is when the sun is shining." Stated otherwise: The sooner, the better, even if things are currently going well.

Two Assumptions

As we consider concrete strategies for bolstering our own marriage, we'll adopt two background assumptions.

Compatibility

The first assumption is that we have at least a basic level of raw compatibility with our spouse. The psychologist Ellen Berscheid defines *compatibility* as the extent to which the partners facilitate each other's pursuit of important goals. Some partners, Berscheid argues, are simply incompatible. In such cases, "no amount of negotiation or 'conflict resolution skills,' no amount of relationship counseling or 'working on' the relationship, may produce compatibility."

There are two reasons why partners might be incompatible. First, they might lack sufficient *motivation* to align their thoughts, feelings, and behaviors. Deep dedication to facilitating a partner's pursuit of important goals requires significant accommodation and sacrifice. Even if the partners' goal pursuits are aligned most of the time, inevitably there will be situations in which one partner's preferences are misaligned with the other's, and building a compatible relationship requires that the two of them develop an understanding about whose goals to prioritize in such situations.

Second, the partners might lack the *ability* to align their thoughts, feelings, and behaviors. "It is undoubtedly one of the saddest facts of human affairs in general, and of interpersonal relationships in particular, that motivation without ability isn't enough," Berscheid observes. The partner of an avid tennis player might lack the hand-eye coordination required to make a match enjoyable, or the partner of an amateur philosopher might lack the linear intellect that makes philosophical debates productive. "In such cases, where motivation and/or ability to make (or not make) the relevant responses is absent," Berscheid argues, "one can predict that the relationship will become *less close,* although it may become *more compatible.*"

Indeed, there are three possible resolutions to such cases. First, one or both partners may relinquish incompatible goals altogether; the amateur philosopher might replace philosophy with a different hobby. Second, one or both partners might develop additional skills or resources to achieve the incompatibility-inducing goals without the other person's help; the amateur philosopher might try to work through certain philosophical debates as a solo activity. Third, one or both partners might find a substitute partner to facilitate the pursuit of the incompatibility-inducing goals; the amateur philosopher might pursue those debates with a colleague from work. All of these resolutions should increase harmony in the relationship by eliminating a source of incompatibility, although this harmony will have been purchased at the cost of rendering the partner irrelevant for the goals in question, thereby reducing the closeness of the relationship.

Here, again, development complicates things. Just because two partners are compatible now doesn't mean that they'll be compatible forever, given changing goals, skills, preferences, obligations, and so forth. An individual might change, for example, because she has achieved a goal (graduating from medical school), because she has jettisoned a goal (abandoning her goal to become a doctor), or because she discovers a new goal (wanting to act in movies). "We are not the same persons this year as last," observes Somerset Maugham, "nor are those we love. It is a happy chance if we, changing, continue to love a changed person." It is possible that changes will increase the compatibility of our marriage, but it is also possible that they will do just the opposite.

Openness

The second assumption is that we're open to having our spouse perceive us as we really are. The self-expressive marriage revolves around authenticity—around having our spouse develop deep understanding of our current and authentic selves. But maybe we would rather have them perceive us as better than we really are. Psychologists have explored this question for decades, discovering that we are happiest when our partner views us with a blend of accuracy and idealization.

There's a lot of truth in the playwright George Bernard Shaw's observation that "love is a gross exaggeration of the difference between one person and everybody else." When we're in love, our perceptions of our beloved tend to accentuate the positives and eliminate the negatives. And this generous bias is linked to greater marital satisfaction over time.

The psychologist Sandra Murray has conducted a series of studies demonstrating the power of rose-colored glasses, including one in which couples reported on their satisfaction seven times during their first three years of marriage. As shown in the chart on the next page, idealization predicted greater marital satisfaction over time. In Murray's words, "seeing a less-than-ideal partner as a reflection of one's ideals predicted a certain level of protection against the corrosive effects of time: People who initially idealized their partner the most experienced no decline in satisfaction." Our tendency to idealize our spouse is also linked to *our spouse's* greater satisfaction, suggesting that the positive effects of idealization exist not only in the mind of the idealizer but also extend to the overall tenor of the marriage.

The psychologists Lisa Neff and Benjamin Karney distinguish between global and specific forms of accuracy versus bias in spouses' perceptions of each other. Global perceptions capture spouses' overall evaluation of the partner by assessing agreement with items like

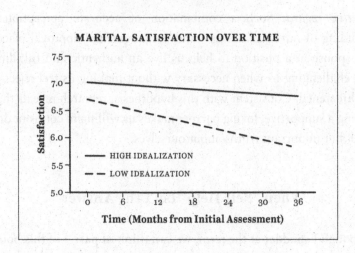

"I feel positively about my spouse." Specific perceptions capture spouses' evaluations of their partner on particular dimensions, including intellectual ability, physical attractiveness, social skills, and organizational skills.

Two longitudinal studies of newlyweds revealed that the most fulfilling marriages, especially for wives, were those characterized by idealization (positive illusions) in global assessments but accuracy in specific assessments. It's much easier to falsify specific perceptions than global ones—a partner's faux pas at a party can serve as concrete evidence he or she lacks social grace, but not that he or she is a bad person. As such, we can globally idealize our partner without much risk of encountering clear disconfirming evidence, but we are well served to be accurate about our partner's specific qualities to avoid disappointment as the evidence rolls in.

Psychologists are still unpacking precisely how accuracy and bias in spouses' perceptions influence relationship well-being. My own hypothesis is that we are happiest when our spouse accurately perceives both our actual self and our authentic self, but only if he or she views these qualities with the orientation toward warmth and acceptance that the psychologist Carl Rogers calls *unconditional positive regard*. Such a combination of accurate perception—including of our weaknesses—and nonjudgmental approval places our spouse in a position to help us live an authentic and fulfilling life, challenging us when necessary without making us feel rejected or threatened. Consistent with this hypothesis, research reveals that having a supportive, loving partner makes us willing to confront difficult but important truths about ourselves.

When "Self-Help" Isn't the Answer

Although I shudder at the term, we can think of part 4 of this book as a form of marital *self-help*—these are do-it-yourself strategies for marital improvement. They require a sober reflection on what we're asking of our marriage and whether we're investing enough time and psychological energy for it to meet these expectations. They also require that, once we've done this reflection, we are willing and able to take some initiative to increase the chances that our marriages will meet our expectations. What they don't require is the involvement of a clinical professional.

But these strategies aren't panaceas. Couples enduring serious difficulties should probably explore opportunities for professional help, including marital therapy.

In addition, not all marriages can be saved, nor should they be. Any marriage characterized by systematic physical or psychological abuse, for example, likely should end. More generally, if we're enduring serious problems in the marriage, we should probably force ourselves to answer difficult questions: Despite the current challenges, is there still a foundation of love here? Are we hopeful that we can get back to a happier place? Are we still providing a nurturing environment for our children? Is there some realignment that can get us back to easing rather than blocking each other's path to happiness and fulfillment?

Some spouses are best served by finding a safe—and, ideally, civil—way to extricate themselves from the marriage. For the rest of us, there are ways to attempt to make our marriage stronger before taking drastic measures.

Supply and Demand

At its core, the all-or-nothing theory of marriage is a supply-and-demand model: Are the two of us investing enough resources—and the right kinds of resources—to meet the needs we're seeking to fulfill through the marriage? This analysis offers three types of strategies for improving marriage. We can (1) try to get more mileage out of our available resources, (2) invest additional resources in pursuit of large rewards at the summit, or (3) recalibrate expectations to stave off disappointment. The first two of these strategies focus on the supply side (either by enhancing efficiency or increasing investment), whereas the third focuses on the demand side (by descending Mount Maslow or otherwise asking less of the marriage).

In exploring these strategies, we'll rely on the best work in the interdisciplinary field of *relationship science*. In contrast to philosophical and artistic investigations—and in contrast to self-proclaimed "relationship experts" who peddle their guesses as established facts—relationship scientists generate falsifiable hypotheses and test them with data.

Because science is a process—we'll know more tomorrow than we do today, and some of the things we currently think are true will turn out to be false—our goal is not to suggest that any specific strategy is sure to succeed. There are no guarantees or one-size-fits-all solutions. But scientific understanding of what makes relationships succeed or fail is far ahead of where it was even a few decades ago. We can leverage these insights to adopt an empirically informed way of thinking about relationships, adapting them for our own unique circumstances to develop a strategy that works for us.

We start by considering strategies that involve modest changes from the status quo. These strategies are unlikely to yield massive increases in marital quality but are likely to produce substantial increases with little investment—to offer good value. Call them "lovehacks."

9.

Lovehacking

> Mystery is not about traveling to new places but about looking with new eyes.
>
> —Marcel Proust

Lovehacks involve tweaking how we think about our partner and relationship. They can provide good bang for the buck—notable improvement in marital quality for modest investment.

"To rescue a long-term relationship from complacency and boredom," observes the philosopher Alain de Botton, "we should try to locate the good and the beautiful beneath the layers of habit and routine. We may so often have seen our partner pushing a buggy, arguing with a toddler, crossly berating the electricity company and returning home defeated from the workplace that we have forgotten that dimension in him or her that remains adventurous, impetuous, cheeky, intelligent, and above all else, alive." That everyday life is consumed with mundane logistics surrounding carpooling or spending decisions certainly doesn't help. Lovehacking involves a deliberate effort to see the beautiful underneath the anger and disappointment and boredom—to look with (appreciative) new eyes.

Lovehacking isn't the most powerful of the strategies we'll

explore; it isn't sufficient to make a marriage flourish. But it is the easiest, and it doesn't require that we lower our expectations. And, if done right, it can make a real difference, especially if we want to ensure that our marriage doesn't deteriorate before we can carve out the mental bandwidth required for deeper, more dedicated attention.

Time, the Life Cycle, and Life Events

There are many reasons why we might struggle to find the time and psychological resources to make significant additional investments in the quality of our marriage. Perhaps we're logging extreme hours to establish ourselves in a new career or piecing together two or three jobs to make ends meet. Perhaps we have two children under the age of three. Perhaps our mother is dying of cancer, and we're barely able to keep our sorrow at bay long enough to think about anything else.

As the psychologists Arthur and Elaine Aron observe in their Commentary on our *Psychological Inquiry* Target Article, demands on our time and psychological resources are not randomly distributed throughout the life cycle. "The early years of marriage correspond for most Americans to a life stage devoted to raising children and simultaneously to developing one's career." The writer Samantha Shanley refers to the early parenting years as "Phase I" of family life: "the part where we make babies and slog through the first years of child rearing with one eye open and the other imitating sleep." As the kids get more self-sufficient, she suggests, a crucial new phase dawns. For Shanley and her husband, "this new phase . . . was like coming off a long winter and waiting to see if the leaves would grow back on the trees: Either two parents figure out how to come back together and have some kind of refreshed marriage after that insulated, self-propelled procreation frenzy, or they don't." Getting to this new phase, however, requires that we keep our marriage from capsizing during Phase I.

Of course, not all circumstances that pull time and energy away from the marriage are linked to the life cycle. In our professional lives, we might be stressed by a client deadline, conflicts with coworkers, or a short-staffed team. In our personal lives, we might be consumed with a sibling's drug addiction, a stability-threatening family squabble, or an unexpected lawsuit. If such events have a much stronger effect on one spouse than the other, they provide an opportunity for the less affected spouse to provide crucial social support. But if they reverberate throughout the marriage, or if either spouse is unwilling or unable to occupy the relevant support role (provider or recipient), it's unlikely that the marriage will flourish. In such circumstances, we are probably better served by seeking to hold the marriage afloat until life gets simpler—to lovehack rather than to go all in.

Lovehacks

Lovehacks have three defining features. First, they don't take much time. Second, they don't require any coordination with, or cooperation from, our spouse. Third, they don't require that we modulate our expectations.

Although all the lovehacks we'll discuss here have received some level of empirical support, the quantity of relevant research is sometimes limited. In addition, not all lovehacks will be effective for any given individual. Considering an array of lovehacks maximizes the odds that at least one of them will appeal to almost everybody. But, more important, these specific examples illustrate a more general way of thinking about how to implement quick-and-dirty procedures to benefit our marriage; we can use them as jumping-off points for developing our own lovehacks.

Our discussion centers around two sets of lovehacks. The first set focuses on countering weaknesses in our marriage and the second focuses on savoring strengths.

Countering Weaknesses

All relationships go through difficult periods. If these periods coincide with life-cycle or life-event stressors, the threat to the relationship can be severe. Indeed, successful versus unsuccessful conflict management—how we think about and behave in conflict-relevant situations—is the factor that most reliably distinguishes successful from distressed marriages. Some reactions are like a can of kerosene, others like a bucket of water. Let's consider four lovehacks that can help us mitigate the damage of potentially destructive circumstances.

MAKING EXTERNAL, TEMPORARY ATTRIBUTIONS FOR NEGATIVE PARTNER BEHAVIORS

In everyday life, partners do some things and not others—our spouse might greet us affectionately but forget to ask us about a major meeting at work—and we must make sense of why they behaved as they did. In doing so, we develop an explanation, attributing this particular behavior to a more general cause.

Our approach to making attributions in our marriage influences how we feel about the relationship as a whole, ultimately affecting our interactions with our spouse and the long-term quality of the marriage. To illustrate how adopting certain attributions for our spouse's negative behavior can influence relationship well-being, the psychologists Thomas Bradbury and Benjamin Karney use the example of our spouse arriving late for an important event. Our attributions vary in the extent to which they explain his or her behavior as having been caused by internal versus external causes (locus of causation) and by stable versus temporary causes (stability of causation).

As we consider these four types of attributions in the table on the next page, we won't be surprised to learn that some of them tend to be better for our relationship than others. In particular, the tendency to make internal and stable attributions for our spouse's negative behaviors (upper-left quadrant) predicts greater distress about those behaviors and greater deterioration in relationship quality over time. The tendency to make external and temporary attributions for such behaviors (lower-right quadrant) does just the opposite, reducing distress about the behavior in question and promoting the well-being of the relationship over time.

		LOCUS OF CAUSATION	
		Internal	External
STABILITY OF CAUSATION	Stable	"My spouse was late because he is a thoughtless jerk."	"My spouse was late because his crappy car broke down again."
	Temporary	"My spouse was late because he forgot to set his alarm."	"My spouse was late because he got stuck in traffic."

Being more intentional about our attributions gives us an opportunity to look with new eyes. Countless times over the course of a day, a year, or a marriage, we generate an explanation for why our partner enacted a given behavior. Perceiving our partner's motives with precise accuracy has value, but doing so is virtually impossible, and the tendency to misperceive benign motivation as malignant can trigger an escalating cycle of conflict and negativity.

If we're confident that our partner is, by and large, a decent person who wants to do well by us, there's a strong argument that we should seek to make attributions that give him or her the benefit of the doubt. When the causes of a given behavior are ambiguous, we are likely to be happier, and our relationship stronger, if we assume that our partner has good intentions. One approach is to train ourselves to adopt an if-then rule like this: *If* I start feeling frustrated or angry about something my spouse did (or didn't do), *then* I will take a few seconds to consider other explanations for his or her behavior.

REAPPRAISING CONFLICT

Even if we adopt external, temporary attributions for our partner's negative behaviors, some amount of conflict will seep into virtually every marriage.

One promising way of mitigating the damage is to reappraise, or reinterpret, the conflict. In one reappraisal procedure—the *marriage hack*, which my colleagues and I recently developed—spouses think about a conflict in their marriage from the perspective of a neutral third party who wants the best for all involved.

To test whether this lovehack can strengthen relationships, we recruited 120 married couples from the Chicago area. Every four months for two years, each partner separately reported on the couple's biggest recent fight. In the second year of the study, we implemented the marriage hack intervention. All couples continued reporting on their biggest conflict every four months, but the half of them assigned to the marriage hack condition wrote for an additional seven minutes on the twelve-month, sixteen-month, and twenty-month questionnaires—for a total of twenty-one additional minutes of writing across the year.

For each seven-minute interlude, participants wrote for two to three minutes in response to each of three prompts. The first was designed to help participants adopt the perspective of a neutral, benevolent third party:

1. Think about the specific disagreement that you just wrote about having with your partner. Think about this disagreement

with your partner from the perspective of a neutral third party who wants the best for all involved; a person who sees things from a neutral point of view. How might this person think about the disagreement? How might he or she find the good that could come from it?

Adoption of this third-party perspective can be helpful, but it's especially useful if we're able to do so in real time as conflict is brewing. "While the information is there for all to read," observes Alain de Botton, "it has a cunning habit of being unavailable to us in moments of crisis. . . . We are undone by the sheer speed with which disappointments occur and by our inability to pause and rerun the tape, to rise above the fray and shift the focus away from recrimination and towards an identification of the true sources of our hurt and fear."

For this reason, we included a second and a third prompt. The second prompt was designed to help participants identify challenges in adopting such a third-party perspective during conflicts in their everyday lives:

2. Some people find it helpful to take this third-party perspective during their interactions with their romantic partner. However, almost everybody finds it challenging to take this third-party perspective at all times. In your relationship with your partner, what obstacles do you face in trying to take this third-partner perspective, especially when you're having a disagreement with your partner?

The third prompt was designed to help participants conquer the challenges they identified regarding the adoption of such a third-party perspective:

3. Despite the obstacles to taking a third-party perspective, people can be successful in doing so. Over the next four

months, please try your best to take this third-party perspective during interactions with your partner, especially during disagreements. How might you be most successful in taking this perspective in your interactions with your partner over the next four months? How might taking this perspective help you make the best of disagreements in your relationship?

The couples in this study exhibited the same downward trajectory in marital quality that reliably emerges in longitudinal research. However, the marriage hack eliminated this downward trajectory. Participants in the two groups exhibited similar rates of decline in marital quality during the first year, but the trajectories diverged once the intervention started at the beginning of the second year. Whereas the downward trajectory continued unabated among participants in the control condition, it disappeared among those in the marriage hack condition, in part because those participants felt less upset and angry about their marital conflicts.

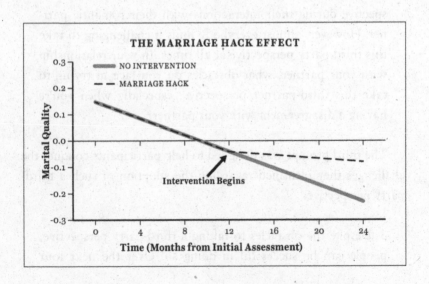

THE MARRIAGE HACK EFFECT

NO INTERVENTION
MARRIAGE HACK

Marital Quality

Intervention Begins

Time (Months from Initial Assessment)

MITIGATING INSECURITY

A third promising lovehack targets the sorts of relationship-undermining insecurities to which people with low self-esteem are especially vulnerable. The psychologist Denise Marigold developed an *abstract reframing* procedure to help low-self-esteem individuals accept rather than doubt compliments from their partner. As we've seen, such individuals tend to be self-protectively skeptical of signs that their partner loves them, which helps them minimize the pain if it turns out that that's not actually the case. Marigold's procedure circumvents this skepticism by having people think about a compliment from their partner not as relevant to a concrete, isolated event, but rather as an abstract, general statement about their worthiness of admiration.

Participants in one experiment were prompted to bring to mind a compliment they had received from their partner. They then responded to one of three prompts:

1. *No-intervention condition*: "Describe the event in the space below."
2. *Concrete reframing condition*: "Describe exactly what your partner said to you. Include any details you can recall about where you two were at the time, what you were doing, what you were both wearing, etc."
3. *Abstract reframing condition*: "Explain why your partner admired you. Describe what it meant to you and its significance for your relationship."

Two weeks later, participants reported how secure they felt in their relationship, responding to items like "I am confident that my partner will always want to look beyond my faults and see the best in me" (1 = *not at all true*; 7 = *completely true*). As shown in the chart on the next page, and in accord with other research, people with lower self-esteem tended to feel less secure in their relationship in the no-intervention condition, an effect that also emerged in the concrete reframing condition. But this adverse effect of low self-esteem disappeared among participants in the abstract reframing condition. It seems that those of us who struggle with low self-esteem can overcome our destructive self-protectiveness, and experience greater feelings of security in our relationship, when we respond to compliments from our partner by considering why he or she admires us and what the compliment signifies about the relationship.

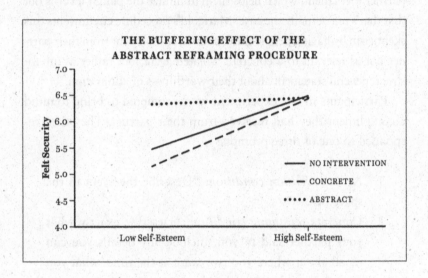

ADOPTING A GROWTH MIND-SET

We have wide latitude in considering whether problems in our marriage are fixable. According to the psychologist Raymond Knee, people with strong *destiny beliefs* think that partners either are or are not "meant to be." They view conflict and other relationship difficulties as indicators that they may simply be incompatible with their partner. People with strong *growth beliefs*, in contrast, think that partners can cultivate a high-quality relationship by working and growing together. They view conflict and other relationship difficulties as opportunities to develop a stronger relationship.

Pop quiz: Does Elizabeth Gilbert subscribe to destiny or growth beliefs? From *Eat Pray Love*, a clue:

> One thing I do know about intimacy is that there are certain natural laws which govern the sexual experience of two people, and that these laws cannot be budged any more than gravity can be negotiated with. To feel physically comfortable with someone else's body is not a decision you can make. It has very little to do with how two people think or act or talk or even look. The mysterious magnet is either there, buried somewhere deep behind the sternum, or it is not. When it isn't there (as I have learned in the past, with heartbreaking clarity) you can no more force it to exist than a surgeon can force a patient's body to accept a kidney from the wrong donor.

The science is clear that holding strong destiny beliefs is perilous, and I wouldn't be surprised if Gilbert's extreme adherence to such beliefs played a role in her divorces. The issue isn't that people who believe in romantic destiny are always less satisfied than people who don't; indeed, when things are going smoothly, such individuals can be especially satisfied. The issue is that people who believe in romantic destiny tend to become unhappy quickly when relationships go through challenging times. Consequently, they are at greater risk for breakup. And, of course, going through challenging times is virtually inevitable in a long-term relationship.

In a 2007 article titled "Vengefully Ever After," the psychologists Jeni Burnette, Lauren Scissors, and I investigated the role of destiny beliefs in the forgiveness process. Across experimental and longitudinal studies, we found that people tend to be especially unforgiving of their partner's transgressions when they are feeling insecure about how much he or she cares for them and when they hold destiny beliefs about relationships. It seems that, when we're encountering relationship difficulties, destiny beliefs are linked to a tendency to be pessimistic or to give up rather than to be understanding and work on the relationship.

Now consider growth beliefs. The journalist Ada Calhoun captures the spirit of the growth mind-set: "It is easy for people who have never tried to do anything as strange and difficult as being married to say marriage doesn't matter, or to condemn those who fail at it, or to mock those who even try. But there is so much beauty in the trying, and in the failing, and in the trying again." She continues: "Epic failure is part of being human, and it's definitely part of being married. It's part of what being alive means, occasionally screwing up in expensive ways. And that's part of what marriage means, sometimes hating this other person but staying together because you promised you would. And then, days or weeks later, waking up and loving him again, loving him still."

Adopting a growth mind-set allows us to look with new eyes at relationship difficulties. Yes, difficulties are unpleasant, and some of them might even point to major incompatibility with our partner. But, assuming there's a deep thread of goodness in the relationship, it's constructive to think of difficulties not only as unpleasant circumstances to be endured, but also as opportunities to learn about each other and to deepen the relationship.

The scientific literature doesn't include any studies seeking to help people adopt a growth mind-set regarding difficulties in their relationship, but perhaps we can mine Knee's self-report measure of growth beliefs to generate ideas. This measure assesses agreement with items like "A successful relationship evolves through hard work and resolution of incompatibilities" and "Challenges and obstacles in a relationship can make love even stronger." One promising option for approaching our relationship in a growth mind-set is to take a few minutes every month to think about ways in which such statements are true, ideally focusing on instances in our own lives when, for example, overcoming an obstacle made a relationship stronger.

Savoring Strengths

Minimalist lovehacks that help people cope with challenges can provide superb value, but managing challenges isn't everything. All decent relationships also enjoy good times. Some couples are excellent at savoring their strengths, whereas others tend to get distracted, failing to appreciate how fortunate they are. Let's consider four lovehacks that can help us savor.

MAKING INTERNAL, STABLE ATTRIBUTIONS FOR POSITIVE PARTNER BEHAVIORS

We saw earlier that making external, temporary attributions for our spouse's negative behaviors is linked to elevated relationship quality. It turns out that the inverse is true regarding our spouse's positive behaviors: Rather than separating our spouse from the behavior and treating it as a one-off event, relationships benefit when we link our spouse to the behavior and treat it as generally characteristic of him or her—when we make internal, stable attributions.

Consider the example of our spouse bringing us a surprise gift. Here, again, our attributions vary in the extent to which they explain his or her behavior as having been caused by internal versus external causes (locus of causation) and by stable versus temporary causes (stability of causation). As we consider these four types of attributions in the table on the following page, it's clear once again that some of them are likely to be better for our relationship than others. In particular, the tendency to make internal and stable attributions for our spouse's positive behaviors (upper-left quadrant) predicts greater happiness about those behaviors and greater improvement in relationship

		LOCUS OF CAUSATION	
		Internal	**External**
STABILITY OF CAUSATION	**Stable**	"My spouse brought me a surprise gift because he's a kindhearted man."	"My spouse brought me a surprise gift because his mom is always nagging him to do so."
	Temporary	"My spouse brought me a surprise gift because he was feeling guilty about starting a fight with me yesterday."	"My spouse brought me a surprise gift because he wanted to regift a vase a client had given him."

quality over time. The tendency to make external and temporary attributions for such behaviors (lower-right quadrant) does just the opposite, diminishing happiness about the behavior and undermining the well-being of the relationship over time.

As with our spouse's negative behaviors, we typically have a good deal of latitude for explaining our spouse's positive behaviors. Making internal, stable attributions for what we have witnessed—attributing our spouse's behavior to his or her general kindheartedness or his or her long-standing love for us—is linked to greater personal happiness and marital well-being. Here, again, one approach is to train ourselves to adopt an if-then rule like this: *If* my partner does—or tries to do—something that benefits me (or doesn't do something that harms me), *then* I will take a few seconds to focus on an internal, stable explanation for his or her behavior.

CULTIVATING GRATITUDE

A second lovehack for savoring strengths is the cultivation of gratitude. In recent years, a number of psychologists, including Sara

Algoe, Amie Gordon, Emily Impett, and Samantha Joel, have conducted research demonstrating the power gratitude for strengthening emotional bonds in close relationships. Algoe argues that gratitude serves as a "booster shot" for romantic relationships.

People tend to experience higher gratitude on days when their partner does something thoughtful for them, and such gratitude predicts elevated relationship quality the next day. In fact, when one partner experiences elevated gratitude on a given day, *both partners* experience positive relationship outcomes. In the long run, people who experience elevated levels of gratitude also experience stronger relationship commitment and are less likely to break up.

Several experiments suggest that deliberate efforts to increase our own feelings of gratitude hold promise for improving our relationships and our overall well-being. In one study, participants who were randomly assigned to write and deliver a letter of gratitude to somebody they had not properly thanked previously were happier over the subsequent month than participants who were randomly assigned to a control condition in which they wrote about their earliest memories every night for a week. In another study, participants assigned to "count their blessings" were happier with their life as a whole—both according to their own and their spouse's ratings of their happiness—than participants who were assigned to a no-intervention control condition.

A third study sought to induce gratitude toward a romantic partner in particular. Participants were randomly assigned to one of three conditions:

1. *No-intervention condition.* Participants didn't partake in a writing procedure.
2. *Own investment condition.* Participants first wrote about "the various ways in which they had invested in the relationship." They then wrote about one particularly significant investment they had made and described why this investment was so significant.

3. *Partner investment (gratitude) condition.* Participants performed the same procedures as in the own investment condition, except they wrote about their partner's investments in the relationship—and the significance thereof—rather than their own.

Next, all participants completed measures of gratitude toward their partner and commitment to the relationship. As illustrated below, relative to participants in the no-intervention or the own investment condition, participants in the partner investment condition exhibited greater gratitude toward their partner and greater commitment to their relationship.

This work identifies the sorts of procedures we can use to perform a gratitude-enhancing lovehack in our own marriage. The partner investment condition didn't use any convoluted or time-consuming procedures. All of us can find a few minutes per week—before going to bed or while showering, perhaps—to think about

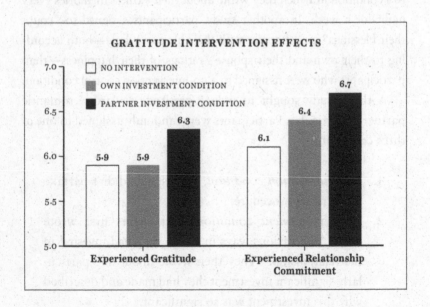

GRATITUDE INTERVENTION EFFECTS

NO INTERVENTION
OWN INVESTMENT CONDITION
PARTNER INVESTMENT CONDITION

ways in which our spouse has invested in our marriage. Doing so has the potential not only to bolster our gratitude and relationship commitment, but also to increase our overall happiness. And here's the kicker: Because our own experience of gratitude tends to predict *our partner's* warm treatment toward us, our decision to pursue a gratitude-increasing lovehack can increase our partner's positivity toward us, potentially launching a virtuous cycle of mutual gratitude, kindness, and commitment.

Of course, working to bolster our own sense of gratitude for our partner isn't the only gratitude-related lovehack available. We can also do little things to *express* our gratitude. Such activities can be cheap if money is scarce—we can leave a brief note of thanks in our spouse's underwear drawer, for example. Or they can be easy if time is scarce. I leveraged this latter option at a dark moment in my marriage.

Alison and I had agreed not to get each other gifts for Valentine's Day. We shared the view that it's a made-up holiday that corporations like Hallmark created so they could exploit humanity's better nature to make more money. Or, at least, I'd *thought* we shared that view. It turns out that failing to do anything for my wife on that particular Valentine's Day was a rather grave error. Alison and I were pretty disconnected during the postpartum period, which made my failure to buy a gift strike her as a lack of love and appreciation. Not a complete fool, I had made a mental note of a decadently expensive sweater she'd admired, and, shortly after our own personal Valentine's Day massacre—no deaths, but lots of tears—I had it overnighted to her, along with a brief note: "I appreciate you." I was pleasantly surprised by how far that gift went in mitigating the damage from the giftlessness of the previous day. It didn't eliminate our problems, of course—no gift could do that—but Alison loves that sweater, which she still calls the "I appreciate you" sweater.

CELEBRATING TOGETHER

A third lovehack for savoring strengths involves helping each other celebrate life's achievements and successes. Inspired by the poet John Milton's observation in *Paradise Lost* that "good, the more communicated, more abundant grows," the psychologists Shelly Gable and Harry Reis observe that social support is about much more than helping each other through hard times. These scholars have built a program of research demonstrating the power of delighting in good news together. In particular, communicating with our partner about personal positive events—that is, engaging in *capitalization attempts*—is linked to positive emotions and mental health, beyond any effect of the events themselves. Such capitalization attempts are also linked to greater feelings of trust, intimacy, and satisfaction in the relationship. And the positive effects emerge not only for the partner doing the disclosing, but also for the listener.

These salutary effects are especially strong when the listener responds in an enthusiastic, celebratory manner rather than in a quietly supportive manner or in a manner that focuses on the potential downsides of the positive event. Enthusiastic responses are beneficial because they convey the listener's shared joy in the event and appreciation of the personal significance of the event for the discloser.

Preliminary evidence suggests that we can readily learn to apply enthusiastic, celebratory responding to our partner's capitalization attempts. In one study, couples were randomly assigned either to a condition in which they were trained, briefly, on how to enact such responses or to a no-intervention condition. Then, every evening over the subsequent week, the partners took turns discussing their most important personal positive event that day. Couples who had been trained in enthusiastic, celebratory responding—trained to ask questions about the event, show positive emotion about it, and generally be engaged and constructive during the interaction—tended to experience greater love for each other following those nightly discussions.

AFFECTIONATELY TOUCHING

A fourth lovehack for savoring strengths—affectionate touch—is particularly promising for helping *our partner* look with new eyes. In one experiment, conducted by the psychologists Brittany Jakubiak and Brooke Feeney, couples watched a video together. Before the video began, the partners were separated to complete questionnaires. At that point, the experimenter gave one of two sets of instructions to the partner about how to behave with the participant while they watched the video together:

1. *No touch condition.* The experimenter instructed the partner to sit near the participant but to avoid touching him or her and "not to reciprocate any touch the [participant] initiated."
2. *Affectionate touch condition.* The experimenter instructed the partner to touch the participant in a "warm, comfortable, and positive way," such as by holding hands or putting an arm around the participant.

After watching the video together, the participant completed a questionnaire indicating how secure and trusting they felt in the relationship, such as their level of agreement with statements like "Right now, I am confident that my partner will always love me." As hypothesized, participants whose partner had been instructed to touch them felt more secure and trusting in the relationship than did participants whose partner had been instructed not to touch them. Perhaps surprisingly, this difference emerged even in a condition in which the experimenter informed the participant that the partner's touching behavior (or lack thereof) had been determined by the study protocol, which suggests that a partner's touch is beneficial even if we know that it isn't a spontaneous expression of affection.*

In Praise of Efficiency

Given the primacy of the marital bond in America today, many of us will be uncomfortable acknowledging that we simply aren't able or willing right now to invest significant additional time and psychological energy to improve the relationship (the sorts of all-in strategies we'll discuss in the next chapter). That discomfort is misguided.

Although it's not always simple to implement lovehacks effectively, doing so provides an efficient method for keeping our marriages afloat during challenging or busy times, and they do so without requiring that we lower our marital expectations. There are times when we simply lack the ability or the motivation to make hefty additional investment, and there's no shame in doing little things to make the relationship a bit stronger than it would be otherwise.

That said, when things ease up and the circumstances allow for hefty investment, the rewards can be enormous. Let's consider some promising ways to go all in.

---

* Additional research demonstrates that affectionate touching also increases spouses' levels of oxytocin, a hormone linked to affiliation, especially in the context of supportive interaction with a loved one.

10.

Going All In

We went to the Musée d'Orsay, and I wept looking at
Caillebotte's Planers, that sublime rendering of sunlight
on wood and bare skin, just as I had when I first saw the
painting all those years before. We walked and we slept
and we drank. We made a new mark on the city.

—Erin White

When Erin was twenty-four, she met Chris, the woman she
would eventually marry. "Chris introduced me to myself,"
Erin reports. "At first I was startled; at first I demurred. Oh, no, I
wanted to say. I think you are mistaken. But she wasn't. By the time
we were in Paris, I had stopped asking myself how she knew. By the
time we were in Paris, I had learned how to just enjoy myself. Which
is exactly what we did."

Erin was twenty-five on that trip. A few years later, when their
first daughter arrived, she decided to become a full-time mother.
She derived great joy from this role, but she also struggled with it.
"The tedium and isolation of stay-at-home motherhood is a story as
old as water, but in every generation we are caught off guard by its
oddities, its strains. We can't imagine anyone ever being as stunned
by love and boredom as we are."

The marriage changed: "I hadn't married Chris because I wanted to be her partner in domestic endeavor; I had married her because when she kissed me, my body said *stay*. But now that we had become so focused on our responsibilities, I wasn't as interested in kissing Chris as I once had been. I was more interested in telling her what she owed me. . . . I devoted myself to my children and I relegated my marriage to the realm of domestic management and scorekeeping."

Chris finally convinced her that they should go back to Paris for her fortieth birthday. But, in Erin's words: "From the moment we arrived, Paris was lovely, and I was sad. . . . I couldn't stop thinking about the girl I had been when we were here before: the girl who would rather go to a bar than a museum; who bought sexy bras at Aubade, not little-girl tights at Monoprix." On the second day, Chris suggested that they revisit the hotel they'd stayed in fifteen years earlier—to get a drink and take a picture that would match the one hanging in their bedroom. Feeling disconnected, Erin declined.

Chris was hurt, and Erin felt guilty. They had a painful conversation, and Erin softened. "I'm so sorry," she said. "And—you're very beautiful." They ordered a bottle of wine and continued to break down the wall that had grown between them. "I was careful, and I could feel Chris being careful too. But it was not awkward. It was the opposite of awkward, really. . . . After that, our days in Paris passed quickly—slowly, luxuriously, too."

The chill that had blown in slowly over the years dissipated, and the two of them rediscovered what made their relationship great. With continued attention, there's a good chance that they'll be able to sustain their rekindled warmth for the long run.

Surviving versus Thriving

Chapter 9 discussed lovehacks—cost-efficient strategies that we can use to make our marriage a bit stronger without requiring that we lower our expectations. Chapter 11 will discuss strategies that we can use to try to reduce the undue pressure that many of us place on our marriage. Neither of these sets of strategies is oriented toward achieving the flourishing marriage available in the self-expressive era—the *all* version of the all-or-nothing marriage. This much more ambitious goal—which involves regular, prolonged summits, along with sensible descents as circumstances require—is the focus of the present chapter. How can spouses build a marriage that doesn't just survive, but thrives?

The psychologists Brooke Feeney and Nancy Collins have a theory. They begin with a quote from Maya Angelou, the author, poet, and civil rights activist: "My mission in life is not merely to survive, but to thrive; and to do so with some passion, some compassion, some humor, and some style. Surviving is important. Thriving is elegant." Feeney and Collins examine how we can achieve this sort of elegance through our relationships.

Their theory identifies two pathways to thriving. First, "individuals thrive . . . when they are able to cope successfully with adversities, not only by being buffered from potentially severe consequences of adversity when it arises, but also by emerging from the experience as a stronger or more knowledgeable person." For example, we can emerge with a "heightened sense of mastery, increased self-regard, a greater sense of purpose in life, and more meaningful social bonds." Second, "individuals thrive . . . when they are able to fully participate in opportunities for fulfillment and personal growth through work, play, socializing, learning, discovery, creating, pursuing hobbies, and making meaningful contribution to community and society."

Happily, neither of these pathways to thriving requires a trip to Paris. Discretionary money and good child care options make things easier, but they're certainly not necessary.

Creating Time

A prerequisite for thriving through marriage is that we dedicate sufficient time and attention to the relationship. Life is filled with things that scream loudly—pressing deadlines, household responsibilities, anxious children, ill parents—and, most of the time, our marriage isn't one of them. Many of us wind up treating quality time with our spouse as a luxury to be enjoyed when all the necessities of life have been addressed—if that ever happens.

But it's possible to reverse, or at least mitigate, that mind-set. Rather than treating everything else as the priority and squeezing our marriage into the pockets of leftover time, we can seek to do the opposite. Given the psychological and physical benefits of a successful marriage, there's an argument to be made that, where possible, we should make quality time for the marriage even if doing so requires that we transfer to a less stressful job or live in a home with dust bunnies or enroll our kids in fewer activities.

Carpe Diem

As busy as we are, most of us could carve out some additional quality time for our spouse. In *I Know How She Does It: How Successful Women Make the Most of Their Time*, the author Laura Vanderkam tracked hourly time logs from 1,001 days in the lives of full-time working mothers. Vanderkam focused on a select group of women who earn at least $100,000 per year, so we need to be careful about generalizing her results to other people. That said, full-time working mothers aren't exactly a group with endless free time on their hands, and their time logs offer some potentially useful lessons for the rest of us. After all, 61 percent of working Americans in 2015 reported that they didn't have enough time to do the things they want to do, and 90 percent of working mothers reported feeling rushed some of or all the time.

And yet, we might have more leisure time than we think. Vanderkam clocked her own schedule during a year when she gave birth to her fourth child (the oldest was seven). She and her husband work full-time, and both travel for work. They have a nanny and family help, but still—these are busy people. At the end of the year, she crunched the numbers in her time log. "If I wanted to construct a narrative of craziness," she reports, "I had moments that would qualify. I pumped breast milk in Amtrak bathrooms. I was up from 11:30 P.M. to 2 A.M. with the baby one night before getting on an early flight to Tampa, Fla., where I was giving a speech. I logged hours doing laundry—sheets, blankets, pillows—as a brutal stomach bug worked its way through the gastrointestinal tracts of all four children. To catch up, I worked late at night. I worked on weekends. I worked on vacations." But, she continues, "there was plenty of evidence of a calmer life. I got eight massages. I went for long weekend runs (constituting some of the 232.75 hours I spent exercising). I went out to dinner with friends. I spent evenings after the kids went to bed sitting out on the porch, reading fashion or gossip magazines. (My reading total: 327 hours flat. It could have been 'War and Peace.' It wasn't.)"

Most of us overestimate how much we work, and the overestimates are particularly large among people who claim to work the most. Americans who claim to work thirty-five to fifty-four hours per week tend to overestimate by about five hours per week on average, whereas those who claim to work seventy-five or more hours per week overestimate by about twenty-five hours per week. And we spend a staggering amount of time watching television. According to a Neilson report in 2016, we watch an average of five hours per day, excluding the ninety minutes we spend looking at our smartphones. It's not as if we could turn every one of those minutes into quality engagement with our spouse—and many of us aren't interested in packing as much into our daily lives as Vanderkam or the women in her book—but many of us could carve out at least some of the time for that purpose.

None of this is to suggest that we're not busy or that all people overestimate how busy they are or that Vanderkam's conclusions apply equally across the social-class spectrum. But the reality is that many of us have more leisure time than we think we do. And that's good news, because it means that we can make an effort to be more mindful about how we use our time.

Serendipity

Since they were babies, both of my children have had a sleepover at their grandparents' house on one weekend night each week, gone from perhaps from 4 P.M. one day until 9 A.M. the next. Although the grandparents usually end up shell-shocked and in need of a seven-hour nap, they love these long visits, as do the kids. And it's not lost on the grandparents (our parents) that they are giving Alison and me a big chunk of childless time every weekend. We typically don't do anything fancy with the time—perhaps we indulge ourselves with the world's greatest pizza* and then watch a movie at home—and many of these date nights are unmemorable.

But every month or two, I'm struck by how much we have to say to each other. Maybe one of us had an awkward interaction with a friend or a notable success at work, and with the chaos of daily life, we just never mentioned it. Yet at the restaurant, or on the couch, with no interruptions and no kid-induced early morning awaiting us, the conversation transforms from mundane to significant. These conversations make a big difference in how close we feel to each other.

Perhaps the most notable feature of these conversations is that they aren't about topics that we had been waiting to discuss. We don't arrive at the dinner with a conversational agenda. The unrushed time affords serendipitous connection.

Frank Bruni, the *New York Times* columnist, argues that "quality time" is a myth—that there's no way we "can plan instances of extraordinary candor, plot episodes of exquisite tenderness, engineer

---

* Union Pizzeria in Evanston, Illinois.

intimacy in an appointed hour." He observes that "people tend not to operate on cue. At least our moods and emotions don't. We reach out for help at odd points; we bloom at unpredictable ones. The surest way to see the brightest colors, or the darkest ones, is to be watching and waiting and ready for them."

Bruni and his extended family of twenty take a weeklong beach vacation every year. He used to arrive a day or two late or leave a day or two early because, let's face it, a week of family time can feel interminable. But now he goes for the whole time. "With a more expansive stretch," he writes, "there's a better chance that I'll be around at the precise, random moment when one of my nephews drops his guard and solicits my advice about something private. Or when one of my nieces will need someone other than her parents to tell her that she's smart and beautiful. Or when one of my siblings will flash back on an incident from our childhood that makes us laugh uncontrollably, and suddenly the cozy, happy chain of our love is cinched that much tighter."

Bruni is right, and his insight applies to marriage. If we're happy to tread water, an attentive hour per month may be sufficient. But if we're seeking something extraordinary—a profound sense of connection—there's no substitute for significant dedicated time. When Erin and Chris revisited Paris, they had a major breakthrough, but it's unlikely that they would have had it without the expansive time the vacation afforded—or that that trip will be sufficient to sustain their marital intimacy for the long run. As they return to their daily lives, they'll need to continue to find dedicated time for each other.

Attention

A crucial element of time together is that the people involved are not only in each other's presence, but also present. Spending a four-hour stretch together when all parties are looking at their own electronic devices most of the time can be enjoyable, but it's a poor recipe for fostering deep intimacy. My aunt, whose five-decade marriage was one for the ages, used to tell her husband: "You're either having dinner with your phone or with me, not with both of us." And she's onto something: Spouses who spend more time together engaged in actual conversation tend to be happier than those who spend less. Spouses who pursue more leisure activities together—including outdoor activities, sports, card games, and travel—are at reduced risk of divorce.

We've seen that people tend to become less happy in their marriage once they have their first child, and that this transition-to-parenthood penalty has gotten stronger over time. A primary reason for these effects is that the baby's arrival decreases the amount of quality time that spouses spend together. One nationally representative study assessed how frequently wives "had spent time alone with their husbands in the previous month either engaged in an activity or talking." The transition to parenthood significantly reduced the frequency of such activities, and this reduction largely accounted for the transition-to-parenthood decline in marital satisfaction.

Being present means focusing our full attention, or at least most of it, on the current interaction. Those of us seeking to maximize the quality of our marriage by engaging in shared activities with our partner are well served to remember the wisdom of the philosopher and activist Simone Weil: "Attention is the rarest and purest form of generosity."

Her Majesty

The idea that spending dedicated time together is required to build a successful marriage in the self-expressive era has an important corollary: The investment of quality time together over the years can build up a store of relationship capital, which can serve as a partial buffer against the lack of quality time together in the present.

In a sense, each relationship develops its own unique culture over time—its own norms, beliefs, and jokes. This miniculture influences how we respond to events in real time. For example, spouses who have accrued a large number of positive shared experiences over time tend to be buffered against the distressing effects of day-to-day conflict in their marriage. More generally, spouses in a successful marriage can leverage their shared culture to achieve a sort of emotional shorthand that can help them stay connected even when time together is scarce.

Alison and I are partial to the phrase *bellyful of wine*.

We first used that phrase in our first months of dating. I took it from "Her Majesty," Paul McCartney's hidden, twenty-three-second gem at the end of the Beatles' *Abbey Road* album. In the playful lyrics, McCartney wants to tell Queen Elizabeth that he loves her, but doing so requires that he get "a bellyful of wine." When I wanted to tell Alison that I loved her, that I was grateful for her, that I admired her, and that she made me happy, I would sing those lyrics. Over time, *bellyful of wine* became an efficient means of expressing a terabyte of affection.

This phrase is part of a broader suite of idiosyncratic references—to bad song lyrics or inadvertently obscene things our kids have said—that help keep us bonded and playful when time together is scarce. Building our little culture took countless thousands of hours over many years, but sustaining it doesn't always require extensive time in the present.

Nourishing the Self-Expressive Marriage

Building and sustaining a high-quality marriage almost always requires that we make a deliberate effort to cultivate our relationship skills. In *The Art of Loving*, the philosopher and psychoanalyst Erich Fromm rejects the romantic idea that love is a magical event that the fates mysteriously bestow upon us. "People think that to *love* is simple," he observes, "but that to find the right object to love—or to be loved by—is difficult." Fromm, in contrast, favors the idea that love—which he defines in terms of care, responsibility, respect, and knowledge—is a skill that we must cultivate. "The first step to take," he argues, "is to become aware that *love is an art*, just as living is an art; if we want to learn how to love we must proceed in the same way we have to proceed if we want to learn any other art, say music, painting, carpentry, or the art of medicine or engineering."

Nobody would seek to be successful at playing the violin by waiting for the right instrument to come along, but many of us seek to be successful at relationships by waiting for the right partner to come along. Fromm is correct that we would be better served by cultivating our ability to love—to become skilled, mature, and self-aware relationship partners.

There's no single recipe for learning how to love, just as there's no standard formula that can enrich every marriage. But relationship science has matured enough to offer some general principles. Let's consider three sets of strategies we can use if we want to nourish our marriage in the self-expressive era—strategies linked to communication, responsiveness, and play.

Communication

A defining feature of the self-expressive marriage is that spouses facilitate each other's self-discovery and personal growth, a process that is especially challenging because each self is unique. Married life provides many clues about our spouse's actual and ideal selves—such as when we watch him or her become more immersed in social activism than in meditation—but the most important pathway for achieving mutual insight is effective communication, especially the self-disclosure of emotionally significant or self-relevant information.

Greater self-disclosure is linked to higher relationship quality. In one study, the psychologist Ronald Rogge randomly assigned couples either to a no-intervention control condition or an intervention condition that "drew partners' attention to current behavior in their relationship and encouraged them to decide for themselves if their behavior was constructive or destructive." In this intervention condition, the spouses "were introduced to the idea that regular everyday events—particularly those captured in commercial films—could be used as prompts" to help them work on relationship awareness and maintenance. Spouses watched a relationship-themed movie together and then spent an hour responding to a preassigned set of questions about it. The questions were about relationship conflict, expectations, social support, and forgiveness. Then, each week over the next month, they viewed a different relationship-themed movie and discussed the same set of questions. Relative to participants in the no-treatment condition, participants in the intervention condition were about half as likely to separate or divorce over the next three years (13 versus 24 percent).*

Talking about highly conflictual issues in the relationship is more challenging, especially if the conversations happen in a climate of anger and frustration. The psychologist John Gottman, having conducted extensive research in which he videotapes distressed and nondistressed couples discussing conflictual topics in their relationship, has compiled a suite of communication behaviors that reliably distinguish between successful and unsuccessful marriages. Four particularly damaging behaviors are criticism (characterizing the conflict in terms of a fundamental flaw in our spouse), defensiveness (counterattacking rather than engaging with our spouse's concern), contempt (engaging in insulting, mocking, or hostile behavior), and stonewalling (clamming up when our partner raises a concern). In general, it's beneficial for each partner to try to respond generously when the other behaves badly, as doing so avoids the escalating cycles of negative reciprocity characteristic of unhealthy relationships.

---

* This study included two additional conditions, both of which were much more labor-intensive than the minimalist movie-viewing condition described here. Those more intensive conditions were also beneficial when compared to the no-intervention condition, but no more so than the movie-viewing condition.

This conclusion echoes the wedding advice given to the Supreme Court justice Ruth Bader Ginsburg by her mother-in-law: "In every good marriage, it helps sometimes to be a little deaf." Or, in Ginsburg's own words: "When a thoughtless or unkind word is spoken, best tune out."

Despite the timeless wisdom in these insights, the truth is that most forms of communication are beneficial in some circumstances but destructive in others. The psychologists Nickola Overall and James McNulty have demonstrated that the effects of particular conflict-relevant communication strategies on relationship well-being are more complicated than they initially appear. These scholars situate the realm of possible communication behaviors within the two-dimensional space depicted on the following page. *Intent of communication* specifies whether our communications express goals and motivations that are similar to and cooperative with our partner's versus contrasting to and opposing our partner's. *Directness of communication* specifies whether our communications are direct versus indirect with regard to both the problem at hand and how to achieve change. The figure provides examples of the four general types of communication encompassed by this two-dimensional space.

It's easy to see why communications characterized by *direct cooperation* (upper-left quadrant), such as offering solutions, tend to be beneficial. But the other three forms of communication can also be beneficial under some circumstances. For example, although communications characterized by *direct opposition* (upper-right quadrant), such as expressing anger, tend to be harmful when they are excessive or when our partner is incapable of resolving the problem, they can be beneficial when they are proportionate to the severity of the problem or when our partner is capable of resolving the problem. Although communications characterized by *indirect opposition* (lower-right quadrant), such as inducing guilt, tend to be harmful when our partner resents the implied obligation or is resistant to change, they can be beneficial when inducing guilt sensitizes

		INTENT OF COMMUNICATION	
		Cooperation	Opposition
DIRECTNESS OF COMMUNICATION	Direct	• Reasoning and negotiation • Outlining the causes and consequences of the problem • Offering solutions and exploring alternatives • Weighing up pros and cons • Generating solution-oriented discussions	• Criticizing • Derogating and blaming the partner • Expressing anger and irritation • Demanding or commanding change • Adopting a domineering and nonnegotiable stance
	Indirect	• Softening conflict • Expressing love and affection • Using humor • Minimizing the problem • Emphasizing positive aspects of partner or relationship • Conveying optimism for improvement • Restraining negative reactions	• Attempts to induce guilt and sympathy by appealing to partner's love and relationship obligations • Emphasizing expressions of hurt and sadness • Conveying dependence or powerlessness

our partner to our hurt feelings and he or she is comfortable with our vulnerability. Although communications characterized by *indirect cooperation* (lower-left quadrant), such as using humor, tend to be harmful when they leave serious problems unaddressed, they can be beneficial when they reduce our partner's defensiveness in a manner that helps us work through the problem together.

If we think in terms of amount rather than type of communication, more communication is linked to marital well-being, but there are exceptions. Some people like to process the relationship regularly, whereas others prefer to take the general goodness of the relationship as an article of faith without doing deep emotional work to unpack every disagreement or miscommunication. Indeed, a key feature of effective communication is understanding when our spouse doesn't want to talk and, more generally, understanding that he or she is entitled to some privacy.

Responsiveness

A second set of all-in strategies is linked to responsiveness—the manner in which partners attend to and support each other's goals and needs. Responsiveness consists of three core components: *Understanding* involves "comprehending the partner's core self (e.g., needs, desires, strengths, weaknesses, etc.)." *Validation* involves "respect for or valuing of the partner's view of the self." *Caring* involves "expressing affection, warmth, and concern for the partner's well-being."

One reason why being a responsive partner isn't a straightforward task is that, even in a climate of goodwill, achieving understanding is far trickier than it sounds. It's not always clear what our own goals and needs are in a given situation, much less what our partner's goals and needs are. Developing veridical and shared understanding can take years of getting to know one another—not to mention close attention in the moment, especially in situations that are psychologically complex. (Every once in a while, a meltdown can facilitate communication, as when Alison's Valentine's Day anguish helped me understand what she was going through. It also helped me enhance her wardrobe.)

The diagram on the next page illustrates a prevailing perspective on responsiveness, from the psychologists Harry Reis and Shelly Gable, on how the three components—understanding, validating, and caring—influence partners' experiences in response to their interactions or other eliciting events. The process kicks off when the

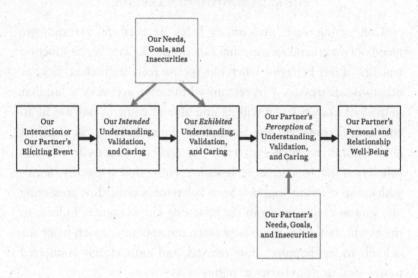

two of us interact or when our partner experiences an eliciting event, such as a stressful experience at work (see the first, leftmost box in the diagram). Ideally, we intend to be responsive—to be understanding, validating, and caring in response (second box)—and we follow through on these intentions though verbal and nonverbal behaviors (third box). Our partner perceives our behaviors (fourth box), which promotes his or her personal and relational well-being (fifth box).

Of course, just because we're immersed in a responsiveness-relevant situation doesn't mean that we'll intend to or actually behave responsively, or that our partner will perceive as responsive the behaviors that we intended as such. One cause of unresponsive behavior is that each of us possesses an idiosyncratic set of needs, goals, and insecurities (see the top and bottom boxes in the diagram). Perhaps we fear intimacy and, consequently, become anxious when our spouse is vulnerable. Or perhaps we're desperate for intimacy and, consequently, become overresponsive—even intrusive or controlling—when we have the opportunity for deep connection. Or perhaps our spouse, fearing abandonment, self-protectively perceives our behavior as less responsive than it actually was.

Conquering such insecurities helps us perform a responsive blend of two crucial relationship functions. The *safe haven* function consists of our behavior when our spouse feels frightened, sick, or otherwise distressed. "To remain within easy access of a familiar individual known to be willing and able to come to our aid in an emergency," observes the psychiatrist John Bowlby, "is clearly a good insurance policy—whatever our age." Serving as an effective safe haven involves attentive listening, conveying sympathy or empathy, and offering support. Such behavior is critical in predicting our spouse's recovery from the upsetting circumstance. Indeed, to the extent that we're responsive when our spouse is upset, he or she is likely to feel happier, more relaxed, and more closely connected to us—and to sleep better at night.

The *secure base* function consists of our behavior when our spouse has opportunities to explore and take risks. "All of us, from the cradle to the grave," observes Bowlby, "are happiest when life is organized as a series of excursions, long or short, from the secure base provided by our attachment figure(s)." Serving as an effective secure base involves encouraging our partner to explore and take risks, giving him or her sufficient space for doing so, and being available if he or she needs reinforcement or time to regroup. Such behavior is critical in promoting our spouse's personal growth. When Alison concluded that it was time to leave her executive position at the only company she'd ever served—even without another job lined up—my emotional and financial support helped her take the leap.

Play

A third set of all-in strategies is linked to play. Indeed, although conflict is a dominant emphasis in relationship science and marital therapy, *boredom*—feeling like the relationship is in a rut—can be every bit as dangerous for the relationship. A central pathway through which married couples can hold boredom at bay is to keep things interesting and fun—that is, to play together.

Socializing

People tend to be happier in marriages in which the spouses' social networks overlap a lot rather than a little. Experimental research by the psychologist Richard Slatcher demonstrates that certain types of socializing together are especially relationship-enhancing. In one study, couples had a forty-five-minute double date with another couple whom they'd never met before. By random assignment, half of these double dates involved games (Jenga!) and a task that facilitates self-disclosure, whereas the other half involved small talk. In the self-disclosure task, participants took turns responding to questions like "For what in your life do you feel the most grateful?"; those in the small-talk condition took turns responding to questions like "When was the last time you walked for more than an hour? Describe where you went and what you saw." Not surprisingly, the couples in the first condition liked each other more than the couples in the second condition, and were more likely to meet up with them again following the study. But the key finding for our purposes is that the couples in the former condition also felt closer to *their own partner*.

A subsequent study again manipulated whether couples were assigned to a forty-five-minute date characterized by either the self-disclosure or the small-talk task, but it also manipulated whether participants had the date by themselves or with another couple. This study design allowed Slatcher to test whether the self-disclosure task benefited the relationship more on a double date than on a date for just the two partners. The results were intriguing: When it came to feelings of satisfaction in the relationship, the self-disclosure task was beneficial regardless of whether the couple was on a double date or by themselves. But when it came to feelings of romantic passion, the self-disclosure task was especially beneficial in the double-date condition. In short, socializing with our spouse and other people can stoke the romantic fire in our marriage, but only if the socializing is fun and intimate.

Novel and Exciting Activities

Whether socializing with our spouse involves other people or not, we can pursue a vast range of activities together. When we're first dating a new person, we often generate fun ideas for shared activities, but we tend to get lazier as the relationship becomes more familiar. That's too bad, because engaging in novel and exciting activities together can keep our relationship fresh, satisfying, and passionate.

Most of the research in this tradition derives from Arthur and Elaine Aron's *self-expansion theory*, which suggests that people have a fundamental motivation to expand the self (to grow) and that a central pathway through which they do so is by engaging in new and stimulating activities with their romantic partner.

In a study from the psychologist Amy Muise, relationship partners completed questionnaires about their relationship for twenty-one consecutive days. They reported how much self-expansion they experienced each day by completing items like: "How much did being with your partner result in you having new experiences?" and "How much did being with your partner expand your sense of the kind of person you are?" They listed activities like shucking oysters for the first time, taking ballroom dancing lessons, and taking a road trip. When participants reported greater self-expansion on a given day, both they and their partner reported experiencing greater sexual desire in—and greater satisfaction with—the relationship. They were also 36 percent more likely to have sex that day.

In a follow-up study, a randomized experiment, Muise had participants complete baseline measures and then assessed their relationship quality and their sexual desire seventy-two hours later.

Immediately after completing the baseline measures, she assigned participants to one of three conditions:

1. *No-Intervention Condition*: Participants didn't read an article.
2. *Comfort Condition*: Participants read an experimenter-created article (designed to look like media coverage of scientific research) extolling the relationship-enhancing power of engaging in routine and comfortable activities together.
3. *Self-expansion Condition*: This condition was the same as the comfort condition, except that the article extolled the relationship-enhancing power of novel and exciting activities, not routine and comfortable activities.

In both of the intervention conditions, participants were encouraged to engage in the relevant type of behavior with their partner over the next seventy-two hours.

Participants assigned to the self-expansion condition did indeed engage in more novel and exciting activities together during that time interval. And, as illustrated in the chart on the following page, doing so mattered. Relative to the control condition, both the self-expansion and the comfort manipulations bolstered relationship quality—and by about the same amount (left side of chart), but only the self-expansion manipulation significantly bolstered sexual desire (right side of chart).

As compelling as such results are, it's not immediately clear how we can apply them in our own relationship; it's not like we can write a compelling mock article and convince ourselves that it's real. Fortunately, researchers have also conducted user-friendlier interventions. The psychologists Kimberley Coulter and John Malouff randomly assigned couples either to engage in novel and exciting activities together—a ninety-minute activity for each of four consecutive

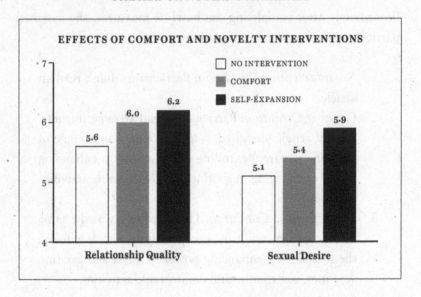

weeks—or to a no-intervention control condition. Relative to couples in the control condition, those in the intervention condition experienced greater excitement in their relationship and greater relationship satisfaction at the end of the study—and four months later.

A study by the psychologist Charlotte Reissman included a more stringent control condition. All couples made a list of activities that they view as exciting and a separate list of activities that they view as pleasant. They were then assigned to engage in either an exciting or a pleasant activity for ninety minutes for each of ten consecutive weeks. Relative to couples in the pleasant condition, couples in the exciting condition were happier in their relationship at the study's conclusion.

What counts as a novel and exciting activity? The possibilities are practically infinite, and each couple's preferences are idiosyncratic. The only rules are (1) that it's an activity that both partners are happy to try and (2) that it takes us out of the mundanities of everyday life. Taking the time to develop a list of such activities with our spouse, and pursuing such activities every week or so, can yield significant benefits for our relationship.

Sex and Romance

Speaking of exciting activities, sex with our spouse can be a particularly delicious form of play. In many cases, such as when we
adopt dominant and submissive roles or dress in risqué costumes,
sex is quite literally play. But even more garden-variety sex, as long
as it's mutually enjoyable, involves a healthy dose of play.

And yet, sustaining a mutually fulfilling sex life is hard. Sexual
desire tends to decrease as relationship duration increases, but lack
of novelty isn't the only cause. As we've seen, another major factor
involves shifting registers between the mundane and the sexy. In the
words of Alain de Botton:

> The qualities demanded of us when we have sex stand in sharp
> opposition to those we employ in conducting the majority of
> our other, daily activities. Marriage tends to involve—if not
> immediately, then within a few years—the running of a house-
> hold and the raising of children, tasks that often feel akin to
> the administration of a small business and that draw upon
> many of the same bureaucratic and procedural skills, includ-
> ing time management, self-discipline, the exercising of author-
> ity and the imposition of rules upon recalcitrant others. . . .
> Sex, with its contrary emphases on expansiveness, imagina-
> tion, playfulness and a loss of control, must by its very nature
> interrupt this routine of regulation and self-restraint.

As the years pass, even those of us for whom the sex is mutually
pleasurable tend to have diminished desire and less frequent sex.
These issues can be surmounted, but doing so can be a challenge,
especially because we frequently forget, when we're not currently
aroused, how pleasurable sex is. As noted by the economist George
Loewenstein, this *empathy gap* helps "explain why couples fail to
initiate sex despite ample past experience showing that it will be

pleasurable if they do. . . . Rules of thumb, such as 'have sex nightly, regardless of immediate desire,' may provide a better guide to behavior than momentary feelings."

For many couples, having sex every night is overkill. Although more frequent sex is generally linked to greater relationship satisfaction, once per week seems sufficient; more sex than that appears to have no additional benefit. But Loewenstein's broader insight is profound: Because our spontaneous desire for sex declines as the novelty of the relationship fades, and because life is busy and tiring, many of us fail to initiate sex even when doing so would have been physically pleasurable and emotionally connective—even when we would have been glad we'd done so. We settle for activities, like channel-surfing or reading, that take less initiative but also are much less beneficial for the relationship, and much less fun.

"Even people who look forward to being sexual with their partner must go through a transition from responsibility to pleasure," observes the sex therapist Esther Perel. "This is a difficult transition for many of us. There are two internal transitions that must occur before you can think about entering an erotic space: Professional→Partner, then Partner→Lover. Eroticism at home requires active engagement and willful intent; it doesn't just happen. It requires that you create your own demarcation between pragmatism and pleasure and that you cultivate a space where a sense of intrigue and curiosity can emerge."

Perel recommends several procedures for such cultivation. First, we can build anticipation throughout the day. Anticipating a sexy interlude that evening can fill the day with mischievous intrigue. One option is to send an afternoon text akin to "cue up the Marvin Gaye when you get home," or, less obliquely, "I can't wait to get you naked tonight." Second, as we transition from the day to the evening, we should connect with our partner first. Before we open the mail, take the dog for a walk, or turn on the news, we should probably give our partner a kiss and ask him or her about the day. Even if the kiss is more tender than hot, it facilitates the Professional→Partner transition. Third, we can carve out time for activities that facilitate the Partner→Lover transition. We can play the Marvin Gaye, open a bottle of wine, or replace electric light with candlelight—or perhaps all of the above. As the wine kicks in, we can start singing along, perhaps using the wine bottle as a faux microphone. Irresistible, right?

Of course, getting into the mood won't be sufficient if the sex itself is unsatisfying. Dan Savage, author of the sex and relationships advice column "Savage Love," offers a guiding philosophy for people who want to sustain a satisfying sex life for the long run. According to this philosophy, we should strive to be "good, giving, and game," or GGG. *Good* means being sexually skilled. *Giving* means being sexually generous, ensuring that we are giving every bit as much time and pleasure to our partner as he or she is giving to us. *Game* means being up for anything, within reason.

The first two *G*'s (good and giving) are pretty straightforward, but it's worth unpacking the third—how does being game for sexual adventure influence relationship quality? Researchers have begun investigating this issue, with positive early results. In one study, the communications researchers Tricia Burke and Valerie Young examined *sexual transformations*—changing our sexual behavior for our partner. They found that our frequency of engaging in sexual transformations predicts our partner's relationship satisfaction without influencing our own. That means our sexual transformations are a collective win for the couple—our partner is happier and we are no less happy. If both of us engage in frequent sexual transformations, both can be happier.

Of course, the "within reason" caveat regarding being game has vast interpretational latitude. Is spanking within reason? Asking your partner to tie you up and scold you for being disobedient? A threesome with a neighbor? There are no universal answers to such questions. The crucial element is to ensure the full consent of both partners, even as both are making a concerted effort to be open-minded about sexual exploration. As we consider what our boundaries are, it's worth recalling research by the psychologist Brad Sagarin demonstrating that couples engaging in sadomasochistic sexual role play—activities like bondage, flogging, and spanking—tend to experience significant increases in relationship closeness from beforehand to afterward.

Whether we're pursuing kinky or vanilla sex, the psychologists Gurit Birnbaum and Harry Reis have shown that we tend to experience greater desire when our partner is responsive toward us. In one study, participants discussed a recent positive or negative event with their partner and then reported how responsive—understanding, validating, and caring—he or she had been during the discussion. The two of them were then given five minutes alone together and encouraged to "engage in an intimate interaction with each other, such as holding hands, kissing, hugging, making out." Participants were allowed to stop the interaction at any point, and they were assured that the experimenter would knock before reentering the room. Participants who reported that their partner had been highly responsive during the discussion task also reported that they experienced greater sexual desire during the "intimate interaction" task. This link between perceived partner responsiveness and sexual desire also emerged when sexual desire was rated by objective coders who viewed a videotape of the intimate interaction task (yes, participants knew they were being recorded).

The Perils of Going All In

The benefits of these all-in strategies surrounding communication, responsiveness, and play don't come without risks. At the most basic level, the time and psychological effort we invest in bolstering our marriage are resources that we are not investing elsewhere—in our jobs or our children, for example. But there are also subtler, more complex issues to consider.

Revealing Incompatibility

This chapter began with Erin and Chris back in Paris, rekindling their fire. In more ways than one, their story has a happy ending. But success wasn't guaranteed; indeed, within the first two days of the trip, the dominant experience was heartache. It was possible that the trip to Paris could have harmed the relationship rather than helping it.

Recall *Blue Valentine*, the Derek Cianfrance drama we mentioned in chapter 1. Dean (Ryan Gosling) and Cindy (Michelle Williams) are struggling. Six years in, the shine has come off their marriage. Cindy is dedicated to her job, and the two of them are busy raising her daughter (his stepdaughter). A recent low point occurred when Cindy left the gate unlocked, and their dog was killed by a car.

Sensing that the marriage is deteriorating, Dean is determined to reconnect. He calls a romantic theme hotel, with Cindy cleaning nearby, to make a reservation for that night: "Hello, I want to see if I can reserve a room for the night. . . . I have a gift certificate. . . . What's our options?" Then to Cindy: "They have Cupid's Cove."

Over her protestations, he continues to explore their options at the motel: "What else? That's it?" Then to Cindy: "There's a Future Room. . . . Will you make the decision, please?"

"I'm on call tomorrow. I can't go."

"Baby, please listen to me for a second. . . . Listen to me for one second, would you stop cleaning for one minute? I'm asking you. Please. Let's get outta here, we gotta get outta here. We have to get out of this house. Let's go get drunk and make love." He reserves the Future Room.

Despite his failure to listen to her objections, his motivations are good. He wants the two of them to feel close and connected like they used to. Unfortunately, their spontaneous visit to the Future Room turns into a debacle.

En route to the motel, Cindy runs into her ex-boyfriend at a liquor store, which makes Dean jealous and provokes an argument.

By the time they get to the hotel, Cindy is struggling to get into the right headspace for a fun night of drunken sex. They fight. The alcohol makes things worse. She resists his advances, and his efforts at seduction become aggressive. She yells at him to cut it out, that he's hurting her. Although he's certainly not a sympathetic character in that moment, his response is poignant: "What do you want? How much rejection am I supposed to take?"

Things deteriorate from there. The two of them have a glimmer of reconciliation before the film ends, but the relationship has been severely damaged, and divorce appears likely. We can imagine an alternate reality—call it *The Notebook*—in which Dean's efforts at reconnection helped them rediscover what they loved about each other in the first place. Had he listened better or been less clumsy in his seduction efforts, or had Cindy welcomed his seduction and returned his desire, the Future Room could have been ground zero for their marital renaissance.

But it wasn't. That's a risk we take when we go all in. Dean and Cindy's marriage wasn't especially strong before the Future Room episode, but it was holding up okay. There were few signs of imminent rupture, and the marriage may have been able to persist like that for the long run. But Dean wanted more. He wanted the two of them to love and crave each other as they used to, and he was willing to sacrifice his time, money, emotional energy, and self-esteem to get back there. In doing so, he made himself vulnerable to rejection, and he exposed deep flaws in the relationship. That's a risk of going all in rather than settling, complacently, for an adequate marriage.

Unhealthy Goals

Thus far, our discussion of self-expression has been content-free. But, in reality, self-expressive goals are *about something*. By and large, the core goals underlying self-expression are productive and good, or at least harmless. But there are exceptions. Perhaps our spouse is so focused on expanding his or her perspective on the world that he or she is willing to sacrifice his or her health, or the health of others, in the pursuit of additional perspective—such as by ingesting dangerous drugs or pursuing extreme sports.

Consider the descent of Kurt Cobain—the epochal lead singer of Nirvana—into drug-fueled self-destruction. Cobain, saddled with the "voice of his generation" label, cherished the authenticity characteristic of the self-expressive era: "I'd rather be hated for who I am, than loved for who I am not." The heartbreaking documentary *Montage of Heck* drives home how Courtney Love—Cobain's wife and a rock star in her own right—supported his drug use and social withdrawal, tendencies that led to his suicide in 1994.

In Praise of Slow Cooking

Such risks are real, and we neglect them at our own peril. But fixating on them is to see the trees instead of the forest. When we zoom out, we see the power of going all in. "Relationships can provide us with tremendous benefits, including better mental and physical health," observe the psychologists Thomas Bradbury and Benjamin Karney. "If you want to reap these benefits, you have to make your relationship a priority in your life. Few of us are lucky enough to have great relationships without putting forth some real effort, over a sustained period of time."

When we invest heavily in our marriage, spending the time and psychological energy to develop and sustain a deep connection, we can achieve something magnificent. Our marriage can provide a level of "profound happiness, serenity, and richness of the inner life" that would have been virtually out of reach in the past.

Of course, it's also possible to overburden our marriage, and there are many effective—and sometimes fun—ways of releasing some of the pressure. Call them recalibrations.

11.

Recalibrating

The only book I ever threw away—and I threw it high
over the rooftops of Boston from an elevated train
platform—was Abraham Maslow's book on self-
actualization.

—John Gottman

The psychologist John Gottman may be the most influential
marriage researcher of all time. He developed or refined some
of the most compelling procedures for understanding marital dynamics, helping to ground this research topic in rigorous scientific
methodology and identifying some of the most important qualities
distinguishing distressed from nondistressed marriages.

When the psychologist James Coan—a friend of mine who is
also a former student and collaborator of Gottman's—alerted me to
Gottman's train platform incident, I was surprised. But, after reading Gottman's *The Marriage Clinic*, I developed greater insight into
his perspective, along with a healthy dose of appreciation for it:

There are many marital therapists who have high expectations for what is possible in marriage. . . . I am not opposed

to such views, but I personally take a different one. I am a "plumber." . . . I have often described my goal as fostering the "good enough marriage." I am likely to think a marriage is good enough if the two spouses choose to have coffee and pastries together on a Saturday afternoon and really enjoy the conversation, even if they don't heal one another's childhood wounds or don't always have wall-socket, mindblowing, skyrocket sex.

Coan, who knew that I was working on this book, channeled Gottman's critique of Maslow for me: "He'd agree with you that it's possible to build a great marriage, but he also feels that the pursuit of 'great' often stresses people out and causes more conflict and disappointment than it resolves." Gottman is right—looking to the summit makes profound fulfillment possible, but it also increases the likelihood that our partner will disappoint us.

In America, *settling* is a dirty word. We owe it to ourselves, the culture tells us, to look for excellence rather than adequacy, for good-as-hell rather than good enough. But even those of us seeking to develop a terrific marriage recognize that expecting sixty years of unmitigated bliss is a tall order. Even in successful marriages, there are difficult periods. Working through those periods can get the marriage back on track, but rarely overnight. And it can be a slog if the challenges are due to longer-term circumstances, like the economic stress triggered by an involuntary unemployment or the sleepless nights triggered by a newborn baby. Adding the disappointment of failing to live up to lofty expectations—our own and our spouse's—can exacerbate the stress, potentially placing the marriage at existential risk.

As with lovehacks, these *recalibration* strategies are especially helpful when we can't figure out a way to go all in and are looking to hold our marriage afloat for the time being. In contrast to lovehacks, recalibration strategies focus on the "demand" rather than the "supply" side—they involve temporarily asking less of our marriage, especially regarding higher-altitude needs, rather than trying to use our limited resources more efficiently.

The Conjugal Crucible

Expectations regarding higher-altitude needs can be stifling, especially when the marriage isn't fulfilling them. Alison and I learned this lesson the hard way.

Both individually and together, we struggled with our transition to parenthood in September of 2009. After enduring a brutal pregnancy and a surgical delivery, Alison was a pale shade of her vibrant self. For my part, after spending thousands of hours supporting her through her suffering—more than a hundred of them in the hospital—I was sapped. I had also built up a thick layer of armor so I could take care of things without melting down; I was able to endure as long as I didn't have to feel anything (other than sympathy). Ideally, the two of us would have greeted the newborn phase with a larger stock of fortitude, but, obviously, we didn't get to choose.

I was the weaker link. Alison had taken a parental leave from work, but I hadn't. And suddenly, I had no time for anything other than the absolutely essential work tasks—teaching my classes, helping to run my department, fulfilling my editorial obligations. Tasks like idea generation and writing, founts of wellness for me, disappeared overnight.

The next year was awful. I was among the 25 percent of men who exhibit notable symptoms of postpartum depression. The lowest moment came in May of 2010. The three of us—Alison, the baby, and I—had flown to Seattle to visit Adam, my lifelong best friend, and his young family. Visiting Adam had always afforded adventure and revelry, and I discovered that adding babies to the mix eliminated all that. Taking plane flights had always provided time for thinking, reading, and writing, and I discovered that plane trips with a baby are a bit different. Most important, traveling with Alison had always been fun and romantic, and I discovered that I was unable to find her through my postpartum haze.

On that trip, she and I decided to forget about Mount Maslow's summit. Seeking bliss through the marriage—particularly looking to each other for assistance with personal growth and self-expression—just made things worse. So we just stopped trying. We put our heads down and focused on putting one foot in front of the other.

That approach worked. The disappointment became less acute. And, eventually, we rediscovered each other. We still weren't ready for the summit, but we started looking to the middle altitudes again, and the marriage provided a deep emotional connection again. When Alison lobbied for a second kid, I was slack-jawed but ultimately receptive. Because we'd overhauled our expectations, reorganizing much about the way we approached our family life and our marriage, the newborn period was easier the second time around.

It took a few years—and we didn't force it—but we eventually got back to the summit. At first, the ascents were rare and brief, but they allowed us to grow and explore and push for more again. After years of a "good enough marriage," we started to pursue the *all* marriage again—longer, more frequent summits, alongside a flexible lowering of expectations when necessary.

Our experiences during those difficult years point to a more general truth: The tendency of contemporary Americans to place so much responsibility for our social and psychological fulfillment on one relationship turns the marriage into something of a crucible. The sense of obligation can become oppressive, especially when it involves not only *behaving* in a specific way, but also *feeling* a certain way. When the crucible starts getting too hot, it's worth considering whether we can turn down the temperature.

Fallow periods can result from either of two causes, even in a generally strong marriage. First, spouses might confront challenging but temporary circumstances that interfere with their ability to promote each other's higher-altitude need fulfillment. Second, spouses might confront an incompatibility in personality or preferences that interferes with the ability to promote each other's higher-altitude need fulfillment for the long run, albeit in a limited set of domains.

In *The New "I Do,"* the couples therapist Susan Pease Gadoua and the journalist Vicki Larson explore distinct types of marriage that can optimize the relationship under this second set of circumstances. These marriages focus on specific goals rather than on adopting all the expectations of contemporary marriage norms. Gadoua and Larson consider, for example, the parenting marriage, the safety marriage, and the covenant marriage—distinct and limited marital structures built around specific priorities. "What if society revisited purpose-driven marriages and deemed them acceptable, or, preferably, even better than love-driven marriage? Rather than expecting one person to meet all your needs, you might ask a spouse to meet a few, and you'd be encouraged to get other needs met in other ways or with other people or in some combination."

I don't favor the either/or contrast in Gadoua and Larson's analysis because I believe that the breadth of acceptable approaches to marriage is vast; as long as spouses are compatible, communicate well, and are willing and able to invest sufficient resources for the marriage, the sky's the limit. That said, I agree that many of us— perhaps most—would benefit from considering ways that we might ask less of our marriage. Such recalibration won't make our marriage flourish at the summit, but it can buy some time and goodwill to get us through fallow periods.

Increasing Independence

My wife has a friend who is happily married, but there's an issue: The friend loves to travel while her husband doesn't. One option would be for her to give up traveling, and another would be for him to travel with her despite his distaste for it. But they wisely pursue a third option—she travels on her own or with other people. This arrangement might be challenging for some couples, as it requires trust and the willingness to sacrifice time together. But it's the sort of arrangement that can help spouses pursue autonomy and personal growth, even where they're incompatible.

Bolstering the Self

Our identities tend to become linked to our relationship in subtle but powerful ways. The psychologist Chris Agnew has shown that people who are highly committed to their relationship, relative to those who are less committed, spontaneously use more plural pronouns (*we, us, our*) when describing the relationship. The psychologist Arthur Aron has shown that, when people in a relationship have to make rapid decisions about whether they possess a trait, such as extraversion, they have a harder time when one of them possesses the trait than if both or neither of them possess it. Because we tend to develop a shared identity with our partner, we sometimes get confused when having to make fast judgments about which of us possesses a given quality.

This shared identity leaves us at risk for feeling unmoored if the relationship starts to falter. In collaboration with the psychologists Erica Slotter and Wendi Gardner, I conducted a study in which participants reported on their self-concept clarity ("I have a clear sense of who I am and what I am") every two weeks for six months. The self-concept clarity of participants whose relationships remained intact increased over time, whereas the self-concept clarity of participants whose relationships ended declined immediately and remained low throughout the subsequent months of the study.

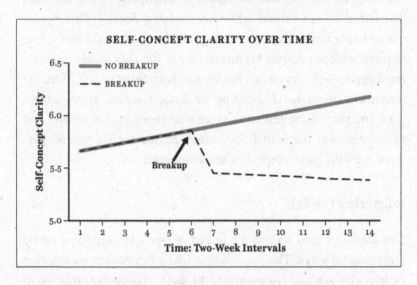

SELF-CONCEPT CLARITY OVER TIME

There are many benefits of merging our sense of identity with our partner. But even setting aside what would happen if the relationship were to end, there are also many benefits of developing and sustaining our own independent identity. This is the idea underlying Shel Silverstein's illustrated book *The Missing Piece Meets the Big O*, which argues that we are best equipped to love when we come from a place of completeness rather than from a place of incompleteness—that optimal relationships emerge when two fully functioning people seek to experience the world together rather than when two partially developed people look to each other to become whole.

None of us is completely whole, of course, but successful efforts to move ourselves in that direction will help us live fulfilling lives. For present purposes, the key point is that it's possible to ask too much of our marriage, especially in terms of self-discovery and self-expression. Independent efforts along these lines can simultaneously foster personal growth and reduce the burden we are placing on our marriage.

Living Apart Together

Whether to provide a sense of autonomy and completeness, or, more prosaically, to avoid fighting over the dishes, one path that a surprisingly large number of married Americans are pursuing is to live in separate residences. As of 2014, 3.5 million married Americans—3 percent of all married couples—lived separately, an arrangement that scholars call *living apart together* and that the documentary filmmaker Sharon Hyman calls *apartnering*.

Many couples live apart for practical reasons, like career opportunities or military deployments. And many who might want to live apart eschew that option due to the expense of supporting two residences instead of one. But, for people who live apart by choice, the decision can be every bit as much oriented toward strengthening the relationship as it is toward bolstering the partners' individual fulfillment. In *Living Happily Ever—Separately*, Lise Stryker Stoessel "tells the story of how my husband and I renewed our marriage and rescued our family from the potential tragedy of divorce, *by living separately.*"

We met Frank Bruni, the *New York Times* columnist, in chapter 10. In a 2013 column, he considers the delights of living apart from his long-term partner: "*Moving in with each other*: that's supposed to be the ultimate prize, the real consummation. You co-sign a lease, put both names on the mailbox, settle on a toothpaste and the angels weep. But why not seize the intimacy without forfeiting the privacy? Establish a different rhythm? One night with him, one night with a pint of Chubby Hubby and 'Monday Night Football' or a marathon of 'Scandal,' my wit on ice, my stomach muscles on hiatus, my body sprawling ever less becomingly across the couch. Isn't *that* the definition of having it all?"

The limited scientific research on the topic doesn't provide a clear answer to this question, but it does provide ample evidence that people who live apart can have excellent relationships. In one study, the sociologist Charles Strohm showed that Americans who live apart perceive just as much emotional support from their partner as those who live together. Research by the psychologist Birk Hagemeyer suggests that some people benefit more than others from living apart. In particular, those of us with relatively independent or avoidant personalities are more likely than the average person to be involved in living-apart relationships (especially after age forty), and with good reason. Although having an independent personality predicts lower relationship quality on average, that's not the case when people live apart. And although spending more time with one's partner is linked to greater relationship satisfaction among independent people who live apart, it is linked to *lower* relationship satisfaction among independent people who live together. (Among people with a more interdependent personality, spending more time together predicts greater relationship satisfaction in both types of living arrangement.) It appears that highly independent people feel stifled by lots of time with their partner, a problem that appears to be mitigated by living apart.

The New "I Do" discusses the pros and cons of living-apart-together relationships. The pros include reduced likelihood of feeling emotionally claustrophobic or of fighting about things like messiness and housework, greater flexibility to pursue independent interests, and increased likelihood that time together feels special rather than routine. The cons include an increased likelihood of feeling jealous or suspicious, reduced access to physical and sexual contact, and the threat that the independence afforded by living in separate residences might cause the partners to grow apart.

What about people who have children? Well, if the children are from previous relationships, living apart can be a sensible way of blending families without fighting over who used up the hot water or who finished the Raisin Bran—or, more seriously, over divergent family traditions and incompatible disciplinary philosophies. If the children are from the current relationship, then the decision to live apart is especially tricky and consequential, but it's clear that some people can make it work. In a 2014 article in *The Huffington Post*, Claire (last name withheld) reported on her atypical marriage to David, providing a proof-of-concept illustration. She lives with the three sons from her previous marriage—aged twenty, eighteen, and fifteen—and her six-year-old son with David. "We live separately," Claire writes, "because if we lived together, it would ruin our relationship. . . . David can be who he is and I can be who I am and we can do what we do best—laugh, have fun, enjoy each other. We're not dragged down by the day to day problems of life."

Outsourcing

Increasing our independence, perhaps by bolstering the self or by living apart, is one avenue through which we can relieve some of the pressure on a marriage. Another is through satisfying some of our social needs outside of the marriage—or, in MBA-speak, through "outsourcing" to others (or to our self) the need fulfillment that contemporary Americans typically seek through marriage.

A Diversified Social Portfolio

Having a robust social network is a surprisingly strong predictor not only of psychological health, but also of physical health, including longevity. A meta-analysis by the psychologist Julianne Holt-Lunstad reveals that people with high scores on broad measures of social integration—marital status, social network size, and social network participation—are about half as likely to die in a given follow-up interval (say, ten years) as people with low scores. This effect is larger than the effects of well-known predictors of mortality like smoking and obesity. It looks like having a strong social network is, quite literally, a lifesaver.

A growing scientific literature investigates the value of having a *diversified* social portfolio—one in which we have various significant others in our lives who relate to us in distinct ways and help us meet distinct needs. In a study by the psychologist Elaine Cheung, participants nominated up to four people who would be especially effective in helping them manage each of seven sorts of emotional experience: cheering up sadness, calming down anger, calming down anxiety, capitalizing upon happiness, amplifying anger, reducing guilt, and reducing embarrassment. Cheung used these nominations to calculate three measures of participants' social portfolios: (1) *breadth*, or the number of emotional experience types for which participants listed at least one partner, (2) *redundancy*, or the average number of partners listed for each emotional experience type, and (3) *specialization*, or the proportion of significant others whom participants listed as helping them regulate precisely one type of emotional experience, such as having a friend who helps us calm our anxiety but doesn't serve any of the other emotion-regulating functions. Both breadth and specialization, but not redundancy, predicted psychological well-being, suggesting that, all else equal, having a number of social support specialists can be preferable to relying on one or two generalists.

Ongoing research that I am pursuing with Cheung and others reveals that having a specialized portfolio also promotes one's own and one's partner's happiness in the relationship. In this nine-month study, breadth and specialization also predicted a decreased likelihood of breakup. In addition, as illustrated in the chart on the next page, having a highly specialized social portfolio protected participants from the typical decline in relationship well-being over time.

Developing and sustaining a diversified social network also has

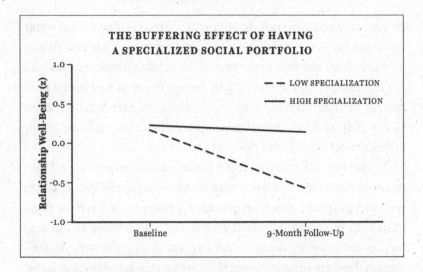

THE BUFFERING EFFECT OF HAVING A SPECIALIZED SOCIAL PORTFOLIO

costs. Close relationships can promote joy and fulfillment, but they can also inflict pain and burden. Each additional person we're close to is likely to influence us in both positive and negative ways, and maintaining a large network of intimates requires significant investments of time and energy. In addition, as we reallocate to other relationships some of the time and energy that we had previously invested in our marriage, we may become somewhat less attached to our spouse. This isn't a reason for us to stay tethered to our spouse at all times, but it is a reason to ensure that we're continuing to invest time and energy in our marriage even as we seek to cultivate an array of other close social connections.

Sexual Alternatives

One of the most vivid and important differences between marriages and (nonmarital) best friendships is that, in most circumstances, only the former involves sex. The sexual component of marriage adds an additional dimension of pleasure but also a level of complexity that can unravel an otherwise strong marriage.

It's unlikely that our sexual cravings and preferences will align precisely with our spouse's. In almost all marriages, one person wants sex more frequently than the other, an asymmetry that can change direction from one year to the next. And, holding frequency aside, it's not especially common for our full, deepest expression of sexual preferences to align precisely with our spouse's, in part because, as we saw in chapter 3, our sexual cravings are often insubordinate to our philosophical, moral, and political preferences.

Sexual fantasies are frequently bound up in domination and submission. They can involve transgression—inappropriate sex acts with inappropriate people or in inappropriate places. Even for those of us with more vanilla sexual preferences, succumbing to our sexual desires involves being vulnerable and losing control. And although there are some common themes that characterize Americans' sexual fantasies, there's also enormous variation from one person to the next. Is it any wonder that sex is a major area of conflict in American marriages?

Let's imagine that we are in a marriage with somebody whom we continue to love and respect, but for whom we have lost our sexual desire. We have been to couples therapy. We have worked hard to heat up the marriage, even forcing ourselves to initiate sex that we don't want because we know how important it is to our spouse. Or perhaps we're the more ardent one, feeling chronically undersexed and hurt by our spouse's lower (or lack of) interest in having sex with us. What should we do?

There's a range of reasonable answers to this question, and I'd encourage anybody inclined to engage seriously with them to read some of the essays edited by the journalist Cathi Hanauer in *The Bitch Is Back*. Should we resign ourselves to weekly sex for the next several decades out of a sense of obligation (Grace O'Malley's essay)? Should we try to enjoy a sexless marriage (Hazel McClay's essay)? Should we initiate divorce proceedings (Claire Johnson's essay)?

Might there be options for keeping the otherwise strong marriage intact while mitigating, or perhaps even obviating, the sex problem?

In accord with the recalibration emphasis in this chapter, we'll focus not on how to improve our sex life with our spouse (we discussed that in chapter 10) but rather on how to take some of the pressure off the marriage—how to mitigate feelings of sexual disappointment.

Masturbation

An ancient option, which has gone steroidal in the Internet era, is masturbation. Let there be no doubt: Having satisfying sex with our spouse is, under most circumstances, more appealing than having satisfying sex with ourselves. And yet, one spouse's disappointment with the other's lack of desire is likely to be much more acute if he or she has no other outlet for orgasm. Masturbation won't quell the feelings of rejection, but it can make the sexual deprivation more bearable, thereby reducing the urgency and intensity of the disappointment. In general, unless we have a moral or religious reason to object, we should probably welcome our spouse's masturbation, especially in cases where we know we are less interested in sex than he or she is.

Masturbation can serve another important function in marriage— it can allow us to indulge those elements of our sexual desires that we would rather not bring into the conjugal bed. If our fantasy involves oral sex with Vladimir Putin or an illicit escapade with our doctor in a broom closet, it might be best to indulge that fantasy in our mind's eye rather than with our spouse. The same goes for cruel or socially stigmatized sex acts, such as being paraded around town on all fours while our master holds the leash. Some people will act out such fantasies in their marriage, and, assuming they avoid prison and don't traumatize strangers, we should tip our hats to them. But many of us will be wary of bringing this sort of sex play into our relationship with the person who is also our primary source of emotional support and the coparent of our children.

Discussions of masturbation often transition into discussions of pornography, and with good reason. As we know from books like

A Billion Wicked Thoughts—in which the neuroscientists Ogi Ogas and Sai Gaddam imposed coherence on Internet searches—people, especially men, like pornography (news flash!). Meanwhile, we're on the cusp of a pornography revolution—one that makes the experience much more immersive than the photos and videos that have traditionally been the norm.

Perhaps the most radical development in this space is the advent of virtual reality porn. In a *Vocativ* article titled "Here's What It's Like to Binge on Virtual Reality Porn," the journalist Tracy Clark-Flory reports on Traffic Jam 2016, a VR porn conference in San Francisco. She had diverse experiences there, but perhaps this one best illustrates the weird potential of this new medium: "There was a naked woman lying on a four-poster bed in front of me with her legs held up to her chest like she was practicing her cannonball. I looked down, and I had a pair of tanned, rock-hard abs. I also had a penis."

Okay, so perhaps adopting the role of the other gender isn't for everybody. And yet, this example helps illustrate the staggering range of pornographic options that VR places within reach. It won't be long before developers have built enough scenes that almost all of us could find one that would tickle the naughtiest recesses of our minds.

Would masturbating to VR porn count as infidelity? All of us have to make our own rules as masturbation technology increasingly approximates actual sex, and it's wise to reach a mutual understanding with our spouse about what's acceptable.

As we're contemplating those complexities, let's make things even trickier: Sexbots are coming. It's as if a friendlier version of the Basic Pleasure Model replicant from Ridley Scott's *Blade Runner*—like the one played by Daryl Hannah—will be hanging out in our closet, always ready for action. Here, again, is an option for taking some of the sexual pressure off of the marriage, albeit one that further blurs the boundaries between masturbation and sex in a way that requires clear spousal communication.

While we're at it, it's also worth discussing whether to use emerging sex technologies to add some heat *within* the marriage, especially when we're apart from our spouse. This is the sort of all-in strategy that's more relevant to chapter 10, but, as long as we're discussing technology and sex, let's take a brief detour. Consider the efforts of Suki and Brian Dunham, the married couple who founded OhMiBod, a sex-toy company. One of their products is a remote-control vibrator worn by a woman and controlled by her partner—from anywhere in the world. This product exemplifies an emerging field called, no joke, *teledildonics*. Perhaps the most groundbreaking idea in this space is that both partners will wear a device on their genitals—such as Kiiroo's Onyx (for him) and Pearl (for her)—that reacts in real time to the movements of the other person. When she inserts the Pearl in Topeka, he feels the pressure from her vagina in Tokyo. Combine this device with real-time video, and you're pretty close to full-on sex with your spouse while you're six thousand miles away.

Consensual Nonmonogamy

If you felt squeamish while reading the masturbation section, you might want to skip this section altogether. Here we'll explore *consensual nonmonogamy*, a second avenue through which people—at least those without moral or religious objections—can dial down some of the pressure on their marriage by seeking sexual fulfillment with another person.

Before we consider consensual nonmonogamy in detail, we need to appreciate that it's a high-risk option. It's a good path for some couples, and, in some cases, it can save an otherwise loving and emotionally committed marriage in which one or both spouses feel imprisoned by the lack of sexual freedom. But it can cause unbearable, and often unanticipated, anguish, especially if one spouse consents to adopt a consensually nonmonogamous norm only at the behest of the other.

Consider David and Lana, who married young and sustained a loving relationship with plenty of enjoyable sex together. After about a decade, though, Lana started experiencing intense cravings for certain sexual experiences that she couldn't get within the marriage: "I still had these unmanageable X-rated fantasies pretty much nonstop." David reluctantly agreed to open up the marriage, but doing so haunted him. "Our open-marriage trial didn't last long," he told *New York* magazine. "I found it completely unbearable. Devastating. But I wasn't going to put her on a leash like some dog. The only option was to break up the marriage and co-parent. The idea of divorce killed me, but her sleeping with other men was even more brutal than that." David soon remarried, and happily so. Lana, who has remained single, adores his second wife. As far as we can tell, the three of them are excellent parents to David and Lana's three children. And yet, we're well served to remember David's ultimate assessment of their foray into consensual nonmonogamy: "If I could do it any differently, I would have probably divorced Lana before she started having sex with other men. All that shit—um, it's a strong word but I'll use it—'damaged' me in a way that might never be quite repaired."

Indeed, consensual nonmonogamy is a relatively extreme approach to recalibration. It's often wise to start with an approach more on the scale of finding a tennis buddy or a monthly dinner date. Still, we'll consider consensual nonmonogamy in some detail because of the recent surge of interest in the topic, both among social scientists and in society at large, and because it is the optimal option for some couples.

THREE TYPES

Consensual nonmonogamy is "a relational arrangement in which partners agree that it is acceptable to have more than one sexual and/or romantic relationship at the same time." It's not cheating or infidelity because it is, by definition, consensual. It's a lifestyle choice that the spouses, both consenting adults, have made willingly, and it typically involves rules that the two partners hammer out for themselves. Perhaps it's okay to have sex with other people, but only when traveling for work—or not more than three times with any one person. Or perhaps it's okay to have sex with other people, but only if both partners are present, as in a threesome or an orgy. Or perhaps, following the timeless wisdom of the film *Pretty Woman*, it's okay to have sex with other people, but not to kiss them on the mouth.

There are three major types of consensual nonmonogamy. As defined by the psychologist Terri Conley, an *open relationship* refers to an arrangement "in which a couple pursues independent sexual relationships outside of their primary dyad." *Swinging* refers to an arrangement "in which a couple engages in extradyadic sex, usually in parties or other social settings where both partners are in attendance." *Polyamory* refers to an arrangement in which individuals have "consensual loving and romantic relationships with more than one partner."*

Polyamory in America has become more prevalent in recent decades, in part as a result of the 1997 publication of *The Ethical Slut*, in which the family therapist Dossie Easton and the sex educator Janet Hardy redefine a *slut* as "a person of any gender who has the courage to lead life according to the radical proposition that sex is nice and pleasure is good for you." The book provides self-help advice for successful polyamorous relationships, including on issues

---

* In *The Truth* (p. 167), Neil Strauss observes there are three major polyamorous relationship structures: (1) "Having a primary partner, with each person free to negotiate or enter into separate secondary and tertiary relationships." (2) "Creating a triad, in which three people are romantically involved. This can take the form of three people in an equal relationship (a 'triangle'); one person simultaneously dating two others who are not as close to each other (a 'V'); or a couple sharing the same secondary." (3) "Forming a group relationship of four or more people."

like scheduling, jealousy, and, for the neophytes among us, etiquette for group-sex encounters.

THE PHILOSOPHY UNDERLYING CONSENSUAL NONMONOGAMY

Conley identifies five principles of consensual nonmonogamy, some of which apply especially to polyamory:

1. "One person should not be expected to meet all of the needs of their partners."
2. "Anticipating that sexual attraction for one's partner will exist, unwaveringly, over the course of a given relationship is unrealistic."
3. "Engaging in multiple loving relationships (including romantic or sexual relationships) with others is healthy and beneficial."
4. "Communication and openness with all partners are the keys to ethical and successful multiple relationships."
5. "Learning how to most effectively talk about relationships and scheduling time to talk about relationships is crucial for polyamory."

As these principles make clear, polyamory typically involves a blend of all-in strategies like extensive communication and recalibration strategies like eschewing the expectation that one partner will meet all of our needs.

When Amelia Earhart, the legendary aviator, agreed to marry her publicist, George Putnam, in 1931, she told him that "I shall not hold you to any midaevil code of faithfulness to me nor shall I consider myself bound to you similarly. . . . I cannot guarantee to endure at all times the confinements of even an attractive cage." Neil

Strauss, the journalist and unlikely lothario who wrote *The Game*, describes in *The Truth* his earnest pursuit of a fulfilling romantic relationship arrangement that would support his needs for both intimacy and freedom. "I wonder why I feel like I can't handle marriage, but I can handle fatherhood," he writes. "I think this is because it's not the responsibility I mind, it's the exclusivity. You can raise a child and still have one or two or ten other children."

As he begins his search, he develops four criteria for the type of relationship he wants:

1. "It can't be sexually exclusive, which rules out monogamy."
2. "It has to be honest, which rules out adultery."
3. "It has to be capable of developing romantic and emotional attachment, which rules out being a permanent bachelor."
4. "It has to be capable of evolving into a family with healthy, well-adjusted children, which rules out unstable partners and lifestyles."

Midway through his search, here's his analysis: "Whether it's Nicole or Sage, Anne or Veronika, each woman is a wonderful world unto herself. And monogamy? It's like choosing to live in a single town and never traveling to experience the beauty, history, and enchantment of all the other unique, wonderful places in the world. Why does love have to limit us?"

It looks like this question has greater resonance for younger than for older Americans. A 2016 survey from the polling firm YouGov posed this question: "On a scale where 0 is completely monogamous and 6 is completely non-monogamous, what would your ideal relationship be?" Across age groups, more than half of the participants responded 0 (completely monogamous), but, as shown in the chart on the next page, the majority gets paper-thin as the participants get younger. If these results represent generational shifts more than aging processes, which seems plausible, a larger and larger proportion of American adults will, in the coming decades, view consensually nonmonogamous relationships as ideal.*

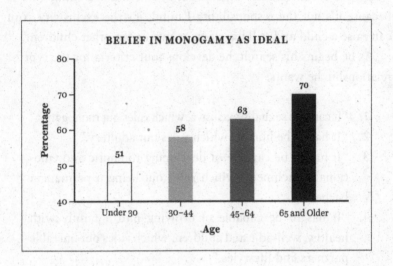

CONSENSUAL NONMONOGAMY AND RELATIONSHIP QUALITY

Conley has leveraged scientific methods to compare consensually nonmonogamous and monogamous relationships. She seeks to test society's widespread assumption that "people in modern society are psychologically or relationally advantaged by monogamy relative to other relationship styles."

Before discussing her findings, we need to appreciate that such a comparison is inherently fraught. One issue is that, for ethical and practical reasons, no studies have employed experimental research methods in which the researcher randomly assigns couples to adopt

---

* Even polygamy—legally marrying more than one partner—has witnessed a surge in public support in the twenty-first century. To be sure, most Americans remain opposed to polygamy, but the percentage of Americans who find it morally acceptable grew from 7 percent in 2003 to 16 percent in 2015.

either a monogamous or a nonmonogamous norm. As such, the best available research compares couples who have *self-selected* to adopt a monogamous or a nonmonogamous norm for their relationship—but, of course, variables that correlate with such a decision (say, a desire for sexual variety) could also, and independently, influence relationship quality. A second issue is that not all people in "monogamous" relationships are actually monogamous—some cheat. Despite this complexity, the most appropriate comparison between monogamous and nonmonogamous relationships involves the norm the partners adopt—their agreement or understanding regarding the rules governing their sexual exclusivity—rather than the behaviors they enact. The other option, which would compare all consensually nonmonogamous relationships (regardless of how successful they are) to the subset of monogamous relationships that omits couples enduring a major transgression, would produce a biased comparison.

Those complexities aside, the available evidence suggests that couples who adopt a consensually nonmonogamous norm have primary relationships that are, on average, every bit as strong as those who adopt a monogamous norm.* In the most ambitious study to date, Conley recruited more than two thousand participants who were thirty-nine years old on average (range: twenty-five to seventy-eight) and who responded affirmatively to this question: "Right now, are you romantically or sexually involved with one or multiple partners?" Participants were defined as monogamous if they responded affirmatively to this question: "Have you and your partner agreed to be monogamous?" Conley provided participants with a definition: "By monogamy we mean that you have agreed to have a sexual and romantic relationship with only one person. This may include a specific conversation about monogamy or may be implied in your relationship."

---

* The limited evidence regarding the effects on children suggests that what is crucial is not the marital norm per se, but rather the stability, love, and attention the children experience. In other words, whether the home environment is stable and loving rather than chaotic and unresponsive is more important for a child's well-being than whether the adults in that household are monogamous rather than consensually nonmonogamous.

Participants who responded in the negative to the monogamy question were categorized as consensually nonmonogamous, and they were retained in the study if they responded affirmatively to this question: "Do you have a 'primary' partner? That is, do you have one romantic partner you are more substantially committed to than any other partners you might have?" These participants reported which of three categories best characterizes their relationship: open relationship, swinging, or polyamory.

For all participants in the study, the sole or primary partner was of the other gender (men with women; women with men), which simplifies comparisons to the gender structure of heterosexual marriages. In the final sample, 1,507 participants were in monogamous relationships and 617 were in consensually nonmonogamous relationships. The average duration of the relationship with their (sole or primary) partner was ten years. In the consensually nonmonogamous group, about half were in polyamorous relationships, with the remaining half about equally split between open relationship and swinging.

Conley compared the relationship quality of monogamous participants (with their sole partner) to that of consensually nonmonogamous participants (with their primary partner). As shown on the next page, the two groups were virtually identical in terms of relationship satisfaction, commitment, and passion. Perhaps surprisingly, consensually nonmonogamous participants reported lower jealousy and higher trust than their monogamous counterparts, differences that were small but statistically significant. These results align with those from other studies: Relationship quality (with the sole or primary partner) tends to be comparable in monogamous and consensually nonmonogamous relationships, and the dissimilarities that do exist suggest that consensually nonmonogamous relationships have slightly higher relationship quality.*

---

* When comparing the forms of consensual nonmonogamy, polyamorous participants tend to have higher relationship quality than open or swinging relationships.

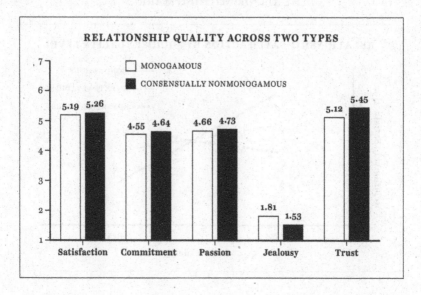

Such conclusions apply on average, but the available evidence (as preliminary as it is) suggests that some people are better suited to monogamous relationships and others are better suited to consensually nonmonogamous relationships. In one study, participants who varied in their level of *sociosexuality*—their interest in and willingness to pursue sexual activity without an emotional connection—reported on their current relationship structure (monogamous or consensually nonmonogamous) and their relationship satisfaction. They also reported whether they had actually engaged in *extradyadic sex*—sex with somebody other than their primary partner. All participants in consensually nonmonogamous relationships had engaged in extradyadic sex, as did some of those in ostensibly monogamous relationships; that is, some were unfaithful. As shown in the chart on the next page, greater sociosexuality is linked to lower relationship satisfaction among individuals in monogamous relationships (especially those who have been faithful), but it was linked to slightly *higher* relationship satisfaction among individuals in consensually nonmonogamous relationships. Indeed, individuals

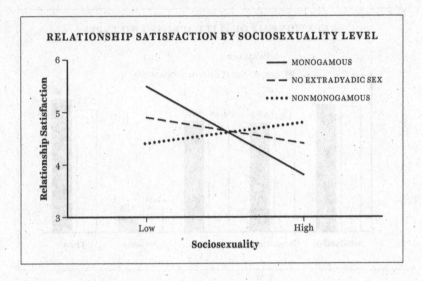

RELATIONSHIP SATISFACTION BY SOCIOSEXUALITY LEVEL

who are high in sociosexuality were most satisfied in the relationship when it was consensually nonmonogamous.

Of course, dyadic relationships are plenty complex, and adding additional people to the relationship can vastly increase the complexity. Navigating this terrain typically requires a great deal of self-insight, empathy, and communication skill, not to mention the willingness to spend a whole lot of time working through relationship issues. There's a strong norm in the poly community to respond to a partner's love for another person with *compersion* rather than with jealousy—with happiness that the partner is enjoying the other relationship—but doing so is easier said than done.

In *The Truth*, Neil Strauss becomes involved in simultaneous live-in relationships with three attractive women, but the situation rapidly mutates from fantasy to nightmare. On one evening, he becomes increasingly unhinged as everybody ends up jealous and upset. Midway through the evening: "I'm locked in a game of emotional chess that's far out of the depth of someone who's experienced nothing but monogamy all his life." By the end: "The only woman still talking to me in the car is the GPS navigation system, who speaks for all of us when she says, 'Recalculating.'"

The Debate about Whether Monogamy Is "Realistic"

Advocates of consensual nonmonogamy frequently argue that monogamy isn't realistic. This argument derives from certain principles regarding the essential nature of humanity's psychological architecture. There are many variations of these principles, but they align in the view that humans didn't evolve to spend sixty years of their lives—many of them postmenopausal—with only one sex partner.

The psychologist Christopher Ryan and physician Cacilda Jethá provide one variation of this idea in *Sex at Dawn*, arguing that sexual possessiveness was rare in preagricultural societies. In hunter-gatherer societies, resources were generally shared. And because there was no notable wealth to pass down from one generation to the next, concerns about paternity were modest. Sex was promiscuous and playful, even serving to increase group cohesion. Such arguments diverge from other, more traditional arguments in evolutionary psychology, which suggest that humans have evolved strong tendencies to monopolize a partner's resources, such as a man's tendency to experience strong sexual jealousy as a means of avoiding cuckoldry or a woman's tendency to experience strong emotional jealousy as a means of avoiding having the father of her children invest resources elsewhere. But these various arguments align in emphasizing that humans have achieved reproductive success through nonmonogamy, albeit perhaps furtively.

Many scholars and public intellectuals share the view that nonmonogamy is in our genes. And they're right. Erica Jong, in her mega-selling 1973 novel *Fear of Flying*, elegantly articulates this view: "You expected *not* to desire any other men after marriage.

And you expected your husband not to desire any other women. Then the desires came and you were thrown into a panic of self-hatred. . . . Did anyone ever tell you that maybe it had nothing whatever to do with your husband?"

But this perspective glosses over the fact that pair-bonding, too, is in our genes. Just as we have evolved to crave sex with gorgeous, charismatic people we've never slept with before, we have also evolved to sustain a long-term, loving relationship with one sexual partner. And, as we've seen, we often do so by engaging in the motivated derogation of potential alternatives—finding fault with partners who might otherwise tempt us.

The central point is this: Humans are cultural animals, and our mating psyche is flexible. Is monogamy realistic? Of course it is. Millions of people have till-death-do-us-part monogamous marriages that are immensely fulfilling.* But there's no question that the human mating psyche also includes substantial proclivities toward nonmonogamy, and cultivating a healthy nonmonogamous relationship is also realistic. Monogamy is the optimal relationship arrangement for many couples, but not for all. And, for otherwise loving couples whose sex life isn't sufficiently fulfilling, or who crave additional romantic passion, some form of consensual non-monogamy might be the healthiest option—not only for each partner's individual fulfillment, but also for the emotional tenor and stability of the marriage.

"Too many people start off in relationships by putting the moral emphasis in the wrong place, smugly mocking the urge to stray as if it were something disgusting and unthinkable," observes Alain de Botton. "But in truth, it is the ability to stay that is both wondrous and worthy of honour, though it is too often simply taken for granted and deemed the normal state of affairs. . . . Spouses who

---

* After Neil Strauss's wild escapades in *The Truth*, he ultimately settles on monogamy, concluding that "the security of the cage is better than the freedom of the wild."

remain faithful to each other should recognise the scale of the sacrifice they are making for their love and for their children, and should feel proud of their valour."

If we elect to adopt a monogamy norm in our own marriage, we should probably appreciate the magnitude of that commitment. We should consider either what other things we're willing to forgo in our marriage or what additional investments we're willing to make for the arrangement to be fulfilling, perhaps including efforts to keep our bodies fit and, in some cases, to have sex even when we'd rather not.

Descending Mount Maslow

All these strategies—bolstering the self, living apart, diversifying our social portfolio, masturbating, and pursuing consensual nonmonogamy—illustrate the broader idea that one promising means of improving a marriage is to ask less of it. Few of us will elect to adopt the normative marriage structure of 1950, much less 1750, but we can fruitfully resurrect or adapt some features of those earlier marriage structures for our own marriage. Maybe we're no longer in love with our spouse romantically, and maybe our conversations lack intellectual sizzle, but we admire our spouse's integrity and appreciate his or her dedication to the children. Maybe the sexual passion has faded and we prefer socializing separately rather than together, but we appreciate the familiarity and stability of married life and the placidity of a low-conflict relationship. Maybe an ill-fated trip to Seattle has convinced us that we shouldn't expect self-expression through the marriage until the kids are older.

These considerations surround the role of expectations—should we keep our sights locked at the top of Mount Maslow, seeking a spectacular marriage despite the fact that such lofty expectations increase our risk of disappointment? As these two tweets—which

Couples who are demanding of their marriage are more likely to have deeply satisfying unions than those who lower their expectations.

Expectations are resentments waiting to happen.

landed in my Twitter feed minutes apart on May 22, 2016—make clear, major thinkers in the relationships space offer virtually incompatible answers to this question.

The all-or-nothing theory of marriage provides a promising means of reconciling such contradictory advice. It suggests that having high expectations regarding our marriage's ability to fulfill our higher-altitude needs is beneficial when it can actually do so, but harmful when it can't.

Upon reading our *Psychological Inquiry* Target Article, the psychologist James McNulty leveraged a preexisting longitudinal study of newlyweds to investigate this idea. Specifically, he tested the hypothesis that high expectations benefit the relationship when problems in the marriage are benign, but harm the relationship when problems are serious.

McNulty assessed newlyweds' expectations by asking them to report how important certain relationship dynamics are to them—things like showing affection and maintaining independence. Spouses who viewed these dynamics as extremely important were scored as having high expectations. McNulty assessed the severity of their marital problems by asking participants to report the extent to which potential problem areas in their marriage (sex, decision-making, etc.) tend to cause problems in their own marriage.

The chart below illustrates changes in marital satisfaction across the first four years of marriage as a function of expectations and relationship problems. Not surprisingly, spouses were able to sustain high levels of marital satisfaction if problems were benign (left side of chart), but not if problems were serious (right side of chart). Of central interest here, however, is that high expectations strengthened this effect: Spouses experiencing benign problems were happier when they had higher rather than lower expectations, whereas spouses experiencing serious problems were happier when they had lower rather than higher expectations. In short, as suggested by the all-or-nothing theory, it seems that spouses with high expectations regarding higher-altitude need fulfillment have especially fulfilling marriages if the relationship functions smoothly, but especially unfulfilling marriages if it doesn't.

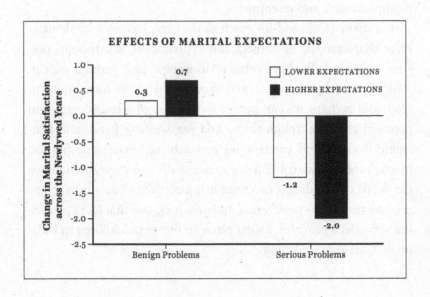

Of course, marriages go through stages. Maybe we're willing to endure mediocre or infrequent sex for a few years while the kids are young, albeit with the hope that the fire will return once everybody's sleeping through the night. Maybe we're willing to endure a few years without spending enough time together while we're both working full-time and pursuing our education, albeit with the hope that we'll have a lifetime of dinners and leisure together once the chaotic stretch subsides. Maybe we're willing to endure arguments after being evicted from our apartment during an economic downturn, albeit with the hope that the fighting will subside once we get our feet back underneath us.

In Praise of Good Enough

I don't share John Gottman's distaste for the pursuit of self-actualization through marriage, but I do share his view that there's no shame in pursuing the "good enough marriage." Lofty expectations can help us achieve marital bliss, but they can also produce disappointment and resentment.

For many of us, and for much of the time, having a stable marriage characterized by respect and appreciation is sufficient, perhaps even ideal. We have other relationships, and perhaps we can achieve our deepest connections through them. We have books to read, and perhaps we can pursue our voyage of self-discovery and personal growth through them. And yes, we have hands and electronic devices, and perhaps we can achieve sexual gratification through them. If we fulfill many of our needs elsewhere, perhaps we can focus on building a marriage in which each of us works to appreciate the other's preferences and priorities, one that lacks pizzazz but serves as a peaceful, loving place for our grandchildren to wake up on Christmas morning.

12.

The Marital Buffet

> People want to be monogamous or promiscuous, they
> want kids or they don't want kids, they want this or they
> want that. For centuries, they had to hide those
> preferences and take everything as a package deal. Now
> you don't have to: It's literally pick and choose. Cut and
> paste the kind of life you want. Family life and love
> relationships are essentially becoming a build-your-own
> model.
>
> —Stephanie Coontz

Americans have never exhibited less agreement about what marriage is all about. This lack of consensus places a significant burden on individuals, and individual couples, as we look to blaze our own path. When there were stronger defaults, there was less pressure to figure out what our marriage would look like. Today, as Leo Tolstoy never said, every married couple must seek happiness in its own way.

But with this burden comes opportunity. That we can have financial security, cohabitation, sex, love, babies, and so forth without being married makes the institution less essential, but also more flexible. We have the freedom to determine what we will—and won't—seek from the marriage, which affords the opportunity to build a relationship that plays to our strengths and circumvents our weaknesses. Neil Strauss captures this new marital zeitgeist: "There isn't just one true and proper way to love, to relate, to bond, to touch. Any style of relationship is the right one, as long as it's a decision made by the whole person and not the hole in the person."

Elements, Not Models

Within a given historical era, broad cultural trends tended to favor a particular type of marriage. Yet even within an era, not everybody seeks the identical features from marriage. "Culture," observes the anthropologist Susan Greenhalgh, "is like a spice rack of ideas and practices from which people choose depending on the menu of opportunities and constraints posed by their environments." That's especially true today.

Imagine removing the overarching marital models—pragmatic, love-based, or self-expressive—and considering their various elements independently. We can select which elements are most sensible to pursue through our marriage in light of our own and our spouse's skills and resources. Will we seek financial security? Emotional warmth? Hot sex? Exciting adventures? Intellectual inspiration? Closeness to God? Coparenthood? Social prestige? Cultural similarity? Sexual monogamy?

Most of us haven't thought seriously about what we're seeking from our marriage. Sure, we're probably looking for love, sex, and companionship. We probably want a partner who brings out the best in us rather than the worst. Maybe we want someone who is stably employed or who has a temperament suited to child-rearing. But these thoughts tend to be vague, and we rarely think about which elements in the marital buffet we're *not* choosing, which is required if we wish to retain sufficient resources for those elements that are most important to us. Chapters 9, 10, and 11 presented three sets of strategies, but the reality is that most of us shouldn't be deciding whether to lovehack *or* go all in *or* recalibrate; we should be using a blend of all three.

The Hybrid Approach

The payoffs of living deliberately in this way are large, but doing so typically requires considerable thought, not to mention extensive conversation and coordination with our spouse. It's a lot of work. Fortunately, the first step is easy.

Implement a Lovehack

Chapter 9 introduced eight lovehacks, four that can help us counter weaknesses in our marriage and four that can help us savor strengths in our marriage. Such procedures require minimal time investment and can be performed without any coordination with our spouse—and yet, they can help us "look with new eyes."

Unlike decisions surrounding going all in or recalibrating, selecting a lovehack doesn't require that we engage in the deliberative process of discerning which elements we'll seek to fulfill through the marriage and which elements we won't. We can simply use our intuition to select a lovehack, ideally one that we'll find relatively easy to implement. The important thing is to avoid getting bogged down in the selection process; we should pick a lovehack right away and get started—today, ideally.

All lovehacks require some nonzero amount of effort—the work involved in deliberately thinking or behaving in a new way rather than in accord with our (bad) habits. This effort isn't particularly time-consuming, but it does require that we set a goal—to make more generous attributions for our spouse's actions, for example—and monitor our behavior to ensure that we're adhering to it, perhaps by setting aside one minute every night to take inventory on how we did that day.

The lovehacks we've discussed have the feature that all of them have received some empirical support. But there's nothing stopping us from making up our own lovehacks. One that I find intriguing, but that hasn't yet been studied yet, involves writing for ten minutes, once per month, about goals and aspirations. Five minutes are dedicated to our own goals—particularly goals, and means of pursuit, linked to our authentic self. The other five minutes are dedicated to thinking about how we can facilitate our spouse's goals, particularly those relevant to his or her authentic self. My guess is that investing the two hours per year that this lovehack requires will provide strong value in terms of relationship well-being.

But this is just one idea; the population of possible lovehacks is infinite. Our job is to start on one that we think will strengthen our marriage without requiring too much effort and to stick with it long enough to give it a chance to work. Ideally, it'll produce noticeable relationship improvement. If it doesn't, we can try a different lovehack.

Take Inventory

Now the real work begins. The two of us must be deliberate about what we will and won't ask of our marriage, and then figure out how the marriage can achieve what we're asking of it. The best place to start is by taking inventory of what we're already asking of our marriage—of the needs and goals we're looking to our marriage to help us fulfill.

In a sense, this task is impossible: We're not always conscious of the things we're asking of our marriage, we might be in denial about how important certain things are to us, and our memory during the list-making process will be imperfect. But let's not get distracted by such concerns, as there's no need for perfection. The goal is to think in a more sophisticated way about whether the requests we're making of our marriage are reasonable in light of what we're investing in it—and about the ways in which we might be well served by seeking to fulfill some elements outside the marriage.

We can start the process by dividing our requests into three categories: (1) needs that we can meet only through our partner; (2) needs that we can meet through our partner or some "other significant other" (OSO), such as a friend or other family member; or (3) needs that we can meet through our partner, through an OSO, or on our own. Let's examine these categories of requests from the perspective of Jasmine, whom we first met in chapter 2. Recall that Jasmine, now forty, is married to James, with whom she has two daughters. She and James both work full-time and are extremely involved parents; they rarely see their friends. They live together, and their marriage is monogamous.

First, let's consider needs or goals that Jasmine can (in her own assessment) meet only through her marriage. Some of these are to develop and sustain a warm emotional climate in the home, serve as the physical and sentimental nexus of a happy and blended extended family, have a partner who is graceful at social events, have a competent coparent, and have a steamy sex life.

Second, let's consider needs or goals that Jasmine is currently looking to meet through her marriage, but that she could also meet through an OSO. Some of these are to receive emotional support when something bad happens at work, celebrate when something good happens at work, debate politics, attend cultural events, and be appreciated for her sense of humor.

Third, let's consider needs or goals that Jasmine is currently looking to meet through her marriage, but that she could also meet either through an OSO or on her own. Some of these are to learn to meditate, generate a long-term career-development strategy, become a kinder person, deepen her relationship with God, and sharpen her logical argumentation skills.

These fifteen examples—five from each category—are idiosyncratic. Our own list will be quite different. Still, Jasmine's list, as far from comprehensive as it is, helps illustrate the number and significance of the goals many of us look to our marriage to help us fulfill. One strategy for helping us identify our list of goals is to think in terms of specific life domains: interpersonal relationships, professional achievement, health and fitness, money management, pleasure, leisure, spirituality, social activism, emotion management, parenting, and so forth.

I suspect that, as for many of us, the process of making the list will cause Jasmine to experience some shock at how much she's asking of her marriage. That's one reason why making the effort to take inventory of such requests is so important. A second reason is that we can consider the list in light of the resources we're investing, using this information to adjust what we're asking of the marriage, the resources we're investing in it, or both.

Assess Resources and Skills

In particular, we can search for places where the psychological return on investment is low—places where the marriage is not doing a particularly good job of fulfilling our higher-altitude needs, or where one of us must invest exorbitant effort to help the other meet certain needs. Once we've done that, we can consider whether we have access to another person, or a solo activity, that can more effectively meet that need—or that could do so if we were to cultivate the outside relationship or solo skill. If we notice that our spouse becomes frustrated whenever we start perseverating about office politics, we might choose to invest in a relationship with a sympathetic coworker. If our nurturant tendencies are stifled by our spouse's independence, we might choose to reach out more than usual to friends who are going through a difficult time (or we could get a puppy).

Although allocating our need-fulfillment efforts across our social network rather than concentrating them in our marriage is typically less efficient (because we tend to have greater physical proximity to our spouse than to others), doing so has important advantages. First, as we've seen, it's unlikely that any one person will have the optimal skill set for all of our needs, so it's wise to leverage the strengths of our broader social network. Second, our spouse will not always be available. He or she may be away on business, enduring a depressive episode, or consumed by studying for the bar exam. If we depend on him or her to help us meet a large proportion of our higher-altitude needs, periods during which he or she is unavailable are likely to be especially challenging for us. Third, our interdependence with our spouse means that stressful periods for us are likely to be stressful for him or her, too. In intact families, when our home is damaged in a hurricane, so is our spouse's; when our child gets suspended from school, so does our spouse's. Shared misery can bring us closer together, but it's risky for those periods when our own personal resources are depleted to be periods when the resources of our primary source of support are also depleted.

Generate a New Plan

Once we've developed a general sense of the needs we're seeking to meet through our marriage—along with an assessment of the skills and resources possessed by ourselves and our OSOs—we can generate a new, more deliberate plan for meeting those needs. For the first set of needs and goals we discussed previously (those we can meet only through our spouse, such as developing and sustaining a warm emotional climate in the household), outsourcing fulfillment to an OSO is not an option. In such cases, we need to evaluate (1) whether there is any amount of effort (from our self, or spouse, or both) that can fulfill this need or goal in the relationship; (2) if so, how much effort it would take; and (3) whether that level of effort investment is worth it. Perhaps we could initiate a conversation about the emotional climate of the household or enter marital therapy to learn more effective conflict-resolution tactics.

If we conclude that the required effort investment is too high, we face an unpleasant choice. If the fulfillment of a particular need—a warm household climate, for example—is absolutely essential, then it might be time to consider the possibility that the marriage is beyond salvation. The other option, which will be preferable in most cases in an otherwise healthy marriage, is to recalibrate. If the insufficiently warm household climate results not from a lack of love but from different styles of handling conflict—perhaps our partner yells and we withdraw—we can consider letting go of that particular need or goal. Perhaps we can work on ourselves, trying to become less conflict-averse and recognizing that the expression of anger and frustration can actually be constructive if it's handled well.

The same logic applies to the second and third sets of needs (those we can also meet through OSOs, and perhaps on our own), although there's a broader range of good options available here. Consider the goal of learning to meditate. In an ideal world, we'd love to embark on this spiritual journey with our spouse, but, alas, he or she simply isn't interested. No problem. We can develop our meditation skills in collaboration with an OSO who likes meditation, or we can do so on our own. Such plans require time and effort independent of our partner, but that's kind of the point—developing independence in ways that facilitate, through more efficient resource use, both partners' need fulfillment.

Working through a similar process for each of the major needs we're looking to our spouse to help us fulfill can make our need fulfillment much more efficient. Because we're playing to the strengths of our partner, our OSOs, and our self, we can achieve much higher levels of overall need fulfillment. And, if we and our spouse leverage our social networks and personal skills more efficiently, our marriage will consist of two better-adjusted people.

Climbing the Mountain

The self-expressive era began more than half a century ago, shattering the love-based, breadwinner-homemaker model of marriage that was ascendant in the 1950s—and dispensing marital chaos. But in recent decades, a new equilibrium has emerged. As more of us seek a form of personal fulfillment oriented toward self-expression and meaning rather than self-esteem and pleasure, as more of us make wise decisions about what we will and won't seek from our marriage, and as more of us find a way to invest the time and energy required to meet our higher-altitude marital expectations, more of our marriages will flourish.

Mountain climbing is a major undertaking. It requires good equipment, extensive training, and strong coordination. It also requires good luck. If a storm rolls in on a summit attempt, the wise strategy is to descend—make the most of the time at base camp and live to summit another day.

Relationship science—marriage's R&D department—has developed some excellent equipment. With training, we can excel at communication, responsiveness, and play. When the storms come, we can descend to safer terrain. When the weather cooperates, we can climb to the summit again. The view is lovely.

NOTES

Preface

ix. *Psychological Inquiry* Target Article: Finkel, E. J., Hui, C. M., Carswell, K. L., & Larson, G. M. (2014). The suffocation of marriage: Climbing Mount Maslow without enough oxygen. *Psychological inquiry, 25*, pp. 1–41.; Finkel, E. J., Larson, G. M., Carswell, K. L., & Hui, C. M. (2014). Marriage at the summit: Response to the commentaries. *Psychological Inquiry, 25*, pp. 120–145.

xiii. across the political spectrum: For an example of a more conservative analysis, see: Murray, C. (2012). *Coming apart: The state of white America, 1960–2010.* New York, NY: Three Rivers Press.; For an example of a more liberal analysis, see: Carbone, J., & Cahn, N. (2014). *Marriage markets: How inequality is remaking the American family.* Oxford, UK: Oxford University Press.

xiv. the all-or-nothing theory of marriage: Finkel, E. J. (2014, February 15). The all-or-nothing marriage. *New York Times.* Retrieved from http://www.nytimes.com/2014/02/15/opinion/sunday/the-all-or-nothing-marriage.html

xiv. *Slate* published a response: Rosin, H. (2014, February 17). The NYT congratulates rich people for having better marriages than poor people. *Slate.* Retrieved from http://www.slate.com/blogs/xx_factor/2014/02/17/new_york_times_all_or_nothing_marriage_article_forgets_about_socioeconomics.html

1. Temperamental but Thrilling

3. voyage of self-discovery: Gilbert, E. (2010). *Eat, pray, love: One woman's search for everything across Italy, India and Indonesia* (p. 30). New York, NY: Riverhead Books.

3. anyone other than myself: Gilbert, E. (2010). (p. 329).

3. higher-stakes, working-class variation: Strayed, C. (2015). *Wild: From lost to found on the Pacific Crest Trail*. London, UK: Atlantic Books.

4. Men, too, are seeking an authentic life: Pappu, S. (2016, June 2). A man goes on a journey. *New York Times*. Retrieved from http://www.ny times.com/2016/06/03/fashion/mens-style/journey-self-discovery.html

4. *The Game*: Strauss, N. (2005). *The game: Penetrating the secret society of pick-up artists*. New York, NY: ReganBooks.

4. *The Truth*, published a decade later: Strauss, N. (2015). *The truth: An uncomfortable book about relationships*. New York, NY: Dey Street.

5. all you have to know is who you are: Strauss, N. (2015). (pp. 369, 217, 347).

5. a cultural universal: Murdock, G. P. (1949). *Social structure*. New York, NY: Free Press.

6. practice polygyny: Gray, P. J. (1998). Ethnographic atlas codebook. *World cultures, 10*, pp. 86–136.

6. an economic and political institution: Coontz, S. (2005). *Marriage, a history: From obedience to intimacy or how love conquered marriage* (p. 5). New York, NY: Viking.

6. primary functions of the marital relationship: Burgess, E. W., & Locke, H. J. (1945). *The family: From institution to companionship*. New York, NY: American Book Company.

7. basic economic and survival needs: Burgess, E. W., & Locke, H. J. (1945).

8. a *love-based* emphasis: Burgess, E. W., & Locke, H. J. (1945).

9. enshrined in popular consciousness: Coontz, S. (2000). *The way we never were: American families and the nostalgia trap*. New York, NY: Basic Books.

10. increasingly postindustrialized: Bell, D. (1973). *The coming of postindustrial society: A venture in social forecasting*. New York, NY: Basic.

10. a *self-expressive* emphasis: Cherlin, A. J. (2009). *The marriage-go-round: The state of marriage and the family in America today*. New York, NY: Alfred A. Knopf.

10. sharing of authentic feelings: Bellah, R., Madsen, R., Sullivan, W., Swindler, A., & Tipton, S. M. (1985). *Habits of the heart: Individualism and commitment in American life* (pp. 107–108). London, UK: Hutchinson.

10. people stopped marrying so young: Kennedy, S., & Ruggles, S. (2014). Breaking up is hard to count: The rise of divorce in the United States, 1980–2010. *Demography, 51*, pp. 587–598.

10. social scientists disagree: Heaton, T. B. (2002). Factors contributing to increasing marital stability in the United States. *Journal of family issues, 23*, 392–409.; Kennedy, S., & Ruggles, S. (2014).; Stevenson, B., & Wolfers, J. (2011). Trends in marital stability. *Research handbook in the law and economics of the family*, pp. 96–108.

11. from the pragmatic to the love-based to the self-expressive eras: Amato, P. R., Booth, A., Johnson, D. R., & Rogers, S. J. (2007). *Alone together: How marriage in America is changing* (p. 70). Cambridge, MA: Harvard University Press.

11. **hierarchy of needs:** Maslow, A. H. (1943, p. 370). A theory of human motivation. *Psychological review, 50,* pp. 370–396.

14. **the core of our identity:** Higgins, E.T. (1987). Self-discrepancy: A theory relating self and affect. *Psychological review, 94,* pp. 319–340.; Markus, H., & Nurius, P. (1986). Possible selves. *American psychologist, 41,* pp. 954–969.; Strohminger N., Newman, G., & Knobe, J. (in press). The true self: A psychological concept distinct from the self. *Perspectives on Psychological Science.*

14. **the sculptor's task:** Gombrich, E. H. (1995). *The story of art* (16th ed.). London, UK: Phaidon Press.

15. **The *Michelangelo effect*:** Drigotas, S. M., Rusbult, C. E., Wieselquist, J., & Whitton, S. W. (1999). Close partner as sculptor of the ideal self: Behavioral affirmation and the Michelangelo phenomenon. *Journal of personality and social psychology, 77,* pp. 293–323.; Rusbult's initial inspiration for the Michelangelo effect metaphor came while reading Lynne Sharon Schwartz's (1980) novel *Rough Strife,* in which two characters are described as serving as "hammer and chisel to each other," à la Michelangelo's sculpting process.

15. *Michelangelo's unfinished captive*: https://commons.wikimedia.org/wiki/File:%27Atlas_Slave%27_by_Michelangelo_-_JBU_02.jpg

16. **misalignment of this sort:** Rusbult, C. E., Finkel, E. J., & Kumashiro, M. (2009). The Michelangelo phenomenon. *Current directions in psychological science, 18,* pp. 305–309.

17. **parents, siblings, neighbors, and friends:** Gerstel, N., & Sarkisian, N. (2006). Marriage: The good, the bad, and the greedy. *Contexts, 5,* pp. 16–21.

18. **how much alone time:** Dew, J. (2009). Has the marital time cost of parenting changed over time? *Social forces, 88,* pp. 519–541.

22. **increase in time-intensive parenting:** Dew, J. (2009).

23. **the proportion of marriages:** Smith, T. W., Son, J., & Schapiro, B. (2015). General social survey final report: Trends in psychological well-being, 1972–2014. Chicago, IL: NORC at the University of Chicago.

23. **richness of the inner life:** Maslow, A. H. (1970). *Motivation and personality,* (p. 99). New York, NY: Harper. (Original work published 1954.)

24. **From 2010 to 2014:** Smith, T. W., Son, J., & Schapiro, B. (2015).

24. **almost twice as strong:** Proulx, C. M., Helms, H. M., & Buehler, C. (2007). Marital quality and personal well-being: A meta-analysis. *Journal of marriage and family, 69,* pp. 576–593.

26. *The Future of Marriage*: Bernard, J. (1982). *The future of marriage* (2nd ed., p. viii). New Haven, CT: Yale University Press.

26. *Domestic Revolutions*: Mintz, S., & Kellogg, S. (1988). *Domestic revolutions: A social history of American family life* (p. xvii). New York, NY: Free Press.

26. *Marriage, a History*: Coontz, S. (2005). (p. 11).

27. Abraham Maslow's lesser-known insights: Aron, A., & Aron, E. N. (2014). Climbing Diotima's mountain: Marriage and achieving our highest goals. *Psychological inquiry, 25*, pp. 47–52.

27. the formerly unhealthy chickens: Dove, W. F. (1935). A study of individuality in the nutritive instincts. *American naturalist, 69*, pp. 469–544.

2. The Pragmatic Marriage

31. experience enough to know what I say: Donald, D. H. (1995). *Lincoln* (p. 27). New York, NY: Simon & Schuster.

32. life was fragile: Fischer, C. S. (2010). *Made in America: A social history of American culture and character.* Chicago, IL: University of Chicago Press.

33. our most distinctive evolved strategy: Baumeister, R. F. (2005). *The cultural animal: Human nature, meaning, and social life.* Oxford, UK: Oxford University Press.

33. cultural evolution: Richerson, P. J., & Boyd, R. (2005). *Not by genes alone: How culture transformed human evolution.* Chicago, IL: University of Chicago Press.; Also see: Mithen, S. J. (1996). *The prehistory of the mind: The cognitive origins of art, religion, and science.* London, UK: Thames & Hudson.

34. human mating tendencies: Eastwick, P. W. (2009). Beyond the Pleistocene: Using phylogeny and constraint to inform the evolutionary psychology of human mating. *Psychological bulletin, 135*, pp. 794–821.

34. altering social roles: Wood, W., & Eagly, A. H. (2002). A cross-cultural analysis of the behavior of women and men: Implications for the origins of sex differences. *Psychological bulletin, 128*, pp. 699–727.

34. used the land more efficiently: Much of the present discussion is adapted from: Diamond, J. M. (1997). *Guns, germs and steel: A short history of everybody for the last 13,000 years.* New York, NY: Random House.

36. forbidding family members from marrying down: Coontz, S. (2005).

36. secularism and rationalism: Inglehart, R., & Welzel, C. (2005). *Modernization, cultural change, and democracy: The human development sequence.* Cambridge, UK: Cambridge University Press.

37. Commercial Revolution: Lal, D. (1998). *Unintended consequences: The impact of factor endowments, culture, and politics on long run economic performance.* Cambridge, MA: MIT Press.

37. dense trading network: Tilly, C. (1997). *Coercion, capital, and European states, AD 990–1992.* Oxford, UK: Blackwell.

37. greater individual autonomy: Hall, J. A. (1989). States and societies: The miracle in comparative perspective. In Baechler, J., Hall, J., & Mann, M. (Eds.), *Europe and the rise of capitalism* (pp. 20-38). Oxford, UK: Blackwell.; Jones, E. L. (1985). *The European miracle: Environments, economies and geopolitics in the history of Europe and Asia* (3rd ed.). Cambridge, UK: Cambridge University Press.; Landes, D. S. (1998). *The*

wealth and poverty of nations: Why some are so rich and some so poor. New York, NY: W. W. Norton & Company.

37. well-functioning marriage: Coontz, S. (2005). (pp. 127–128).

38. the legacy of these influences: Cherlin, A. J. (2009).

38. population of the Plymouth Colony: Plymouth populations, 1620–1690. (n.d.). Retrieved from http://www.histarch.illinois.edu/plymouth/town pop.html

38. average duration of marriages: Mintz, S., & Kellogg, S. (1988). (p. 36).

39. killed in an ambush: Donald, D. H. (1995). *Lincoln.* New York, NY: Simon & Schuster.

39. most rapidly remarrying: Coontz, S. (2005).

39. average of six children: Mintz, S., & Kellogg, S. (1988). (p. 12).; Also see: Philbrick, N. (2006). *Mayflower: A story of courage, community, and war.* New York, NY: Penguin.

40. strong population growth: U.S. Bureau of the Census. (1909). *A century of population growth from the first census of the United States to the twelfth, 1790–1900* (p. 9). Suitland, MD: Author.

41. Immanuel Kant: Kant, I. (1784). What is enlightenment? *On History* (pp. 3–10).

42. the private sphere: Coontz, S. (2005).

42. the male sphere: Arendt, H. (1958). *The human condition.* Chicago, IL: University of Chicago Press.

42. the true woman: Welter, B. (1966). The cult of true womanhood: 1820–1860. *American quarterly,* pp. 151–174.

42. paths that are never the same: De Tocqueville, A. (2003). *Democracy in America* (Vol. 10, p. 697). Washington, DC: Regnery Publishing.

43. their lot in life is different: De Tocqueville, A. (2003). (p. 699).

43. love . . . struck its decisive blow: Coontz, S. (2005).

44. shifted the basis of marriage: Coontz, S. (2005). (p.156).

3. From Pragmatism to Love

46. excited, abnormal, and exhausting condition: Shaw, G. B. (1908). *Getting married.* Retrieved from http://www.gutenberg.org/files/5604/5604-h /5604-h.htm

46. joke would have fallen flat: Coontz, S. (2005). (p. 15).

47. changed beyond recognition: Gordon, R. J. (2016, p. 320). *The rise and fall of American growth: The U.S. standard of living since the Civil War.* Princeton, NJ: Princeton University Press.

47. technological developments: Chandler, A. D. (1977). *The visible hand: The managerial revolution in American business.* Boston, MA: Harvard University Press.; Geddes, P. (1915). *Cities in evolution: An introduction to the town planning movement and to the study of civics.* London, UK: Williams & Norgate.; Landes, D. S. (2003). *The unbound Prometheus: Technological change and industrial development in western*

Europe from 1750 to the present. Cambridge, UK: Cambridge University Press.

47. productivity outpaced population growth: Bernstein, W. J. (2004). *The birth of plenty.* New York, NY: McGraw Hill.; Landes, D. S. (1998).

48. urban rather than rural settings: Greenfield, P. M. (2013). The changing psychology of culture from 1800 through 2000. *Psychological science, 24*(9), pp. 1722–1731. Figure 1.; Greenfield conceptualizes the distinction between rural and urban ecologies in terms of population density, with the dividing line between the two ecologies set at 2,500 people.

48. lifetime fertility for married women: Jones, L. E., & Tertilt, M. (2006). *An economic history of fertility in the US: 1826–1960* (No. w12796). New York, NY: National Bureau of Economic Research.

48. intergenerational wealth flow: Caldwell, J. C. (1976). Toward a restatement of demographic transition theory. *Population and development review, 2*(3/4), pp. 321–366.; Caldwell, J. C. (2005). On net intergenerational wealth flows: An update. *Population and development review, 31*(4), pp. 721–740.

49. working-class family: Cherlin, A. J. (2014). *Labor's love lost: The rise and fall of the working-class family in America.* New York, NY: Russell Sage.

50. the work worlds of husbands and wives: Cherlin, A. J. (2014). (p. 11).

52. rose in motivational priority: Maslow, A. H. (1943). (p. 370).; Also see: Tay, L., & Diener, E. (2011). Needs and subjective well-being around the world. *Journal of personality and social psychology, 101,* pp. 354–365.

52. ability to coordinate daily activities: Coontz, S. (2005). (pp.145–147).; Also see: Burgess, E. W., & Locke, H. J. (1945).; Cherlin, A. J. (1992). *Marriage, divorce, remarriage* (2nd ed.). Revised and enlarged edition (social trends in the United States). Cambridge, MA: Harvard University Press.; Mintz, S., & Kellogg, S. (1988).; McWilliams, J. E. (2006). Marketing middle-class morality. *Reviews in American history, 34,* pp.162–168.

52. heaven on earth: Coontz, S. (2005). (p. 162).

52. haven in a heartless world: Lasch, C. (1976). The family as a haven in a heartless world. *Salmagundi,* pp. 42–55.

53. counterweight to acquisitive values: Mintz, S., & Kellogg, S. (1988). (p. 44).; Also see: Coontz, S. (2005).; Cott, N. F. (1977). *The bonds of womanhood: "Women's sphere" in New England, 1780–1835.* New Haven, CT: Yale University Press.; Jeffrey, K. (1972). The family as utopian retreat from the city: The nineteenth-century contribution. *Soundings,* pp. 21–41.

53. Masculine virtue: Coontz, S. (2005). (pp. 166–168).

54. An undersexed marriage: Celello, K. (2009). *Making marriage work: A history of marriage and divorce in the twentieth-century United States.* Chapel Hill, NC: University of North Carolina Press.; Coontz, S. (2005).

55. acts of caregiving and love: Coontz, S. (2005). (p. 155).
55. The homemaker's labor: Gillis, J. R. (1997). *A world of their own making: Myth, ritual, and the quest for family values.* Cambridge, MA: Harvard University Press.
55. industrial production declined: Blum, J., Cameron, R., & Barnes, T. G. (1970). *The European world: A history* (2nd ed). New York, NY: Little, Brown.
56. concerns with basic survival: Mintz, S., & Kellogg, S. (1988). (p. 149).
56. The philosophy underlying such legislation: Mintz, S., & Kellogg, S. (1988). (p. 144).
57. number of women in the workforce: Cherlin, A. J. (2014). (p. 82).
58. Divorces spiked: Mintz, S., & Kellogg, S. (1988).
58. Americans married for love: Cherlin, A. J. (2014). (p. 95).
58. "end of history": Fukuyama, F. (1989). The end of history? *The national interest, 16*, pp. 3–18.
59. ideal in both practical and moral terms: Sirjamaki, J. (1948). Culture configurations in the American family. *American journal of sociology*, pp. 464–470.; Also see: Coontz, S. (2005).
59. the breadwinner-homemaker marriage was optimally suited: Parsons, T., & Bales, R. F. (1955). *Family, socialization, and interaction process.* New York, NY: Free Press.
59. corporate profits and employee wages: Cherlin, A. J. (2014). (pp. 69, 101–102).
59. Income inequality . . . remained modest: Cherlin, A. J. (2014). (pp. 93, 115).
60. ushered out of the labor force in droves: Coontz, S. (2005). (p. 222).
60. G.I. Bill: Olson, K. W. (1973). The G.I. Bill and higher education: Success and surprise. *American quarterly*, pp. 596–610.
60. most women sought fulfillment through domestic life: Cherlin, A. J. (2014). (p. 69).; Coontz, S. (2005). (p. 223).; Mintz, S., & Kellogg, S. (1988). (pp. 180–181).
60. the domestic life sought by married couples: Weiss, J. (2000). *To have and to hold: Marriage, the baby boom, and social change.* Chicago, IL: University of Chicago Press.
61. nuclear family unit: Unknown Author (1954, May). A man's place is in the home. *McCall's, 81*, pp. 28–34.; Also see: Cherlin, A. J. (2009). (pp. 83–84).; Mintz, S., & Kellogg, S. (1988). (pp. 179–180).
61. family togetherness: Friedan, B. (1963). *The feminine mystique* (pp. 41–44). New York, NY: W. W. Norton & Company.
62. huge growth in affordable houses: Mintz, S., & Kellogg, S. (1988).
62. more and more houses contained amenities: Coontz, S. (2005). (pp.230–231).
62. "the great exception": Mintz, S. & Kellogg, S. (1988). (p. 178).
62. not a documentary: Coontz, S. (2000).
63. Jane Austen's observation: Coontz, S. (2005). Quoted on p.185.

64. social interaction with coworkers: Spurlock J., & Magistro, C. (1998). *New and improved: The transformation of women's emotional culture.* New York, NY: New York University Press.

65. Spouses' daily lives overlapped less than ever: Cancian, F. (1987). *Love in America: Gender and self-development.* Cambridge, UK: Cambridge University Press.; Coontz, S. (2005).; Cott, N. F. (1977). (p. 73).

66. The lenses through which we look: Hansen, K. E., & Pronin, E. (2012). (p. 345) Illusions of self-knowledge. In Vazire, S., & Wilson, T. D. (Eds.), *Handbook of self-knowledge* (pp. 345–362). New York, NY: Guilford Press.; For extensive discussion of self-knowledge, see: Vazire, S., & Wilson, T. D. (Eds.). (2012). *Handbook of self-knowledge.* New York, NY: Guilford Press.

66. other people know us better: Vazire, S. (2010). Who knows what about a person? The self–other knowledge asymmetry (SOKA) model. *Journal of personality and social psychology, 98*(2), pp. 281–300.

66. shameful qualities: Reis, H. T., & Shaver, P. (1988). Intimacy as an interpersonal process. In Duck, S. (Ed.), *Handbook of personal relationships* (pp. 367–389). Chichester, UK: John Wiley & Sons.

66. might feel threatened: Ickes, W., & Simpson. J. A. (2001). Motivational aspects of empathic accuracy. In Fletcher, G. J. O., & Clark, M. S. (Eds.), *Blackwell handbook of social psychology: Interpersonal processes* (pp. 229–249). Oxford, UK: Blackwell.

66. it's difficult for our partner to know: Carlson, E. N., & Kenny, D. A. (2012). Meta-accuracy: Do we know how others see us? In Vazire, S., & Wilson, T. D. (Eds.). (pp. 242–257).

66. *The Lonely Crowd*: Riesman, D., Glazer, N., & Denney, R. (1950). *The lonely crowd.* New Haven, CT: Yale University Press.

66. the cover of *Time* magazine: *Time* magazine cover: David Reisman (1954, September 27). Retrieved from http://content.time.com/time/covers /0,16641,19540927,00.html

67. roots dating to the 1920s: Lewis, S. (1922). *Babbitt.* New York, NY: Harcourt, Brace & Co.

67. soul-crushing pressure to conform: Whyte, W. H., Jr. (1956). *The organization man.* New York, NY: Simon & Schuster.

67. consequences of this decision suggest: Yates, R. (1961). *Revolutionary road.* New York, NY: Atlantic-Little, Brown.

67. dehumanizing venalities of corporate life: Wilson, S. (1955). *The man in the gray flannel suit.* New York, NY: Simon & Schuster.; Also see: Cherlin, A. J. (2014). (p. 106).; Mintz, S., & Kellogg, S. (1988). (pp. 196–197).

68. not unusual for wives: Coontz, S. (2005). (pp. 4).

68. as much housework: Cherlin, A. J. (2009).; Cherlin, A. J. (2014).

68. impervious to superficial remedies: Quoted in Mintz, S., & Kellogg, S. (1988). (p. 199).

68. "Is this all?": Friedan, B. (1963).

69. assertiveness and nurturance are fundamental needs: Baumeister, R. F., & Leary, M. R. (1995). The need to belong: Desire for interpersonal attachments as a fundamental human motivation. *Psychological bulletin*, *117*(3), pp. 497–529.; Cacioppo, J. T., & Patrick, W. (2008). *Loneliness: Human nature and the need for social connection.* New York, NY: W. W. Norton & Company.; Holt-Lunstad, J., Smith, T. B., & Layton, J. B. (2010). Social relationships and mortality risk: A meta-analytic review. *PLoS medicine*, *7*(7), e1000316.; Deci, E. L., & Ryan, R. M. (2000). The "what" and "why" of goal pursuits: Human needs and the self-determination of behavior. *Psychological inquiry*, *11*(4), pp. 227–268.; Schwarzer, R. (Ed.). (2014). *Self-efficacy: Thought control of action.* Park Drive, UK: Taylor & Francis.; Fiske, S. T. (2009). *Social beings: Core motives in social psychology.* Hoboken, NJ: John Wiley & Sons.

70. their primary interest is in the home: Quoted in Coontz, S. (2005). (p. 236).

70. Mars and Venus: Gray, J. (1992). *Men are from Mars, women are from Venus: A practical guide for improving communication and getting what you want in your relationship.* New York, NY: HarperCollins.

70. men and women are . . . from Earth: Carothers, B. J., & Reis, H. T. (2013). Men and women are from Earth: Examining the latent structure of gender. *Journal of personality and social psychology*, *104*(2), p. 385.; Hyde, J. S. (2005). The gender similarities hypothesis. *American psychologist*, *60*(6), pp. 581–592.; Zell, E., Krizan, Z., & Teeter, S. R. (2015). Evaluating gender similarities and differences using metasynthesis. *American psychologist*, *70*(1), pp. 10–20.

70. psychologically androgynous: Bem, S. L. (1977). On the utility of alternative procedures for assessing psychological androgyny. *Journal of consulting and clinical psychology*, *45*, pp. 196–205.; Also see: Spence, J. T., Helmreich, R., & Stapp, J. (1975). Ratings of self and peers on sex role attributes and their relation to self-esteem and conceptions of masculinity and femininity. *Journal of personality and social psychology*, *32*, pp. 29–39.

70. unmitigated forms of assertiveness or nurturance: Bakan, D. (1966). *The duality of human existence: An essay on psychology and religion.* Chicago, IL: Rand McNally.; Helgeson, V. S., & Fritz, H. L. (1998). A theory of unmitigated communion. *Personality and social psychology review*, *2*(3), pp. 173–183.

71. the sex therapist Esther Perel: Perel, E. (2007). *Mating in captivity: Unlocking erotic intelligence.* New York, NY: Harper.

71. turned on at night by the very same: Perel, E. (n.d.). *The secret to desire in a long-term relationship* [Transcript]. Retrieved from http://www.ted.com/talks/esther_perel_the_secret_to_desire_in_a_long_term_relationship/transcript?language=en

71. emotional intimacy and intimate communication: Johnson, S. (2013). *Love sense: The revolutionary new science of romantic relationships.* Boston, MA: Little, Brown.; Johnson, S. The three kinds of sex. (n.d.).

Retrieved from http://www.drsuejohnson.com/the-three-kinds-of-sex; Cupach, W. R., & Comstock, J. (1990). Satisfaction with sexual communication in marriage: Links to sexual satisfaction and dyadic adjustment. *Journal of social and personal relationships*, 7(2), pp. 179–186.

71. sexual desire is frequently insubordinate: Perel, E. (2007).; Also see: de Botton, A. (2012). *How to think more about sex*. New York, NY: Picador.

72. the 1950s was an outlier: Coontz, S. (2016).

72. the end of family history: Coontz, S. (2005). (p. 83).; The "end of history" phrase initially comes from: Fukuyama, F. (1989).

73. less willing to endure an unfulfilling marriage: Coontz, S. (2005). (pp. 240–244).

4. From Love to Self-Expression

74. final episode of *Sex and the City*: (n.d.). Retrieved from http://www.hbo.com/sex-and-the-city/episodes/6/94-an-american-girl-in-paris-part-deux/index.html

76. the increased automation of work tasks: Sellier, A. L., & Avnet, T. (2014). So what if the clock strikes? Scheduling style, control, and well-being. *Journal of personality and social psychology*, 107(5), pp. 791–808.

76. rediscovering the living person: May, R. (1983). *The discovery of being: Writings in existential psychology* (p. 53). New York, NY: W. W. Norton & Company.

76. they must try to answer questions: Kierkegaard, S. (1843). *Fear and trembling*.; see also Nietzsche, F. (1886). *Beyond good and evil.*; Heidegger, M. (1962). *Being and time*. (J. Macquarrie and E. Robinson, Trans.). New York, NY: Harper & Row. (Original work published 1927)

77. experienced as meaningful: King, L. A., Hicks, J. A., Krull, J. L., & Del Gaiso, A. K. (2006). Positive affect and the experience of meaning in life. *Journal of personality and social psychology*, 90, pp. 179–196. Quote from p. 180.

77. live long, healthy lives: Hill, P. L., & Turiano, N. A. (2014). Purpose in life as a predictor of mortality across adulthood. *Psychological science*, 25, pp. 1482–1486.; Kim, E. S., Sun, J. K., Park, N., Kubzansky, L. D., & Peterson, C. (2013). Purpose in life and reduced risk of myocardial infarction among older US adults with coronary heart disease: A two-year follow-up. *Journal of behavioral medicine*, 36, pp. 124–133.

78. roots in existentialism: Nietzsche, F. (1974). *The gay science* (W. Kaufmann, Trans.) (pp. 7, 82). New York, NY: Vintage Books.

78. pursuit of self-discovery: Rogers, C. R. (1951). *Client-centered therapy: Its current practice, implications, and theory*. London, UK: Constable.; Rogers, C. (1961). *On becoming a person: A therapist's view of psychotherapy* (p. 196). New York, NY: Houghton Mifflin.

78. words of the poet E. E. Cummings: Cummings, E. E. (1958). *A miscellany* (G. J. Firmage, Ed.) (p. 13). New York, NY: Argophile Press.

79. staple of self-help books: Dyer, W. (1976). *Your erroneous zones*. New York, NY: Funk & Wagnalls.; Peck, M. S. (1978). *The road less traveled*. New York, NY: Simon & Schuster.; Warren, R. (2002). *The purpose driven life*. Grand Rapids, MI: Zondervan.; For a review, see chapter 4 of: McAdams, D. P. (2013). *The redemptive self: Stories Americans live by* (revised and expanded edition). Oxford, UK: Oxford University Press.

79. there's always Oprah: Clemetson, L. (2001, January 8). Oprah on Oprah. *Newsweek*, pp. 28–48. Quote from p. 45.

79. *relationship* as a social connection: Rank, O. (1996). *A psychology of difference: The American lectures* (p. 79). Princeton, NJ: Princeton University Press.; Kramer, R. (1995). The birth of client-centered therapy: Carl Rogers, Otto Rank, and "the beyond." *Journal of humanistic psychology, 35*(4), pp. 54–110.

80. symbols, information, and people: Bell, D. (1976, May). The coming of the post-industrial society. *The educational forum, 40*(4), pp. 574–579).

80. Postindustrial jobs: Florida, R. L. (2011). *The rise of the creative class, revisited*. New York, NY: Basic Books. See Figure 3.2 on p. 46.

80. transition from an industrial to a postindustrial: Inglehart, R., & Welzel, C. (2005).; Florida, R. (2002). *The rise of the creative class, and how it is transforming work, leisure, community and everyday life*. New York, NY: Basic Books.

80. cultural emphasis shifts: Inglehart, R., & Welzel, C. (2005). (p. 2).

81. people sought fulfillment: Baumeister, R. F. (1986). *Identity: Cultural change and the struggle for self*. Oxford, UK: Oxford University Press.; Baumeister, R. F. (1987). How the self became a problem: A psychological review of historical research. *Journal of personality and social psychology, 52*, pp. 163–176.; Baumeister, R. F., & MacKenzie, M. J. (2014). The value of marriage in the era of the glorified self. *Psychological inquiry, 25*, pp. 53–55.

81. discoveries of the Florentine humanist: Greenblatt, S. (2011). *The swerve: How the world became modern*. New York, NY: W. W. Norton & Company. Quote from p. 16.

82. *rugged individualism* or *utilitarian individualism*: Cherlin, A. J. (2009). (p. 39).

82. individual specialness: Bellah, R., Madsen, R., Sullivan, W., Swindler, A., & Tipton, S. M. (1985). *Habits of the heart: Individualism and commitment in American life*. London, UK: Hutchinson.

82. capturing the essence of expressive self: Thurman, H. (1980, May 4). The sound of the genuine. Baccalaureate address Spelman College. *Spelman Messenger, 96*, pp. 14–15.

82. self-defining life choices: Baumeister, R. F. (1986, 1987).; Giddens, A. (1991). *Modernity and self-identity: Self and society in the late modern age*. Palo Alto, CA: Stanford University Press.

83. Western societies have secularized: Baumeister, R. F., & MacKenzie, M. J. (2014). The value of marriage in the era of the glorified self.

Psychological inquiry, 25(1), pp. 53–55. Quote from p. 53.; Also see: Baumeister, R. F. (1991). *Meanings of life*. New York, NY: Guilford.; For evidence that Americans are becoming less religious, see here: http://www.pewforum.org/2015/11/03/u-s-public-becoming-less-religious/

83. The moral thread of self-actualisation: Giddens, A. (1991). (pp. 78–79).

83. not fulfilled by your marriage: Klinenberg, E. (2012). *Going solo: The extraordinary rise and surprising appeal of living alone*. New York, NY: Penguin. Quote from p. 13.

84. the development of one's authentic self: Kidd, V. (1975). Happily ever after and other relationship styles: Advice on interpersonal relations in popular magazines, 1951–1973. *Quarterly journal of speech*, 61, pp. 31–39. Quote from p. 34.

84. long-term trend toward self-expression: Cancian, F. M., & Gordon, S. L. (1988). Changing emotion norms in marriage: Love and anger in US women's magazines since 1900. *Gender & society*, 2(3), pp. 308–342.

85. best version of myself: Eastwick, P. W., & Hunt, L. L. (2014). Relational mate value: Consensus and uniqueness in romantic evaluations. *Journal of personality and social psychology*, 106, pp. 728–751. Quote from p. 749.

85. self-expressive era has vanquished: Goldin, C. (2014). A grand gender convergence: Its last chapter. *The American economic review*, 104, pp. 1091–1119.

86. inhabit a single sphere: Goldin, C. (2014). Quote from p. 1091.; Also see: Parker, K., & Wang, W. (2013, March 14). Modern parenthood. Pew Research Center. Retrieved from http://www.pewsocialtrends.org/2013/03/14/modern-parenthood-roles-of-moms-and-dads-converge-as-they-balance-work-and-family/

86. work depended less on physical strength: Bell, D. (1999). Preface. In *The coming of post-industrial society: A venture in social forecasting*. With a new introduction by the author. New York, NY: Basic Books.

86. Women today earn about half of professional degrees: Mason, M. A. (2009). Better educating our new breadwinners. In Boushey, H., & O'Leary, A. (Eds.). *The Shriver report. A woman's nation changes everything*. Washington, DC: Center for American Progress.; Cherlin, A. J. (2014).; Data on college graduate rates from U.S. Department of Commerce (1996, 2014). Also see: Rosin, H. (2012). *The end of men: And the rise of women*. New York, NY: Riverhead Books.

86. the middle-class job that grew the most: Aisch, G., & Gebeloff, R. (2015, February 22). The changing nature of middle-class jobs. *New York Times*. Retrieved from http://www.nytimes.com/interactive/2015/02/23/business/economy/the-changing-nature-of-middle-class-jobs.html?_r=0

86. from 1960 to 1990 alone: Ruggles, S. (2015). Patriarchy, power, and pay: The transformation of American families, 1800–2015. *Demography*, 52, pp. 1797–1823. See Figure 8 on p. 1805.

86. male breadwinner family: Ruggles, S. (2015). Figure adapted from Figure 4 on p. 1801.

87. marriages characterized by greater gender equality: Goldscheider, F., Bernhardt, E., & Lappegård, T. (2015). The gender revolution: A framework for understanding changing family and demographic behavior. *Population and development review, 41*, pp. 207–239. Retrieved from https://contemporaryfamilies.org/gender-restabilization/; Carlson, D. L., Miller, A. J., Sassler, S., & Hanson, S. (2016). The gendered division of housework and couples' sexual relationships: A reexamination. *Journal of marriage and family, 78*, pp. 975–995.; Johnson, M. D., Galambos, N. L., & Anderson, J. R. (2016). Skip the dishes? Not so fast! Sex and housework revisited. *Journal of family psychology, 30*, pp. 203–213. Retrieved from https://contemporaryfamilies.org/sex-equalmarriages/

88. marriages had become egalitarian: Rampell, C. (2014, December 9). What men (and women) want in a marriage, today vs. yesterday. Retrieved from https://www.washingtonpost.com/news/rampage/wp/2014/12/09/what-men-and-women-want-in-a-marriage-today-vs-yesterday/

88. "head and master" laws: Head and Master law. (2017, January 20). Retrieved from https://en.wikipedia.org/wiki/Head_and_Master_law

88. Renaissance-Era English common law: Marital rape (United States law). (2017, February 12). Retrieved from https://en.wikipedia.org/wiki/Marital_rape_%28United_States_law%29

88. doubling of the divorce rate: Amato, P. R., & Irving, S. (2006). A historical perspective on divorce in the United States. In Fine, M., & Harvey, J. (Eds.), *Handbook of divorce and relationship dissolution* (pp. 41–58). Hillsdale, NJ: Erlbaum.

88. no-fault divorce: Divorce in the United States. (2017, February 15). Retrieved from https://en.wikipedia.org/wiki/Divorce_in_the_United_States

89. Racial Integrity Act of 1924: Racial Integrity Act of 1924. (2017, February 17). Retrieved from https://en.wikipedia.org/wiki/Racial_Integrity_Act_of_1924

89. same-sex marriage: Coontz, S. (2014, October 13). Why America changed its mind on gay marriage. CNN. Retrieved from http://www.cnn.com/2014/10/13/opinion/coontz-same-sex-marriage/

90. U.S. Supreme Court ruled in 2015: Liptak, A. (2015, June 26). Supreme Court ruling makes same-sex marriage a right nationwide. *New York Times*. Retrieved from http://www.nytimes.com/2015/06/27/us/supreme-court-same-sex-marriage.html?hp&action=click&pgtype=Homepage&module=span-ab-top-region®ion=top-news&WT.nav=top-news

90. Americans approved of same-sex marriage: Jones, R. P. (2014, March 10). The South's stunning embrace of gay marriage. *The Atlantic*. Retrieved from https://www.theatlantic.com/politics/archive/2014/03/the-souths-stunning-embrace-of-gay-marriage/284306; Casselman, B. (2014, November 25). The census doesn't know how many same-sex couples there are. *FiveThirtyEight*. Retrieved from https://fivethirtyeight.com/features/the-census-still-doesnt-know-how-many-same-sex-couples-there-are; McCann, A., & Hickey, W. (2015, June 26). Same-sex marriage: From

0 to 100 percent, in one chart. *FiveThirtyEight*. Retrieved from https://fivethirtyeight.com/datalab/same-sex-marriage-from-0-to-100-percent-in-one-chart

90. marriage has become decreasingly characterized by obligation: Cherlin, A. J. (2004). The deinstitutionalization of American marriage. *Journal of marriage and family*, 66, pp. 848–861.

90. American women married at least once: Ruggles, S. (2015). Figure adapted from Figure 3 on p. 1800.

90. driven primarily by people with less education: Goldstein, J. R., & Kenney, C. T. (2001). Marriage delayed or marriage forgone? New cohort forecasts of first marriage for US women. *American sociological review*, pp. 506–519.; Wang, W., & Parker, K. (2014, September 24). Record share of Americans have never married. Pew Research Center. Retrieved from http://www.pewsocialtrends.org/2014/09/24/record-share-of-americans-have-never-married/#will-todays-never-married-adults-eventually-marry; Thornton, A., & Young-DeMarco, L. (2001). Four decades of trends in attitudes toward family issues in the United States: The 1960s through the 1990s. *Journal of marriage and family*, 63, pp. 1009–1037.

91. Americans married at historically young ages: Ruggles, S. (2015). Figure adapted from Figure 11 on p. 1809.; Also see: Bell, P. (2015, November 6). Young women today are half as likely to be married as in 1940. Pew Research Center. Retrieved from http://www.pewresearch.org/fact-tank/2015/11/11/record-share-of-young-women-are-living-with-their-parents-relatives/ft_11-03-15_womenlivehome_310px/

91. women aged thirty-five to forty-four who had ever cohabited: Manning, W. D., Brown, S. L., & Payne, K. K. (2014). Two decades of stability and change in age at first union formation. *Journal of marriage and family*, 76, pp. 247–260.

91. approval of premarital sex: Wells, B. E., & Twenge, J. M. (2005). Changes in young people's sexual behavior and attitudes, 1943–1999: A cross-temporal meta-analysis. *Review of general psychology*, 9, pp. 249–261.; Also see: Twenge, J. M., Sherman, R. A., & Wells, B. E. (2015). Changes in American adults' sexual behavior and attitudes, 1972–2012. *Archives of sexual behavior*, pp. 44, 2273–2285.

92. American babies born to unwed mothers: Centers for disease control and prevention. Unmarried childbearing. (2016, June 13). Retrieved from http://www.cdc.gov/nchs/fastats/unmarried-childbearing.htm

92. birth rate for unmarried women: Curtin, S. C., Ventura, S. J., & Martinez, G. M. (2014). Recent declines in nonmarital childbearing in the United States. NCHS data brief, no 162. Hyattsville, MD: National Center for Health Statistics.

92. much more likely to be intentional: Sawhill, I. V. (2014). *Generation unbound: Drifting into sex and parenthood without marriage*. Washington, DC: Brookings Institution Press.

92. high levels of respect for the institution: Cherlin, A. J. (2009).

92. more difficult to get divorced: Amato, P. R., et al. (2007). (p. 243). Figure 8.1.

92. Getting married has shifted: Cherlin, A. J. (2004).

93. life stages need to be spliced into the nursery rhyme: Rampell, C. (2015, November 19). For millennials, first comes love—then what? *Washington Post.* Retrieved from https://www.washingtonpost.com/opinions /first-comes-love--then-what/2015/11/19/39eb8186-8f02-11e5-baf4-bdf 37355da0c_story.html?wpmm=1&wpisrc=nl_headlines

92. the eight-year divorce rate: Miller, C. C. (2014, December 1). The divorce surge is over, but the myth lives on. *New York Times.* Retrieved from http://www.nytimes.com/2014/12/02/upshot/the-divorce-surge-is-over -but-the-myth-lives-on.html?_r=2 %2F%2F Justin Wolfers%3A http% 3A%2F%2Fwww.nytimes.com%2F2014%2F12%2F04%2Fupshot% 2Fhow-we-know-the-divorce-rate-is-falling.html%3Fabt&abg=1

94. those without a high school degree: Martin, S. P. (2006). Trends in marital dissolution by women's education in the United States. *Demographic research, 15,* pp. 537–560. doi: 10.4054/DemRes.2006.15.20

94. Benjamin Franklin observed: Franklin, B. (1997). *Autobiography, Poor Richard, and later writings.* Lemay, J. A. L. (Ed.). New York, NY: Library of America.

94. voiced a similar sentiment: Quoted in Popova, M. (2016, June 22). Nietzsche on how to find yourself and the true value of education. *Brain Pickings.* Retrieved from https://www.brainpickings.org/2015/09/30/nietzsche-find -yourself-schopenhauer-as-educator/

95. William James: James, W. (1963). *Psychology.* Greenwich, CT: Fawcett. (Original work published 1892)

95. adult life with broad purpose and a dynamic sense of temporal continuity: McAdams, D. P. (2013). The psychological self as actor, agent, and author. *Perspectives on psychological science, 8,* pp. 272–295. Quotes from p. 272.; For additional discussion of the "social actor" role, see: Becker, E. (1971). *The birth and death of meaning.* New York, NY: Free Press.; Goffman, E. (1959). *The presentation of self in everyday life.* Garden City, NY: Doubleday.; Mead, G. H. (1934). *Mind, self, and society.* Chicago, IL: University of Chicago Press.; Bandura, A. (1989). Human agency in social-cognitive theory. *American psychologist, 44,* pp. 1175–1184.; Erikson, E. H. (1963). *Childhood and society* (2nd ed.). New York, NY: W. W. Norton & Company.; Piaget, J. (1970). Piaget's theory. In Mussen, P. H. (Ed.), *Carmichael's manual of child psychology* (2nd ed., Vol. 1, pp. 703–732). New York, NY: Wiley.; For additional discussion of the "autobiographical author" role, see: Dennett, D. (1992). The self as a center of narrative gravity. In Kessel, F., Cole, P., & Johnson, D. (Eds.), *Self and consciousness: Multiple perspectives* (pp. 103–115). Hillsdale, NJ: Erlbaum.; Hammack, P. L. (2008). Narrative and the cultural psychology of identity. *Personality and social psychology review, 12,* pp. 222–247.; McLean, K. C., Pasupathi, M., & Pals, J. L. (2007). Selves creating stories creating selves: A process

model of self-development. *Personality and social psychology review,* *11*, pp. 262–278.

95. identity that articulates: McAdams, D. P. (2013). (pp. 279, 281).; Also see: Giddens, A. (1991).

95. vary greatly from person to person: Maslow, A. H. (1943). (p. 383).

95. spouse must understand our psychological constitution: McNulty, J. K. (2016). Highlighting the contextual nature of interpersonal relationships. *Advances in experimental social psychology* (pp. 54, 247–315).; Also see: Overall, N. C., & Simpson, J. A. (2013). Regulation processes in close. In Simpson, J. A., & Campbell, L. (Eds.), *Oxford handbook of close relationships* (pp. 427–451). New York, NY: Oxford University Press.

96. threads that bound them together began to fray: Rinaldi, R. (2016). *Fifty shades of free.* In Hanauer, C. (Ed.). *The bitch is back: Older, wiser, and (getting) happier* (pp. 143–152). New York, NY: Morrow. Quotes from pp. 145, 151.

97. the philosopher Arthur Schopenhauer's famous parable: Schopenhauer, A. (1851). *Parerga and Paralipomena* (E. F. J. Payne, Trans.) (Vol. 2, Chapter XXXI). Oxford, UK: Oxford University Press. Quote from p. 651.

97. Sigmund Freud introduced this porcupine idea: Freud, S. (1921). *Group psychology and the analysis of the ego* (J. E. Strachey, Trans.). New York, NY: W. W. Norton & Company.

97. context of intimate relationships: Fincham, F. D. (2000). The kiss of the porcupines: From attributing responsibility to forgiving. *Personal relationships,* *7*(1), pp. 1–23.; Maner, J. K., DeWall, C. N., Baumeister, R. F., & Schaller, M. (2007). Does social exclusion motivate interpersonal reconnection? Resolving the "porcupine problem." *Journal of personality and social psychology,* *92*, pp. 42–55.

97. maintaining a strong sense of security: Murray, S. L., Holmes, J. G., & Collins, N. L. (2006). Optimizing assurance: The risk regulation system in relationships. *Psychological bulletin,* *132*(5), pp. 641–666.

98. desire of the philosopher Howard Thurman: Thurman, H. (1980). (p. 15).

98. self-fulfilling dynamics: Murray, S. L., et al. (2006).; Also see: Clark, M. S., & Lemay, E. P. (2010). Close relationships. In Fiske, S. T., Gilbert, D. T., and Lindzey, G. (Eds.), *Handbook of social psychology* (5th ed., pp. 898–940).; Downey, G., Freitas, A. L., Michaelis, B., & Khouri, H. (1998). The self-fulfilling prophecy in close relationships: Rejection sensitivity and rejection by romantic partners. *Journal of personality and social psychology,* *75*, pp. 545–560.; Mikulincer, M., & Shaver, P. R. (2007). *Attachment in adulthood: Structure, dynamics, and change.* New York, NY: Guilford Press.

98. *attachment avoidance*: Mikulincer, M., & Shaver, P. R. (2007).

99. reduction in avoidant tendencies over time: Arriaga, X. B., Kumashiro, M., Finkel, E. J., VanderDrift, L. E., & Luchies, L. B. (2014). Filling the void: Bolstering attachment security in committed relationships. *Social psychological and personality science,* *5*, pp. 398–406.

100. argued that women can achieve full success: Sandberg, S. (2013). *Lean in: Women, work, and the will to lead.* New York, NY: Random House.; Slaughter, A. (2014, October 10). Why women still can't have it all. *The Atlantic.* Retrieved from http://www.theatlantic.com/magazine/archive /2012/07/why-women-still-cant-have-it-all/309020

101. blamed marital problems on the emotional immaturity: Celello, K. (2009).

101. spent an average of 33.5 hours parenting: Yavorsky, J. E., Kamp Dush, C. M., & Schoppe-Sullivan, S. J. (2015). The production of inequality: The gender division of labor across the transition to parenthood. *Journal of marriage and family,* 77, pp. 662–679.

102. make sure that almost everything gets done: Shulevitz, J. (2015, May 9). Mom: The designated worrier. *New York Times.* Retrieved from http:// www.nytimes.com/2015/05/10/opinion/sunday/judith-shulevitz-mom-the -designated-worrier.html?smprod=nytcore-iphone&smid=nytcore-iphone -share

102. sexual fulfillment: Celello, K. (2009). (pp. 143–144).

102. more insidious set of ideals and aspirations: Hills, R. (2015, August 31). When your sex life doesn't follow the script. *Well blog. New York Times.* Retrieved from http://well.blogs.nytimes.com/2015/08/31 /when-your-sex-life-doesnt-follow-the-script/; Also see: Hills, R. (2015). *The sex myth.* London, UK: Penguin UK.

103. true and honest indices: de Botton, A. (2012). Quote from p. 29.

104. Women's adoption of assertive qualities: Rosin, H. (2012). Also see: Croft, A., Schmader, T., & Block, K. (2015). An underexamined inequality: Cultural and psychological barriers to men's engagement with communal roles. *Personality and social psychology review,* 19, pp. 343–370.; England, P. (2010). The gender revolution uneven and stalled. *Gender & society,* 24(2), pp. 149–166.; Slaughter, A. (2016, March 4). Why women need a men's revolution. ABC News. Retrieved from http://www.abc.net.au/news/2016 -03-04/anne-marie-slaughter-women-and-men-revolution/7221596

104. remarkably unable to adapt: Rosin, H. (2012). (pp. 124–125).

104. reestablish their sense of masculinity: Bosson, J. K., Vandello, J. A., Burnaford, R. M., Weaver, J. R., & Wasti, S. A. (2009). Precarious manhood and displays of physical aggression. *Personality and social psychology bulletin,* 35, pp. 623–634.; Also see: Bosson, J. K., & Vandello, J. A. (2011). Precarious manhood and its links to action and aggression. *Current directions in psychological science,* 20, pp. 82–86.

105. reluctant to enter female-dominated fields: Cherlin, A. J. (2014).; Williams, J. (2010). *Reshaping the work-family debate.* Cambridge, MA: Harvard University Press.; Miller, C. C. (2017, January 4). Why men don't want the jobs done mostly by women. *New York Times.* Retrieved from https://www.nytimes.com/2017/01/04/upshot/why-men-dont-want -the-jobs-done-mostly-by-women.html?hp&action=click&pgtype =Homepage&clickSource=story-heading&module=second-column -region&ion=top-news&WT.nav=top-news&_r=0

105. the drive to self-actualize: Maslow. (1943). (p. 382).

105. manifestation of self-actualizing needs: Maslow. (1943). (p. 383).

105. progress toward self-actualization yields: Maslow, A. H. (1970). Quote from p. 99.

106. Psychologically androgynous individuals: Cheng, C. (2005). Processes underlying gender-role flexibility: Do androgynous individuals know more or know how to cope? *Journal of personality*, *73*, pp. 645–674.; Guastello, D. D., & Guastello, S. J. (2003). Androgyny, gender role behavior, and emotional intelligence among college students and their parents. *Sex roles*, *49*, pp. 663–673.

106. good relationship partners: Peterson, C. D., Baucom, D. H., Elliott, M. J., & Farr, P. A. (1989). The relationship between sex role identity and marital adjustment. *Sex roles*, *21*, pp. 775–787.; Shaver, P. R., Papalia, D., Clark, C. L., Koski, L. R., Tidwell, M. C., & Nalbone, D. (1996). Androgyny and attachment security: Two related models of optimal personality. *Personality and social psychology bulletin*, *22*, pp. 582–597.; Helgeson, V. S. (1993). Implications of agency and communion for patient and spouse adjustment to a first coronary event. *Journal of personality and social psychology*, *64*, pp. 807–816.

106. navigate conflict constructively: Gordon, A. M., & Chen, S. (2016). Do you get where I'm coming from?: Perceived understanding buffers against the negative impact of conflict on relationship satisfaction. *Journal of personality and social psychology*, *110*, pp. 239–260.; Also see: Moorman, S. M. (2011). The importance of feeling understood in marital conversations about end-of-life health care. *Journal of social and personal relationships*, *28*, pp. 100–116.

107. in the *Sex and the City* film: Sex and the City (2008). (n.d.). IMDb. Retrieved from http://www.imdb.com/title/tt1000774/

5. Personal Fulfillment and Marital Commitment

111. *TO HELEN*: Rogers, C. R. (1972). *Becoming partners*. New York, NY: Dell. Dedication.

112. willing and eager for the other to *grow*: Rogers, C. R. (1972). (pp. 28–29). Emphasis in original.

112. the history of the love-based marriage: Coontz, S. (2005). (p. 5).

113. flower-bedecked marriage barges go to pieces: Rogers, A. (1907, September). Why American marriages fail. *The Atlantic Monthly*, pp. 289–297. Quote on p. 292.

113. insufficient love: Coontz, S. (2005). (pp. 201–202).; Carson, W. E. (1915). *The marriage revolt: A study of marriage and divorce*. New York, NY: Hearst's International Library. Quote from p. 377.

114. in the current model of marriage, disaster loomed: Coontz, S. (2005).

114. Marriage, "the obligatory entrée": Quoted in Coontz, S. (2005). (p. 276).

115. if current divorce trends continued: Etzioni, A. (1977). The family: Is it obsolete? *Journal of current social issues, 14*(1), pp. 4–9.

115. investigations into happiness: McMahon, D. M. (2006). *Happiness: A history.* New York, NY: Grove/Atlantic.

115. define *meaning* (or "eudaimonic well-being"): Huta, V., & Waterman, A. S. (2014). Eudaimonia and its distinction from hedonia: Developing a classification and terminology for understanding conceptual and operational definitions. *Journal of happiness studies, 15*(6), pp. 1425–1456.; McGregor, I., & Little, B. R. (1998). Personal projects, happiness, and meaning: On doing well and being yourself. *Journal of personality and social psychology, 74*(2), pp. 494–512.; Ryan, R. M., & Deci, E. L. (2001). On happiness and human potentials: A review of research on hedonic and eudaimonic well-being. *Annual review of psychology, 52*(1), pp. 141–166.; Waterman, A. S. (1993). Two conceptions of happiness: Contrasts of personal expressiveness (eudaimonia) and hedonic enjoyment. *Journal of personality and social psychology, 64*(4), pp. 678–691.

115. suggests that a meaningful life results from: Ryff, C. D. (1995). Psychological well-being in adult life. *Current directions in psychological science, 4*, pp. 99–104. Quote on p. 100.; Also see: Aristotle (1925). *The Nicomachean Ethics* (D. Ross, Trans.). New York, NY: Oxford University Press.

115. Happiness and meaning are linked: Kashdan, T. B., Biswas-Diener, R., & King, L. (2008). Reconsidering happiness: The costs of distinguishing between hedonics and eudaimonia. *The journal of positive psychology, 3*, pp. 219–233. Retrieved from http://dx.doi.org/10.1080/17439760802303044

116. happy life is characterized by ease and pleasure: Baumeister, R. F., Vohs, K. D., Aaker, J. L., & Garbinsky, E. N. (2013). Some key differences between a happy life and a meaningful life. *The journal of positive psychology, 8*(6), pp. 505–516.; Also see: Tov, W., & Lee, H. W. (in press). A closer look at the hedonics of everyday meaning and satisfaction. *Journal of personality and social psychology.*

116. the essence of meaningful engagement: Six by Sondheim. (2016, December 21). In *Wikipedia, the free encyclopedia.* Retrieved February 22, 2017, from https://en.wikipedia.org/wiki/Six_by_Sondheim

117. building a successful, long-lasting marriage: Blumstein, P., & Schwartz, P. (1983). *American couples: Money, work, sex.* New York, NY: Morrow.

119. *fun morality* had emerged: Wolfenstein, M. (1951). The emergence of fun morality. *Journal of social issues, 7*(4), pp 15–25. Quote from pp. 15.

120. vast new apparatus surrounding consumer credit: Calder, L. (1999). *Financing the American dream: A cultural history of consumer credit.* Princeton, NJ: Princeton University Press. Quotes from pp. 4, 5.

120. story not of hedonism run amok: Inglehart, R., and Welzel, C. (2005). (pp. 291–293).; Pinker, S. (2011). *The better angels of our nature: Why violence has declined.* New York, NY: Penguin.

121. a once-stable family equilibrium: Esping-Andersen, G., & Billari, F. C. (2015). Re-theorizing family demographics. *Population and development review*, *41*(1), pp. 1–31. Quotes from p. 6.

122. reflections are both personal and fascinating: Rosin, H. (2012). (p. 74).

123. having stepchildren living in the home: Amato, P. R., et al. (2007). (pp. 82).

123. well-being of each person is incompatible: Rusbult, C. E., Olsen, N., Davis, J. L., & Hannon, P. A. (2004). Commitment and relationship maintenance mechanisms. In Reis, H. T., & Rusbult, C. E. (Eds.), *Close relationships: Key readings* (pp. 287–303). New York, NY: Psychology Press. Quote from p. 287.

124. sexual activities without an emotional connection: Rusbult, C. E., Olsen, N., Davis, J. L., & Hannon, P. A. (2004).; The sexual activity outside the relationship point comes from: Rodrigues, D., Lopes, D., & Smith, C. V. (in press). Caught in a "bad romance"? Reconsidering the negative association between sociosexuality and relationship functioning. *The journal of sex research*.

125. Highly committed participants, in contrast: Johnson, D. J., & Rusbult, C. E. (1989). Resisting temptation: Devaluation of alternative partners as a means of maintaining commitment in close relationships. *Journal of personality and social psychology*, *57*, p. 967.

125. which have been replicated many times: Lydon, J., & Karremans, J. C. (2015). Relationship regulation in the face of eye candy: A motivated cognition framework for understanding responses to attractive alternatives. *Current opinion in psychology*, *1*, pp. 76–80.

125. spouse to meet our needs: Feeney, B. C., & Collins, N. L. (2014). Much "I do" about nothing? Ascending Mount Maslow with an oxygenated marriage. *Psychological inquiry*, *25*(1), pp. 69–79.; Holmes, J. G., & Murray, S. L. (2014). A steep hill to climb: Reconciling the expanding demands of marriage. *Psychological inquiry*, *25*(1), pp. 80–83.; Neff, L. A., & Morgan, T. A. (2014). The rising expectations of marriage: What we do and do not know. *Psychological inquiry*, *25*(1), pp. 95-100.

126. endure costs in our relationship if: Clark, M., & Grote, N. (1998). Why aren't indices of relationship costs always negatively related to indices of relationship quality? *Personality and social psychology review*, *2*, pp. 2–17.; Clark, M. S., Lemay, E. P., Graham, S. M., Pataki, S. P., & Finkel, E. J. (2010). Ways of giving and receiving benefits in marriage: Norm use and attachment related variability. *Psychological science*, *21*, pp. 944–951.

126. providing support: Gleason, M. E. J., & Iida, M. (2015). Social support. In Simpson, J., & Dovidio, J. (Eds.), *APA handbook of personality and social psychology: Interpersonal relationships and group processes* (Vol. 2). Washington, DC: American Psychological Association.; Gleason, M. E. J., Iida, M., Bolger, N., & Shrout, P. (2003). Supportive equity in close relationships. *Personality and social psychology bulletin*, *29*, pp.

1036–1045.; Also see: Raposa, E. B., Laws, H. B., & Ansell, E. B. (2015). Prosocial behavior mitigates the negative effects of stress in everyday life. *Clinical psychological science, 4,* pp. 691–698.
126. no compelling evidence that people bolt: Celello, K. (2009).

6. Marriage at the Summit

128. *like two flowers*: Cutie and the Boxer. (2016, September 28). In *Wikipedia, the free encyclopedia*. Retrieved March 06, 2017, from https://en.wikipedia.org/wiki/Cutie_and_the_Boxer
129. obligated to marry: Perel, E. (2007). Quote on pp. 178–179.
130. more likely today: Celello, K. (2009). (pp. 143–144).
131. significant inequality: US Bureau of Labor Statistics. (2014, December). Highlights of women's earnings in 2013. BLS report, no. 1061. Washington, DC: Author. Retrieved from https://www.bing.com/cr?IG=D16 07E995E6C464AB97A092A7466FC84&CID=152BAD69CC086C82 3ADCA754CD396D3A&rd=1&h=lWQpH27sDhIWGqv_FZBTOX2h v9YPxKUdPdfMGnzdlU&v=1&r=https%3a%2f%2fwww.bls.gov%2 fopub%2freports%2fwomens-earnings%2farchive%2fhighlights-of -womens-earnings-in-2013.pdf&p=DevEx,5054.1; Goldin, C. D. (1991). The role of World War II in the rise of women's employment. *The American economic review*, pp. 741–756.; Ruggles, S. (2015). (pp. 1797–1823).
131. Even as homes: Bianchi, S. M., Milkie, M. A., Sayer, L. C., & Robinson, J. P. (2000). Is anyone doing the housework? Trends in the gender division of household labor. *Social forces*, 79(1), pp. 191–228.
131. fertility rate declined: Fertility rate. (n.d.). Retrieved from https://www .google.com/publicdata/explore?ds=d5bncppjof8f9_&met_y=sp_dyn_tfrt _in&idim=country%3AUSA%3AJPN%3AIND&hl=en&dl=en
131. sex between unmarried: Wells, B. E., & Twenge, J. M. (2005).; Gesselman, A. N., Webster, G. D., & Garcia, J. R. (2016). Has virginity lost its virtue? Relationship stigma associated with being a sexually inexperienced adult. *The journal of sex research*, pp. 1–12.
131. vibrate at 120 hertz: McCann, C. (2016, November 29). Let's get digital. *1843* magazine. Retrieved from https://www.1843magazine.com/design /the-daily/lets-get-digital
132. used a vibrator: Herbenick, D., Reece, M., Sanders, S., Dodge, B., Ghassemi, A., & Fortenberry, J. D. (2009). Prevalence and characteristics of vibrator use by women in the United States: Results from a nationally representative study. *The journal of sexual medicine*, 6(7), pp. 1857–1866.
132. American singles: Wilcox, W. B., Marquardt, E., Popenoe, D., & Whitehead, B. D. (2011). When baby makes three: How parenthood makes life meaningful and how marriage makes parenthood bearable. *The state of our unions: Marriage in America 2011*, pp. 1–59. Retrieved from http://nationalmarriageproject.org/wp-content/uploads/2012/05 /Union_2011. pdf

132. have a baby: Pagnini, D. L., & Rindfuss, R. R. (1993). The divorce of marriage and childbearing: Changing attitudes and behavior in the United States. *Population and development review*, pp. 331–347.

132. stigma of divorce: Celello, K. (2009).; Cott, N. F. (2002). *Public vows: A history of marriage and the nation.* Cambridge, MA: Harvard University Press.; Waite, L. J. (2000). Trends in men's and women's well-being in marriage. *The ties that bind: Perspectives on marriage and cohabitation* (pp. 368–392). Hawthorn, NY: Aldine de Gruyter.

132. greater happiness and meaning: Flood, S. M., & Genadek, K. R. (2016). Time for each other: Work and family constraints among couples. *Journal of marriage and family*, 78(1), pp. 142–164.; Also see: Sullivan, O. (1996). Time co-ordination, the domestic division of labour and affective relations: Time use and the enjoyment of activities within couples. *Sociology, 30*, pp. 79–100. doi:10.1177/0038038596030001006; Milek, A., Butler, E. A., & Bodenmann, G. (2015). The interplay of couple's shared time, women's intimacy, and intradyadic stress. *Journal of family psychology*, 29(6), pp. 831–842.; Also see: O'Leary, K. D., Acevedo, B. P., Aron, A., Huddy, L., & Mashek, D. (2012). Is long-term love more than a rare phenomenon? If so, what are its correlates? *Social psychological and personality science*, 3(2), pp. 241–249.

133. regularly spend: Wilcox, W. B., & Dew, J. (2012). *The date night opportunity: What does couple time tell us about the potential value of date nights?* Charlottesville, VA: The National Marriage Project at the University of Virginia.

133. the overwhelm: Schulte, B. (2014). *Overwhelmed: How to work, love, and play when no one has the time.* New York, NY: Macmillan. Quote from p. 9.

133. spend at work: Jacobs, J. A., & Gerson, K. (2004). *The time divide: Work, family, and gender inequality.* Cambridge, MA: Harvard University Press.; Jacobs, J. A., & Green, K. (1998). Who are the overworked Americans? *Review of social economy, 56*(4), pp. 442–459.

133. married women who work: Amato, P. R., et al. (2007).

133. paid employment: Organisation for Economic Co-Operation and Development. (n.d.). Employment: Time spent in paid and unpaid work, by sex. Retrieved March 06, 2017, from http://stats.oecd.org/index.aspx?queryid=54757

134. intensive child-rearing: Zelizer, V. A. R. (1985). *Pricing the priceless child: The changing social value of children.* Princeton, NJ: Princeton University Press.

135. fathers and mothers: Ramey, G., & Ramey, V. A. (2009). *The rug rat race* (No. w15284). New York, NY: National Bureau of Economic Research.

135. concerted cultivation: Lareau, A. (2011). *Unequal childhoods: Class, race, and family life.* Berkeley, CA: University of California Press.; Also see: Kalil, A., Ziol-Guest, K. M., Ryan, R. M., & Markowitz, A. J. (2016). Changes in income-based gaps in parent activities with young children from 1988 to 2012. *AERA open*, 2(3), 2332858416653732.

135. work new parents do: Miller, C. C. (2015, November 11). Men do more at home, but not as much as they think. *New York Times*. Retrieved from http://www.nytimes.com/2015/11/12/upshot/men-do-more-at-home-but-not-as-much-as-they-think-they-do.html

135. spouses without children: Schor, J. (2008). *The overworked American: The unexpected decline of leisure*. New York, NY: Basic Books.

135. American workers: Expedia.com. (2016, November 15). Work-life imbalance: Expedia's 2016 vacation deprivation study shows americans leave hundreds of millions of paid vacation days unused. Retrieved from http://www.prnewswire.com/news-releases/work-life-imbalance-expedias-2016-vacation-deprivation-study-shows-americans-leave-hundreds-of-millions-of-paid-vacation-days-unused-300362867.html

135. parenting and work trends: Amato et al. (2007).; Bianchi, S. M., Robinson, J. P., & Milkie, M. A. (2006). *Changing rhythms of American family life*. New York, NY: Russell Sage Foundation.

135. how much *spousal time*: Dew, J. (2009). Has the marital time cost of parenting changed over time? *Social forces, 88*, pp. 519–541. doi: 10.1353/sof.0.0273

136. systematic analysis of shared time: Flood, S. M., & Genadek, K. R. (2016). Data from Table 4 on p. 1915. Note: This article also reported in time use trends in 1965, but whereas the 1975, 2003, and 2012 estimates had a 50/50 weekend/weekday split, the 1965 estimates had a 73/27 split, which makes the comparison to the other waves hard to interpret.

138. engage in everyday activities together: Amato, P. R., et al. (2007). (p. 135).

139. early twenty-first century: Amato, P. R., et al. (2007). (p. 54). Adapted from Figure 2.3.

139. Stress is linked: Buck, A. A., & Neff, L. A. (2012). Stress spillover in early marriage: The role of self-regulatory depletion. *Journal of family psychology, 26*, pp. 698–708. doi: 10.1037/a0029260; Demerouti, E., Bakker, A. B., Sonnentag, S., & Fullagar, C. J. (2012). Work-related flow and energy at work and at home: A study on the role of daily recovery. *Journal of organizational behavior, 33*, pp. 276–295. doi: 10.1002/job.760; Finkel, E. J., DeWall, C. N., Slotter, E. B., McNulty, J. K., Pond, R. S., Jr., Atkins, D. C. (2012). Using I[3] theory to clarify when dispositional aggressiveness predicts intimate partner violence perpetration. *Journal of personality and social psychology, 102*, pp. 533–549.

139. stressed American men and women: Cohen, S., & Janicki-Deverts, D. (2012). Who's stressed? Distributions of psychological stress in the United States in probability samples from 1983, 2006, and 2009. *Journal of applied social psychology, 42*, pp. 1320–1334. doi: 10.1111/j.1559-1816.2012.00900

139. elevated stress levels: Amato, P. R., et al. (2007).

140. Nobel Prize–winning cognitive scientist: Simon, H. A. (1971). Designing organizations for an information-rich world. In Greenberger, M. (Ed.), *Computers, communication, and the public interest*. Baltimore, MD: The Johns Hopkins Press. Quote on pp. 40–41.

140. age of information overload: Levitin, D. J. (2014). *The organized mind: Thinking straight in the age of information overload*. New York, NY: Dutton.

140. five exabytes: Lyman, P., & Varian, H. (2004). *How much information? 2003*. Berkeley, CA: University of California at Berkeley. Available at http://groups.ischool.berkeley.edu/archive/how-much-info-2003/

140. estimate from IBM: IBM. (2016, October 31). Bringing big data to the enterprise. Retrieved from https://www-01.ibm.com/software/data/big data/what-is-big-data.html

140. speeding up: Hilbert, M., & López, P. (2011). The world's technological capacity to store, communicate, and compute information. *Science, 332*(6025), pp. 60–65.

141. glances at the smartphone: Schulte, B. (2014). (p. 26).

141. four-second interruption: Altmann, E. M., Trafton, J. G., & Hambrick, D. Z. (2014). Momentary interruptions can derail the train of thought. *Journal of experimental psychology: General, 143*(1), pp. 215–226.

141. three interruption conditions: Stothart, C., Mitchum, A., & Yehnert, C. (2015). The attentional cost of receiving a cell phone notification. *Journal of experimental psychology: Human perception and performance, 41*(4), pp. 893–897.

141. prone to feeling overwhelmed: Schulte, B. (2014). (pp. 25–27).; Hochschild, A., & Machung, A. (2012). *The second shift: Working families and the revolution at home*. New York, NY: Penguin.

142. ability to reflect: Schulte, B. (2014). (pp. 53–54). Quote from p. 53.

142. spouse poignantly observes: Schulte, B. (2014). (p. 46).

142. symmetrical nature of marriage: Gleason, M. E., Iida, M., Bolger, N., & Shrout, P. E. (2003). Daily supportive equity in close relationships. *Personality and social psychology bulletin, 29*(8), pp. 1036–1045.; Also see: Patrick, H. (2014). Ascending Mount Maslow with oxygen to spare: A self-determination theory perspective. *Psychological inquiry, 25*(1), pp. 101–107.

142. our partner's needs: Patrick, H., Knee, C. R., Canevello, A., & Lonsbary, C. (2007). The role of need fulfillment in relationship functioning and well-being: A self-determination theory perspective. *Journal of personality and social psychology, 92*(3), p. 434.

142. dual-career couples: Warner, J. (2013, April 7). The opt-out generation wants back in. *New York Times*. Retrieved from http://www.nytimes.com /2013/08/11/magazine/the-opt-out-generation-wants-back-in.html?page wanted=all

142. the disconnect: Perel, E. (n.d.).

143. early childrearing years: Cancian, F. M. (1987). *Love in America: Gender and self-development*. New York, NY: Cambridge University Press. Quotes from p. 132.

143. mothers of young infants: Twenge, J. M., Campbell, W. K., & Foster, C. A. (2003). Parenthood and marital satisfaction: A meta-analytic review. *Journal of marriage and family, 65*(3), pp. 574–583.

143. capitalist democracies: Glass, J., Simon, R., & Andersson, M. (in press). Parenthood and happiness: Effects of work-family reconciliation policies in 22 OECD countries. *American journal of sociology.*

144. difficulties of every: Popova, M. (2015, October 14). Friedrich Nietzsche on why a fulfilling life requires embracing rather than running from difficulty. *Brain Pickings.* Retrieved from https://www.brainpickings .org/2014/10/15/nietzsche-on-difficulty/

145. alarmed look at: Crouse, K. (2016, August 3). Katinka Hosszu and her husband raise eyebrows at the pool. *New York Times.* Retrieved from http://www.nytimes.com/2016/08/04/sports/olympics/katinka-hosszu-rio -swimming-husband-shane-tusup.html

145. working hard: Celello, K. (2009).; Coontz, S. (2005).

146. relative to meeting lower-altitude needs: Maslow, A. H. (1970). Quote on p. 99.

146. substantial minority of married: Acevedo, B. P., & Aron, A. (2009). Does a long-term relationship kill romantic love? *Review of general psychology, 13,* pp. 59–65.

146. reported their love: O'Leary, K. D., Acevedo, B. P., Aron, A., Huddy, L., & Mashek, D. (2012). Is long-term love more than a rare phenomenon? If so, what are its correlates? *Social psychological and personality science, 3*(2), pp. 241–249.

147. burst into public consciousness: Weiner, J. (2014). *The beak of the finch: A story of evolution in our time.* New York, NY: Vintage.

147. own *40 Years of Evolution*: Grant, P. R., & Grant, B. R. (2014). *40 years of evolution: Darwin's finches on Daphne Major island.* Princeton, NJ: Princeton University Press.

147. Grants' marital dynamics: Weiner, J. (2014, August 4). In darwin's footsteps. *New York Times.* Retrieved from http://www.nytimes.com/2014 /08/05/science/in-darwins-footsteps.html?emc=edit_th_20140805&nl= todaysheadlines&nlid=22989314&_r=0

149. things fell apart: Vulpo, M. (2016, September 20). Watch George Clooney find out Brad and Angelina are divorcing. *E!* Retrieved from http:// www.eonline.com/news/796420/watch-george-clooney-find-out-the-news -that-brad-pitt-and-angelina-jolie-are-divorcing

7. For Richer or Poorer

151. *Postindustrialization brings*: Inglehart, R., & Welzel, C. (2005). (p. 44).

152. survival has been precarious: Inglehart, R., & Welzel, C. (2005). (pp. 23).; Also see: Sen, A. (1999). *Development as freedom.* New York, NY: Oxford University Press.

153. class, race, and gender: Cherlin, A. J. (2009). (pp. 158 and 174).

154. President Barack Obama declared: Remarks by the president on economic mobility. (2013, December 4). Retrieved from https://www.whitehouse .gov/the-press-office/2013/12/04/remarks-president-economic-mobility

154. **American labor market:** Autor, Katz, and Kearney (2006) talked about the "hollowing out" of the economy, and Massey and Hirst (1998) talk about the "hourglass economy."; Pew Research Center. (2015, December 9). The American middle class is losing ground: No longer the majority and falling behind financially. Retrieved from http://www .pewsocialtrends.org/2015/12/09/the-american-middle-class-is-losing -ground/; Casselman, B. (2015, December 9). Most Americans aren't middle class anymore. *FiveThirtyEight.* Retrieved from http://fivethir tyeight.com/features/most-americans-arent-middle-class-anymore

154. **labor unions:** Cherlin, A. J. (2014). (p. 8).; Ruggles, S., et al. (2010).

154. **during the *Mad Men* era:** Carbone, J., & Cahn, N. (2014). *Marriage markets: How inequality is remaking the American family* (p. 14). Oxford, UK: Oxford University Press.; Also see: Cowen, T. (2015, December 26). The marriages of power couples reinforce income inequality. *New York Times.* Retrieved from http://www.nytimes.com/2015/12 /27/upshot/marriages-of-power-couples-reinforce-income-inequality .html?_r=0&nl=todaysheadlines&nlid=22989314; Dokko, J., Li, G., & Hayes, J. (2015). Credit scores and committed relationships. *Finance and economics discussion series 2015-081.* Washington, DC: Board of Governors of the Federal Reserve System. Retrieved from http://dx.doi .org/10.17016/FEDS.2015.081

154. **links between social class and marriage:** Merton, R. K. (1968). *Social theory and social structure.* New York, NY: Simon and Schuster.; Callan, M. J., Kim, H., Gheorghiu, A. I., & Matthews, W. J. (in press). The interrelations between social class, personal relative deprivation, and prosociality. *Social psychological and personality science,* 1948550616673877.

155. **regardless of how wealthy:** Cheung, F., & Lucas, R. E. (2016). Income inequality is associated with stronger social comparison effects: The effect of relative income on life satisfaction. *Journal of personality and social psychology, 110*(2), pp. 332–341.

155. **income data to classify women:** Bramlett & Mosher (2002).; Also see: Dokko, J., Li, G., & Hayes, J. (2015).

155. **eventually divorce:** Raley, R. K., & Bumpass, L. L. (2003). The topography of the divorce plateau: Levels and trends in union stability in the United States after 1980. *Demographic research, 8,* pp. 245–260.

155. **data from 2006 to 2010:** Wang, W. (2015, December 4). The link between a college education and a lasting marriage. Pew Research Center. Retrieved from http://www.pewresearch.org/fact-tank/2015/12/04/educa tion-and-marriage/

155. **understate the magnitude of the inequality:** Goldstein, J. R., & Kenney, C. T. (2001).; Krause, E., Sawhill, I. V., & Reeves, R. V. (2016, November 22). The most educated women are the most likely to be married. Brookings Institution. Retrieved from https://www.brookings.edu/blog /social-mobility-memos/2016/08/19/the-most-educated-women-are-the -most-likely-to-be-married/

155. marriages that remain intact: Amato, P. R., et al. (2007).

157. high-social-class and low-social-class groups: Martin, S. P. (2006). Trends in marital dissolution by women's education in the United States. *Demographic research, 15*, pp. 537–560.

158. four income groups agreed: Trail, T. E., & Karney, B. R. (2012). What's (not) wrong with low-income marriages. *Journal of marriage and family, 74*, pp. 413–427.; Also see: Edin, K. (2000). What do low-income single mothers say about marriage? *Social problems, 47*(1), pp. 112–133.; Lichter, D. T., Batson, C. D., & Brown, J. B. (2004). Welfare reform and marriage promotion: The marital expectations and desires of single and cohabiting mothers. *Social service review, 78*(1), pp. 2–25.; Mauldon, J. G., London, R. A., Fein, D. J., Patterson, R., & Bliss, S. (2002, November). What do they think?: Welfare recipients' attitudes toward marriage and childbearing. Research brief #2. Welfare Reform and Family Formation Project.

158. higher-class Americans: Graham, C. (2016, October 26). The rich even have a better kind of stress than the poor. Brookings Institution. Retrieved from https://www.brookings.edu/2016/02/10/the-rich-even-have-a-better-kind-of-stress-than-the-poor/

160. lack a financial cushion: Maisel, N. C., & Karney, B. R. (2012). Socioeconomic status moderates associations among stressful events, mental health, and relationship satisfaction. *Journal of family psychology, 26*(4), pp. 654–660.

160. threats have grown: Great Recession in the United States. (2017, February 24). In *Wikipedia, the free encyclopedia.* Retrieved March 6, 2017, from https://en.wikipedia.org/wiki/Great_Recession_in_the_United_States

161. shift in risk affects: Cooper, M. (2014). *Cut adrift: Families in insecure times* (p. viii) Berkeley, CA: University of California Press.

161. daily life for poor Americans: Kantor, J. (2014, August 13). Working anything but 9 to 5. *New York Times.* Retrieved from http://www.nytimes.com/interactive/2014/08/13/us/starbucks-workers-scheduling-hours.html; For additional discussion of the challenges of transportation for lower-SES Americans: Cronk, I. (2015, August 9). The transportation barrier. *The Atlantic.* Retrieved from http://www.theatlantic.com/health/archive/2015/08/the-transportation-barrier/399728/

161. insufficient time and psychological bandwidth: Tritch, T. (2015, August 10). Unpredictable work hours, chaotic life. *Taking Note* blog. *New York Times.* Retrieved from http://takingnote.blogs.nytimes.com/2015/08/10/unpredictable-work-hours-chaotic-life/; Heymann, J. (2001). *The widening gap.* New York, NY: Basic Books.; Clawson, D., & Gerstel, N. (2014). *Unequal time: Gender, class, and family in employment schedules.* New York, NY: Russell Sage Foundation.; Presser, H. B. (1995). Job, family, and gender: Determinants of nonstandard work schedules among employed Americans in 1991. *Demography, 32*(4), pp. 577–598.; Presser, H. B., & Cain, V. S. (1983). Shift work among dual-earner couples with children. *Science, 219*(4586), pp. 876–879.; Also see: Hamermesh, D. S.

(2002). Timing, togetherness and time windfalls. *Journal of population economics*, *15*(4), pp. 601–623.; Henly, J. R., Shaefer, H. L., & Waxman, E. (2006). Nonstandard work schedules: Employer-and employee-driven flexibility in retail jobs. *Social service review*, *80*(4), pp. 609–634.; Lambert, S. J. (2012). "Opting in" to full labor force participation in hourly jobs. In Jones, B. (Ed.), *Women who opt out: The debate over working mothers and work-family balance* (pp. 87–102). New York, NY: New York University Press.; Lambert, S. J., Haley-Lock, A., & Henly, J. R. (2012). Schedule flexibility in hourly jobs: Unanticipated consequences and promising directions. *Community, work & family*, *15*(3), pp. 293–315.; Watson, E., & Swanberg, J. (2011). Rethinking workplace flexibility for hourly workers: Policy brief. Washington, DC: WF2010, Georgetown Law, Georgetown University.

162. limited opportunity for engaging in loving: Trail, T. E., & Karney, B. R. (2012).

162. spouse works nights: Presser, H. B. (2000). Nonstandard work schedules and marital instability. *Journal of marriage and family*, *62*(1), pp. 93–110.

162. less able to prioritize their relationship: Emery, L. F., & Finkel, E. J. Unpublished data, Northwestern University.

163. new lower class: Murray, C. (2012).

163. dispositional qualities: Finkel, E. J., DeWall, C. N., Slotter, E. B., Oaten, M., & Foshee, V. A. (2009). Self-regulatory failure and intimate partner violence perpetration. *Journal of personality and social psychology*, *97*, pp. 483–499.; Kelly, E. L., & Conley, J. J. (1987). Personality and compatibility: A prospective analysis of marital stability and marital satisfaction. *Journal of personality and social psychology*, *52*(1), pp. 27–40.; Moffitt, T. E., Arseneault, L., Belsky, D., Dickson, N., Hancox, R. J., Harrington, H., . . . & Sears, M. R. (2011). A gradient of childhood self-control predicts health, wealth, and public safety. *Proceedings of the national academy of sciences*, *108*(7), pp. 2693–2698.

163. a substantial genetic component: Cesarini, D., and Visscher, P. M. (2017). Genetics and educational attainment. *npj Science of learning*, *2*(1), pp. 1–7.

163. gutting the middle class: Frum, D. (2012, February 6). Is the white working class coming apart? *The Daily Beast*. Retrieved from http://www.thedailybeast.com/articles/2012/02/06/charles-murray-book-review.html; Krugman, P. (2012, February 9). Money and morals. *New York Times*. Retrieved from http://www.nytimes.com/2012/02/10/opinion/krugman-money-and-morals.html?partner=rssnyt&emc=rss

163. urban black neighborhoods: Wilson, W. J. (1996). *When work disappears: The world of the new urban poor*. New York, NY: Knopf.

164. poverty influences marital and other outcomes: Chetty, R., Hendren, N., & Katz, L. F. (2016). The effects of exposure to better neighborhoods on children: New evidence from the Moving to Opportunity experiment. *The American economic review*, *106*, pp. 855–902.

165. a fairly typical day: Sullivan, P. (2015, October 9). Work-life balance poses challenges regardless of wealth. *New York Times*. Retrieved from

http://www.nytimes.com/2015/10/10/your-money/work-life-balance-poses
-challenges-regardless-of-wealth.html

165. living a packed life: Schulte, B. (2014). (p. 45.)

165. male industrial worker: Cherlin, A. J. (2014). (p. 111).; Lamont, M. (2000). *The dignity of working men: Morality and the boundaries of race, class, and immigration.* Cambridge, MA: Harvard University Press.

167. privileged who can hope to self-actualize: Feeney, B. C., & Collins, N. L. (2015). A new look at social support: A theoretical perspective on thriving through relationships. *Personality and social psychology review*, *19*(2), pp. 113–147. Quote from p. 135.

8. For Better or Worse

171. Elizabeth Gilbert posted this note on Facebook: Gilbert, E. (2016, July 1). In *Facebook* [Fan page]. Retrieved March 1, 2017, from https://www.facebook.com/GilbertLiz/photos/a.356148997800555.79726.227291194019670/1054602967955151/?type=3&theater%2F%2F; https://www.nytimes.com/2016/07/02/style/elizabeth-gilbert-separation-eat-pray-love.html

171. Gilbert wrote in a follow-up note: Gilbert, E. (2016, September 7). Me & Rayya. In *Facebook* [Fan page]. Retrieved from https://www.facebook.com/GilbertLiz/posts/1107564732658974:0

171. Gilbert had married Nunes: Sittenfeld, C. (2010, January 9). Eat, pray, marry. *New York Times.* Retrieved from http://www.nytimes.com/2010/01/10/books/review/Sittenfeld-t.html?pagewanted=all&_r=0

172. initial Facebook announcement included a positive assessment of their relationship: Gilbert, J. (n.d.). Failing and flying. Retrieved from http://www.poetryfoundation.org/poems-and-poets/poems/detail/48132

172. navigate a dense thicket of challenges: Bradbury, T. N., & Karney, B. R. (2014). *Intimate relationships* (2nd ed.). New York, NY: W. W. Norton & Company. Figure is from p. 485.

173. two major studies suggest that that's not the case: Left panel: Glenn, N. D. (1998). The course of marital success and failure in five American 10-year marriage cohorts. *Journal of marriage and the family, 60*, pp. 569–576.; Right panel: VanLaningham, J., Johnson, D. R., & Amato, P. (2001). Marital happiness, marital duration, and the U-shaped curve: Evidence from a five-wave panel study. *Social forces, 78*, pp. 1313–1341.

174. misremembering their Time 1 satisfaction as being 4.7 when it was actually 5.8: Karney, B. R., & Coombs, R. H. (2000). Memory bias in long-term close relationships: Consistency or improvement? *Personality and social psychology bulletin, 26*(8), pp. 959–970. This study also included a third wave of data collection, ten years after the first follow-up and twenty years after intake. Results were generally consistent with those reported in Figure 9.2, although the bias was a bit less pronounced.; Also see: Ross, M., & Wilson, A. E. (2003). Autobiographical memory and conceptions of self

getting better all the time. *Current directions in psychological science*, 12(2), pp. 66–69.

175. some marriages show even steeper declines: Lavner, J. A., & Bradbury, T. N. (2010). Patterns of change in marital satisfaction over the newly-wed years. *Journal of marriage and family*, 72, pp. 1171–1187.

175. the logic of President John F. Kennedy's 1962 argument: Kennedy, J. F. (1962, January 11). Annual message to the Congress on the state of the union. The American presidency project. Retrieved from http://www.presidency.ucsb.edu/ws/?pid=9082

176. simply incompatible: Berscheid, E. (1985). Compatibility, interdependence, and emotion. In Ickes, W. (Ed.), *Compatible and incompatible relationships* (pp. 143–161). New York, NY: Springer-Verlag. Quotes on pp. 145–146.; Also see: Lewin, K. (1948). *Resolving social conflicts: Selected papers on group dynamics*. New York, NY: Harper & Row.

176. partners might lack the *ability* to align their thoughts: Berscheid, E. (1985). (p. 154).

177. one can predict that the relationship: Berscheid, E. (1985). (p. 154).

177. partner irrelevant for the goals in question: Berscheid, E. (1985). (p. 155).

177. changing, continue to love a changed person: Maugham, W. S. (2001). *The summing up*. New York, NY: Random House.

178. positive effects of idealization: Murray, S. L., Griffin, D. W., Derrick, J. L., Harris, B., Aloni, M., & Leder, S. (2011). Tempting fate or inviting happiness? Unrealistic idealization prevents the decline of marital satisfaction. *Psychological science*, 22(5), pp. 619–626. Quote from p. 619.

179. we can globally idealize our partner: Neff, L. A., & Karney, B. R. (2005). To know you is to love you: The implications of global adoration and specific accuracy for marital relationships. *Journal of personality and social psychology*, 88(3), pp. 480–497.

179. how accuracy and bias in spouses' perceptions influence relationship well-being: Campbell, L., Lackenbauer, S. D., & Muise, A. (2006). When is being known or adored by romantic partners most beneficial? Self-perceptions, relationship length, and responses to partner's verifying and enhancing appraisals. *Personality and social psychology bulletin*, 32(10), pp. 1283–1294.; Swann, W. B., Jr. (2011). Self-verification theory. In Van Lange, P. A. M., Kruglanski, A. W., & Higgins, E. T. (Eds.), *Handbook of theories of social psychology* (Vol. 2, pp. 23–42). Thousand Oaks, CA: Sage.

180. having a supportive, loving partner makes us willing to confront difficult but useful truths about ourselves: Caprariello P. A., & Reis, H. T. (2011). Perceived partner responsiveness minimizes defensive reactions to failure. *Social psychology and personality science*, 2(4), pp. 365–372.; Kumashiro, M., & Sedikides, C. (2005). Taking on board liability-focused information: Close positive relationships as a self-bolstering resource. *Psychological science*, 16(9), pp. 732–739.; Oishi, S., Krochik, M., & Akimoto, S. (2010). Felt understanding as a bridge between close relationships and subjective well-being: Antecedents and consequences

across individuals and cultures. *Social and personality psychology compass*, 4, pp. 403–416.; Weeks, T. L., & Pasupathi, M. (2011). Stability and change self-integration for negative events: The role of listener responsiveness and elaboration. *Journal of personality*, 79, pp. 469–498.

181. relationship scientists generate falsifiable hypotheses: Berscheid, E. (1999). The greening of relationship science. *American psychologist*, 54(4), pp. 260–266.; Finkel, E. J., Simpson, J. A., & Eastwick, P. E. (2017). The psychology of close relationships: Fourteen core principles. *Annual review of psychology*, 68, pp. 383–411.

9. Lovehacking

184. our time and psychological resources: Aron, A., & Aron, E. N. (2014). (p. 48).

184. early parenting years: Shanley, S. (2015, March 29). The truck that sparked our marriage back to life. *Motherlode* blog. *New York Times.* Retrieved from https://parenting.blogs.nytimes.com/2015/03/29/the-truck-that-sparked-our-marriage-back-to-life/

186. conflict management: Gottman, J. M. (1998). Psychology and the study of marital processes. *Annual review of psychology*, 49(1), pp. 169–197.

186. attributions in our marriage: Bradbury, T. N., & Fincham, F. D. (1990). Attributions in marriage: Review and critique. *Psychological bulletin*, 107(1), pp. 3–33.; Jacobson, N. S., McDonald, D. W., Follette, W. C., & Berley, R. A. (1985). Attributional processes in distressed and nondistressed married couples. *Cognitive therapy and research*, 9(1), pp. 35–50.

186. adopting certain attributions: Bradbury, T. N. & Karney, B. R. (2014). (p. 358).

187. external and temporary attributions: Bradbury, T. N., & Fincham, F. D. (1990). Jacobson, N. S., McDonald, D. W., Follette, W. C., & Berley, R. A. (1985).

187. partner's motives: Van Lange, P. A., Ouwerkerk, J. W., & Tazelaar, M. J. (2002). How to overcome the detrimental effects of noise in social interaction: The benefits of generosity. *Journal of personality and social psychology*, 82(5), pp. 768–780.

188. adopt an if-then: For a discussion of if-then decision rules, see: Gollwitzer, P. M. (1999). Implementation intentions: Strong effects of simple plans. *American psychologist*, 54(7), p. 493.

188. the *marriage hack*: Finkel, E. J., Slotter, E. B., Luchies, L. B., Walton, G. M., & Gross, J. J. (2013). A brief intervention to promote conflict-reappraisal preserves marital quality over time. *Psychological science* 24, pp. 1595–1601.

189. cunning habit: de Botton (2012). (p. 118).

191. circumvents this skepticism: Marigold, D. C., Holmes, J. G., & Ross, M. (2007). More than words: Reframing compliments from romantic

partners fosters security in low self-esteem individuals. *Journal of personality and social psychology, 92*(2), pp. 232–248.

192. conflict and other relationship difficulties: Knee, C. R. (1998). Implicit theories of relationships: Assessment and prediction of romantic relationship initiation, coping, and longevity. *Journal of personality and social psychology, 74*(2), pp. 360–370.

193. subscribe to destiny: Gilbert, E. (2010). (p. 294).

193. believe in romantic destiny: Knee, C. R. (1998). (p. 360).

193. especially unforgiving: Finkel, E. J., Burnette, J. L., & Scissors, L. E. (2007). Vengefully ever after: Destiny beliefs, state attachment anxiety, and forgiveness. *Journal of personality and social psychology, 92*(5), pp. 871–886.

194. what marriage means: Calhoun, A. (2015, July 19). The wedding toast I'll never give (updated with podcast). *New York Times.* Retrieved from http://www.nytimes.com/2015/07/19/fashion/the-wedding-toast-ill-never-give.html

194. measure assesses agreement: Knee, C. R., Patrick, H., & Lonsbary, C. (2003). Implicit theories of relationships: Orientations toward evaluation and cultivation. *Personality and social psychology review, 7*(1), pp. 41–55.

196. tendency to make external: Bradbury, T. N., & Fincham, F. D. (1990); Jacobson, N. S., McDonald, D. W., Follette, W. C., & Berley, R. A. (1985). Attributional processes in distressed and nondistressed married couples. *Cognitive therapy and research, 9*(1), pp. 35–50.

197. power gratitude for strengthening: Algoe, S. B. (2012). Find, remind, and bind: The functions of gratitude in everyday relationships. *Social and personality psychology compass, 6*(6), pp. 455–469.; Gordon, A. M., Impett, E. A., Kogan, A., Oveis, C., & Keltner, D. (2012). To have and to hold: Gratitude promotes relationship maintenance in intimate bonds. *Journal of personality and social psychology, 103*(2), pp. 257–274.; Joel, S., Gordon, A. M., Impett, E. A., MacDonald, G., & Keltner, D. (2013). The things you do for me: Perceptions of a romantic partner's investments promote gratitude and commitment. *Personality and social psychology bulletin, 39*(10), pp. 1333–1345.

197. gratitude serves as: Algoe, S. B., Gable, S. L., & Maisel, N. C. (2010). It's the little things: Everyday gratitude as a booster shot for romantic relationships. *Personal relationships, 17*(2), pp. 217–233.

197. higher gratitude on days: Algoe, S. B., Gable, S. L., & Maisel, N. C. (2010); Also see: Gordon, A. M., et al. (2012).; Gordon, C. L., Arnette, R. A., & Smith, R. E. (2011). Have you thanked your spouse today? Felt and expressed gratitude among married couples. *Personality and individual differences, 50*(3), pp. 339–343.

197. one partner experiences elevated gratitude: Algoe, S. B., Gable, S. L., & Maisel, N. C. (2010); Gordon, C. L., Arnette, R. A., & Smith, R. E. (2011).

197. the long run: Gordon, A. M., et al. (2012).

197. letter of gratitude: Seligman, M. E., Steen, T. A., Park, N., & Peterson, C. (2005). Positive psychology progress: Empirical validation of interventions. *American psychologist, 60*(5), pp. 410–421.

197. count their blessings: Emmons, R. A., & McCullough, M. E. (2003). Counting blessings vs. burdens: An experimental investigation of gratitude and subjective well-being in daily life. *Journal of personality and social psychology, 84*(2), pp. 377–389.

198. measures of gratitude: Joel, S., et al., & Keltner, D. (2013).

199. gratitude tends to predict: Kubacka, K. E., Finkenauer, C., Rusbult, C. E., & Keijsers, L. (2011). Maintaining close relationships: Gratitude as a motivator and a detector of maintenance behavior. *Personality and social psychology bulletin, 37*(10), pp. 1362–1375.

200. *capitalization attempts*: Gable, S. L., Reis, H. T., Impett, E. A., & Asher, E. R. (2004). What do you do when things go right? The intrapersonal and interpersonal benefits of sharing positive events. *Journal of personality and social psychology, 87*(2), pp. 228–245.

200. positive effects emerge hot only for the partner: Otto, A. K., Laurenceau, J. P., Siegel, S. D., & Belcher, A. J. (2015). Capitalizing on everyday positive events uniquely predicts daily intimacy and well-being in couples coping with breast cancer. *Journal of family psychology, 29*(1), pp. 69–79.

200. Enthusiastic responses: Gable, S. L., Gonzaga, G. C., & Strachman, A. (2006). Will you be there for me when things go right? Supportive responses to positive event disclosures. *Journal of personality and social psychology, 91*(5), pp. 904–917.

200. trained in enthusiastic, celebratory responding: Gonzaga, G. C., Setrakian, H., Strachman, A. N., & Gable, S. L. (2009). How do I feel when things go right? Positive emotion, partner responsiveness to positive events, and the upward spiral. Unpublished manuscript, eHarmony .com.; For a review of experimental studies, see: Gable, S. L., & Reis, H. T. (2010). Good news! Capitalizing on positive events in an interpersonal context. *Advances in experimental social psychology, 42*, pp. 195–257.

201. affectionate touch: Jakubiak, B. K., & Feeney, B. C. (in press). Affectionate touch to promote relational, psychological, and physical well-being in adulthood: A theoretical model and review of the research. *Personality and social psychology review,* 1088868316650307.

201. partner's touching behavior: Jakubiak, B. K., & Feeney, B. C. (in press). A sense of security touch promotes state attachment security. *Social psychological and personality science,* 1948550616646427.

10. Going All In

203. Erin was twenty-four: White, E. (2016). Her life. My life. In Hanauer, C. (Ed.), *The bitch is back: Older, wiser, and (getting) happier* (pp. 167–178). New York, NY: William Morrow.

205. have a theory: Feeney, B. C., & Collins, N. L. (2015). A new look at social support: A theoretical perspective on thriving through relationships. *Personality and social psychology review, 19*(2), 113–147.

205. a quote from Maya Angelou: Angelou, M. (2011, July 5). In *Facebook* [Fan page]. Retrieved from https://www.facebook.com/MayaAngelou/posts/101 50251846629796

205. heightened sense of: Feeney, B. C., & Collins, N. L. (2015). Quote from p. 115.

205. individuals thrive: Feeney, B. C., & Collins, N. L. (2015). Quote from p. 116.

206. tracked hourly time logs: I know how she does it—How successful women make the most of their time. (n.d.). Laura Vanderkam: books. Retrieved from http://lauravanderkam.com/books/i-know-how-she-does-it/

206. working Americans: Newport, F. (2015, December 31). Americans' perceived time crunch no worse than in past. Gallup. Retrieved from http://www.gallup.com/poll/187982/americans-perceived-time-crunch-no-worse-past.aspx

206. working mothers: Suh, M. (2015, November 2). More full-time working moms say they always feel rushed, spend too little time with their kids. Pew Research Center. Retrieved from http://www.pewsocialtrends.org/2015/11/04/raising-kids-and-running-a-household-how-working-parents-share-the-load/st_2015-11-04_working-parents-07/

207. evidence of a calmer life: Vanderkam, L. (2016, May 14). The busy person's lies. *New York Times.* Retrieved from http://www.nytimes.com/2016/05/15/opinion/sunday/the-busy-persons-lies.html

207. claim to work: Robinson, J., Martin, S., Glorieux, I., & Minnen, J. (2011). The overestimated workweek revisited. *Monthly labor review, 134*(6), pp. 43–53.

207. time watching television: Kafka, P. (2016, June 27). You are still watching a staggering amount of TV every day. *Recode.* Retrieved from http://www.recode.net/2016/6/27/12041028/tv-hours-per-week-nielsen; Also see: Libresco, L. (2016, March 6). Here's how Americans spend their working, relaxing and parenting time. *FiveThirtyEight.* Retrieved from http://fivethirtyeight.com/datalab/heres-how-americans-spend-their-working-relaxing-and-parenting-time/

209. more expansive stretch: Bruni, F. (2015, September 5). The myth of quality time. *New York Times.* Retrieved from http://www.nytimes.com/2015/09/06/opinion/sunday/frank-bruni-the-myth-of-quality-time.html?smprod=nytcore-iphone&smid=nytcore-iphone-share&_r=0

210. together engaged: Kingston, P. W., & Nock, S. L. (1987). Time together among dual-earner couples. *American sociological review*, pp. 391–400.

210. more leisure activities: Hill, M. S. (1988). Marital stability and spouses' shared time: A multidisciplinary hypothesis. *Journal of family issues, 9*(4), pp. 427–451., Also see: Girme, Y. U., Overall, N. C., & Faingataa,

S. (2014). "Date nights" take two: The maintenance function of shared relationship activities. *Personal relationships, 21*(1), pp. 125–149.

210. **become less happy:** Twenge, J. M., Campbell, W. K., & Foster, C. A. (2003). Parenthood and marital satisfaction: A meta-analytic review. *Journal of marriage and family, 65*(3), pp. 574–583.

210. **primary reason:** Hill, M. S. (1988).; Dew, J. P. (2009). Has the marital time cost of parenting changed over time? *Social forces, 88*, pp. 519–541.

210. **transition to parenthood:** Dew, J., & Wilcox, W. B. (2011). If momma ain't happy: Explaining declines in marital satisfaction among new mothers. *Journal of marriage and family, 73*(1), pp. 1–12. Quote from p. 5.

210. **quality of our marriage:** Popova, M. (2016, June 20). Simone Weil on attention and grace. *Brain Pickings.* Retrieved from https://www.brain pickings.org/2015/08/19/simone-weil-attention-gravity-and-grace/

210. **investment of quality time:** Gottman, J. M. (1999). *The marriage clinic: A scientifically based marital therapy.* New York, NY: W. W. Norton & Company.

210. **own unique culture:** Gottman, J. M. (2014). *Principia amoris: The new science of love.* Abingdon, UK: Routledge.

211. **spouses who have accrued:** Walsh, C. M., Neff, L. A., & Gleason, M. E. (in press). The role of emotional capital during the early years of marriage: Why everyday moments matter. *Journal of family psychology.*

211. **rejects the romantic idea:** Fromm, E. (1956). *The art of loving.* New York, NY: Harper & Row.; Also see: Popova, M. (2016, March 22). Philosopher Erich Fromm on the art of loving and what is keeping us from mastering it. *Brain Pickings.* Retrieved from https://www.brain pickings.org/2015/10/29/the-art-of-loving-erich-fromm/

212. **self-disclosure:** Sprecher, S., & Hendrick, S. S. (2004). Self-disclosure in intimate relationships: Associations with individual and relationship characteristics over time. *Journal of social and clinical psychology, 23*(6), pp. 857–877.; Also see: Collins, N. L., & Miller, L. C. (1994). Self-disclosure and liking: A meta-analytic review. *Psychological bulletin, 116*(3), pp. 457–475.

213. **extensive research:** Gottman, J. (2000). *The seven principles for making marriage work: A practical guide from the country's foremost relationship expert.* New York, NY: Harmony Books.

214. **wedding advice:** Ginsburg, R. B. (2016, October 2). Ruth Bader Ginsburg's advice for living. *New York Times.* Retrieved from http://www.nytimes .com/2016/10/02/opinion/sunday/ruth-bader-ginsburgs-advice-for-living.html?emc=edit_th_20161002&nl=todaysheadlines&nlid= 22989314&_r=1

214. **possible communication behaviors:** Overall, N. C., & McNulty, J. K. (2017). What type of communication during conflict is beneficial for intimate relationships? *Current opinion in psychology, 13*, 1–5. The 2 × 2 figure is adapted from Figure 1 in this article.

216. three core components: Reis, H. T., & Gable, S. L. (2015). Responsiveness. *Current opinion in psychology*, 1, pp. 67–71. Quotes from pp. 67–68.; Also see: Clark, M. S., & Lemay, E. P., Jr. (2010). Close relationships. In Fiske, S. T., Gilbert, D. T., & Lindzey, G. (Eds.), *Handbook of social psychology* (5th ed., Vol. 2, pp. 898–940). New York, NY: Wiley.; Reis, H. T. (2007). Steps toward the ripening of relationship science. *Personal relationships*, 14(1), 1–23.; Reis, H. T., Clark, M. S. (2013). Responsiveness. In Simpson, J. A., & Campbell, L. (Eds.), *The Oxford handbook of close relationships* (pp. 400–423). New York, NY: Oxford.; Reis, H. T., Clark, M. S., & Holmes, J. G. (2004). Perceived partner responsiveness as an organizing construct in the study of intimacy and closeness. In Mashek, D. J., & Aron, A. (Eds.), *Handbook of closeness and intimacy* (pp. 201–225). Mahwah, NJ: Erlbaum.; Reis, H. T., & Shaver, P. R. (1988). Intimacy as an interpersonal process. In Duck, S. (Ed.), *Handbook of personal relationships* (pp. 367–389). Chichester, UK: John Wiley & Sons.; Reis, H. T., & Patrick, B. C. (1996). Attachment and intimacy: Component processes. In Higgins, E. T., & Kruglanski, A.W. (Eds.), *Social psychology: Handbook of basic principles* (pp. 523–563). New York, NY: Guilford Press.

216. perspective on responsiveness: Reis, H. T., & Gable, S. L. (2015). (pp. 67–71). Figure adapted from Figure 1.

217. desperate for intimacy: Feeney, B. C. (2004). A secure base: Responsive support of goal strivings and exploration in adult intimate relationships. *Journal of personality and social psychology*, 87(5), pp. 631–648.

217. fearing abandonment: Murray, S. L., Holmes, J. G., & Collins, N. L. (2006).

218. *safe haven* function: Bowlby, J. (1988). *A secure base*. New York, NY: Basic Books.; Feeney, B. C., & Collins, N. L. (2001). Predictors of caregiving in adult intimate relationships: An attachment theoretical perspective. *Journal of personality and social psychology*, 80(6), pp. 972–994.

218. within easy access: Bowlby, J. (1988). (pp. 27).

218. effective safe haven: Collins, N. L., & Feeney, B. C. (2000). A safe haven: An attachment theory perspective on support seeking and caregiving in intimate relationships. *Journal of personality and social psychology*, 78(6), p. 1053.

218. extent that we're responsive: Maisel, N. C., & Gable, S. L. (2009). The paradox of received social support: The importance of responsiveness. *Psychological science*, 20(8), pp. 928–932.

218. sleep better: Selcuk, E., Stanton, S. C., Slatcher, R. B., & Ong, A. D. (2016). Perceived partner responsiveness predicts better sleep quality through lower anxiety. *Social psychological and personality science*, 1948550616662128.

218. *secure base* function: Bowlby, J. (1988). (p. 62).

218. secure base involves: Feeney, B. C., & Thrush, R. L. (2010). Relationship influences on exploration in adulthood: The characteristics and func-

tion of a secure base. *Journal of personality and social psychology*, 98(1), pp. 57–76.

218. conflict is a dominant emphasis: Tsapelas, I., Aron, A., & Orbuch, T. (2009). Marital boredom now predicts less satisfaction 9 years later. *Psychological science*, 20(5), pp. 543–545.

219. social networks: Amato, P. R., et al. (2007). (p. 186).; Also see: Kim, H. J., & Stiff, J. B. (1991). Social networks and the development of close relationships. *Human communication research*, 18(1), pp. 70–91.; Kearns, J. N., & Leonard, K. E. (2004). Social networks, structural interdependence, and marital quality over the transition to marriage: A prospective analysis. *Journal of family psychology*, 18(2), pp. 383–395.; Parks, M. R., Stan, C. M., & Eggert, L. L. (1983). Romantic involvement and social network involvement. *Social psychology quarterly*, pp. 116–131.

219. certain types of socializing together: Slatcher, R. B. (2010). When Harry and Sally met Dick and Jane: Creating closeness between couples. *Personal relationships*, 17(2), pp. 279–297.

219. self-disclosure or the small-talk: Welker, K. M., Baker, L., Padilla, A., Holmes, H., Aron, A., & Slatcher, R. B. (2014). Effects of self-disclosure and responsiveness between couples on passionate love within couples. *Personal relationships*, 21(4), pp. 692–708.

220. exciting activities: Aron, A., Norman, C. C., Aron, E. N., McKenna, C., & Heyman, R. E. (2000). Couples' shared participation in novel and arousing activities and experienced relationship quality. *Journal of personality and social psychology*, 78(2), pp. 273–284.; O'Leary, K. D., Acevedo, B. P., Aron, A., Huddy, L., & Mashek, D. (2012). Is long-term love more than a rare phenomenon? If so, what are its correlates? *Social psychological and personality science*, 3(2), pp. 241–249.

220. *self-expansion theory*: Aron, A., Lewandowski, G. W., Jr., Mashek, D., & Aron, E. N. (2013). The self-expansion model of motivation and cognition in close relationships. In Simpson, J. A., & Campbell, L. (Eds.), *Oxford handbook of close relationships* (pp. 90–115). New York, NY: Oxford University Press.

220. greater self-expansion: Muise, A., Day, L. C., Gere, J., & Impett, E. A. (2017, January). *Expanding your horizons: Self-expanding activities promote desire and satisfaction in romantic relationships*. Data blitz presentation at the Close Relationships Preconference at the Society for Personality and Social Psychology, San Antonio, Texas.

222. greater relationship satisfaction: Coulter, K., & Malouff, J. M. (2013). Effects of an intervention designed to enhance romantic relationship excitement: A randomized-control trial. *Couple and family psychology: Research and practice*, 2(1), pp. 34–44.

222. exciting or a pleasant activity: Reissman, C., Aron, A., & Bergen, M. R. (1993). Shared activities and marital satisfaction: Causal direction and self-expansion vs. boredom. *Journal of social and personal relationships*, 10(2), pp. 243–254.

223. The qualitites demanded of us: de Botton (2012). (pp. 89–90).

223. sex is mutually pleasurable: Laumann, E. O., Gagnon, J. H., Michael, R. T., & Michaels, S. (1994). *The social organization of sexuality: Sexual practices in the United States.* Chicago, IL: University of Chicago Press.

223. *empathy gap*: Loewenstein, G. (1996). Out of control: Visceral influences on behavior. *Organizational behavior and human decision processes, 65*(3), pp. 272–292. Quote from p. 287.

224. more frequent sex: Muise, A., Schimmack, U., & Impett, E. A. (2016). Sexual frequency predicts greater well-being, but more is not always better. *Social psychological and personality science, 7*(4), pp. 295–302.

224. Eroticism at home: Perel, E. (2016, April 12). Rituals to transition from work to play. Retrieved from http://www.estherperel.com/from-work-to-play

225. good, giving, and game: Savage, D. (2007, March 1). Savage love: Wrong and right. *The stranger.* Retrieved from http://www.thestranger.com/seattle/SavageLove?oid=167448

225. frequent sexual transformations: Burke, T. J., & Young, V. J. (2012). Sexual transformations and intimate behaviors in romantic relationships. *Journal of sex research, 49*(5), pp. 454–463.

226. sadomasochistic sexual role play: Sagarin, B. J., Cutler, B., Cutler, N., Lawler-Sagarin, K. A., & Matuszewich, L. (2009). Hormonal changes and couple bonding in consensual sadomasochistic activity. *Archives of sexual behavior, 38*(2), pp. 186–200.

226. partner responsiveness and sexual desire: Birnbaum, G. E., Reis, H. T., Mizrahi, M., Kanat-Maymon, Y., Sass, O., & Granovski-Milner, C. (2016). Intimately connected: The importance of partner responsiveness for experiencing sexual desire. *Journal of personality and social psychology, 111*, pp. 530–546. Study 2. Quote from p. 6.

227. *Blue Valentine*: (n.d.). Retrieved March 7, 2017, from http://www.bluevalentinemovie.com/

229. heartbreaking documentary: Cobain: *Montage of Heck* (2015). (n.d.). IMDb. Retrieved March 7, 2017, from http://www.imdb.com/title/tt4229236/

229. tremendous benefits: Bradbury, T. N., & Karney, B. R. (2014). (p. 448).

229. happiness, serenity, and richness: Maslow, A. H. (1970). (p. 99).

11. Recalibrating

230. *threw away*: Gottman, J. M. (1999). Quote from p. 185.

230. many marital therapists: Gottman, J. M. (1999). (pp. 185–186).

232. symptoms of postpartum depression: Paulson, J. F., & Bazemore, S. D. (2010). Prenatal and postpartum depression in fathers and its association with maternal depression: A meta-analysis. *Jama, 303*(19), pp. 1961–1969.

234. purpose-driven marriages: Gadoua, S. P., & Larson, V. (2014). *The New I Do: Reshaping Marriage for Skeptics, Realists, and Rebels*. Berkeley, CA: Seal Press. Quote from p. 27.

235. committed to their relationship: Agnew, C. R., Van Lange, P. A., Rusbult, C. E., & Langston, C. A. (1998). Cognitive interdependence: Commitment and the mental representation of close relationships. *Journal of personality and social psychology, 74*(4), pp. 939–954.

235. shared identity: Aron, A., Aron, E. N., Tudor, M., & Nelson, G. (1991). Close relationships as including other in the self. *Journal of personality and social psychology, 60*(2), pp. 241–253.; Mashek, D. J., Aron, A., & Boncimino, M. (2003). Confusions of self with close others. *Personality and social psychology bulletin, 29*(3), pp. 382–392.

235. self-concept: Slotter, E. B., Gardner, W. L., & Finkel, E. J. (2010). Who am I without you? The influence of romantic breakup on the self-concept. *Personality and social psychology bulletin, 36*, pp. 147–160. doi:10.1177/0146167209352250

236. equipped to love: Silverstein, S. (2006). *The missing piece meets the big O*. New York, NY: HarperCollins.

237. lived separately: U.S. Census Bureau, Demographic Internet Staff. (2012, May 21). America's families and living arrangements: 2014: Adults (A table series). Retrieved from https://www.census.gov/hhes/families/data/cps2014A.html

237. *living apart together*: Strohm, C. Q., Seltzer, J. A., Cochran, S. D., & Mays, V. M. (2009). "Living apart together" relationships in the United States. *Demographic research, 21*, pp. 177–214.

237. *apartnering*: APARTNERS. (n.d.). Retrieved from http://apartnersthemovie.com/APARTNERS.html

237. I renewed our marriage: Stoessel, L.S. (n.d.). Living happily ever after—separately. Lise Stryker Stoessel. Retrieved from http://www.lisestryker stoessel.com/living-happily-ever-after-ndash-separately.html

237. apart from his long-term partner: Bruni, F. (2013, July 20). Of love and fungus. *New York Times*. Retrieved from http://www.nytimes.com/2013/07/21/opinion/sunday/bruni-of-love-and-fungus.html

238. Americans who live apart: Strohm, C. Q., Seltzer, J. A., Cochran, S. D., & Mays, V. M. (2009).

238. highly independent: Hagemeyer, B., Schönbrodt, F. D., Neyer, F. J., Neberich, W., & Asendorpf, J. B. (2015). When "together" means "too close": Agency motives and relationship functioning in coresident and living-apart-together couples. *Journal of personality and social psychology, 109*, pp. 813–835.

238. cons include: Gadoua, S. P., & Larson, V. (2014). (See chapter 5, especially pp. 128–131).

239. her atypical marriage: Willis, K. (2014, November 13). Why my husband and I would never choose to live together. *Huffington Post*. Retrieved

from http://www.huffingtonpost.com/high50/married-couples-living
-apart_b_6133786.html

239. robust social network: Feeney, B. C., & Collins, N. L. (2015). (p. 121).

239. larger than the effects: Holt-Lunstad, J., Smith, T. B., & Layton, J. B.
(2010). Social relationships and mortality risk: A meta-analytic review.
PLoS Med, 7(7), e1000316.

240. participants' social portfolios: Cheung, E. O., Gardner, W. L., & Anderson, J. F. (2015). Emotionships: Examining people's emotion-regulation
relationships and their consequences for well-being. *Social psychological and personality science*, 6(4), pp. 407–414. Study 2.; Also see: Arm-
strong, B. F., & Kammrath, L. K. (2015). Depth and breadth tactics in
support seeking. *Social psychological and personality science*, 6(1), pp.
39–46.

240. highly specialized social portfolio: Cheung, E. O., Galvin, R., Gardner,
W. L., Carswell, K. L., & Finkel., E. J. (2016). *Putting all your eggs in one
basket? Exploring the trade-off between optimizing individual vs. relationship well-being when seeking a romantic partner for emotion regulation.* Unpublished manuscript. Evanston, IL: Northwestern University.

241. reallocate to other relationships: Drigotas, S. M., & Rusbult, C. E. (1992).
Should I stay or should I go? A dependence model of breakups. *Journal
of personality and social psychology*, 62(1), pp. 62–87.; In a related
study, greater closeness to one's best friend places dating relationships at
greater risk of breakup.; Felmlee, D. H. (2001). No couple is an island: A
social network perspective on dyadic stability. *Social forces*, 79(4),
pp. 1259–1287.

242. engage seriously: Hanauer, C. (Ed.). (2016). *The bitch is back: Older,
wiser, and (getting) happier.* New York, NY: William Morrow.

244. coherence on Internet searches: Ogas, O., & Gaddam, S. (2011). *A billion
wicked thoughts: What the Internet tells us about sexual relationships.*
New York, NY: Penguin.

244. VR porn conference: Clark-Flory, T. (2016, August 1). Here's what it's like
to binge on virtual reality porn. *Vocativ*. Retrieved from http://www.voca
tiv.com/346583/heres-what-its-like-to-binge-on-virtual-reality-porn/

245. *teledildonics*: Palet, L. S. (2014, December 27). The future of sex tech
looks awesome/terrifying. *Ozy*. Retrieved from http://www.ozy.com
/fast-forward/the-future-of-sex-tech-looks-awesome/terrifying/33248;
Gibson, C. (2016, January 14). The future of sex includes robots and
holograms. What does that mean for us? *Washington Post*. Retrieved
from https://www.washingtonpost.com/news/soloish/wp/2016/01/14
/the-future-of-sex-includes-robots-and-holograms-what-does-that-mean
-for-us/?wpisrc=nl_headlines&wpmm=1; McCann, C. (2016, November
29). Let's get digital. *1843* magazine. Retrieved from https://
www.1843magazine.com/design/the-daily/lets-get-digital

246. open up the marriage: Cut, T. (n.d.). Both sides of a breakup: Their open
marriage still makes him want to vomit. *New York*. Retrieved from

http://nymag.com/thecut/2017/01/both-sides-of-a-breakup-an-open
-marriage-made-him-feel-sick.html

246. Consensual nonmonogamy: Conley, T. D., Matsick, J. L., Moors, A. C., & Ziegler, A. (in press). The investigation of consensually non-monogamous relationships: Theories, methods and new directions. *Perspectives on psychological science.*

247. the film *Pretty Woman*: Pretty Woman. (2017, March 6). In *Wikipedia, the free encyclopedia.* Retrieved from https://en.wikipedia.org/wiki/Pretty_Woman

247. three major types of consensual nonmonogamy: Conley, T. D., Ziegler, A., Moors, A. C., Matsick, J. L., & Valentine, B. (2013). A critical examination of popular assumptions about the benefits and outcomes of monogamous relationships. *Personality and social psychology review*, 17(2), pp. 124–141. Quote on p. 126.; For a discussion of the sex party scene in New York circa 2016, see: Wicker, A. (2016, December 16). Will the man running a sex party like a startup be able to leave anyone satisfied? *Quartz.* Retrieved from https://qz.com/865047/new-yorks-sex-party-scene-daniel-saynt-of-socialyte-nylon-and-fashionindie-com-is-attempting-to-disrupt-sin-with-his-sex-party-start-up/

247. *Polyamory*: Also see: Sheff, E. (2014). *The polyamorists next door: Inside multiple-partner relationships and families.* New York, NY: Rowman & Littlefield.

247. more prevalent in recent decades: Easton, D., Liszt, C. A., Dodson, B., Nearing, R., Magazine, L. M., Anapol, D., & Stan Dale, D. H. S. (1997). *The ethical slut: A practical guide to polyamory, open relationships and other adventures.* Emeryville, CA: Greenery Press.; Also see: The Ethical Slut. (2017, March 1). In *Wikipedia.* Retrieved from https://en.wikipedia.org/wiki/The_Ethical_Slut

248. blend of all-in strategies: Conley, T. D., & Moors, A. C. (2014). More oxygen please! How polyamorous relationship strategies might oxygenate marriage. *Psychological inquiry*, 25(1), pp. 56–63. Quote from p. 57.

248. Amelia Earhart, the legendary aviator: Popova, M. (2016, July 23). Amelia Earhart on marriage. *Brain Pickings.* Retrieved from https://www.brainpickings.org/2012/12/11/amelia-earhart-on-marriage/

249. earnest pursuit of a fulfilling romantic relationship: Strauss, N. (2015). (p. 159).

249. criteria for the type: Strauss, N. (2015). (p.161).

249. never traveling: Strauss, N. (2015). (pp. 241–242).

249. ideal relationship: YouGov survey results. (2016, September 23–25). Retrieved March 7, 2017, from https://d25d2506sfb94s.cloudfront.net/cumulus_uploads/document/cqmk3va41c/tabs_OP_Relationships_20160925.pdf

250. society's widespread assumption: Conley, T. D., Ziegler, A., Moors, A. C., Matsick, J. L., & Valentine, B. (2012). A critical examination of popular assumptions about the benefits and outcomes of monogamous

relationships. *Personality and social psychology review*, 17, pp. 124–141. Quote from p. 124.; Conley, T. D., Matsick, J. L., Moors, A. C., & Ziegler, A. (in press). The investigation of consensually non-monogamous relationships.

252. lower jealousy and higher trust: Conley, T. D., Matsick, J. L., Moors, A. C., & Ziegler, A. (in press). The investigation of consensually non-monogamous relationships.

253. greater sociosexuality: Rodrigues, D., Lopes, D., & Smith, C. V. (in press). Caught in a "bad romance"? Reconsidering the negative association between sociosexuality and relationship functioning. *The journal of sex research*.

254. increasingly unhinged: Strauss, N. (2015). (pp. 255, 277).

255. promiscuous and playful: Ryan, C., & Jethá, C. (2010). *Sex at dawn: The prehistoric origins of modern sexuality*. New York, NY: Harper-Collins.; Also see: Lerner, G. (1986). *The creation of patriarchy* (Vol. 1). New York, NY: Oxford University Press, USA.

255. monopolize a partner's resources: Buss, D. M., Larsen, R. J., Westen, D., & Semmelroth, J. (1992). Sex differences in jealousy: Evolution, physiology, and psychology. *Psychological science*, 3(4), pp. 251–255.

255. not to desire: Jong, E. (2013). *Fear of flying: A novel* (40th anniversary reissue). New York, NY: Macmillan. Quote from p. 11.

256. evolved to crave sex: Eastwick, P. W. (2009). Beyond the Pleistocene: Using phylogeny and constraint to inform the evolutionary psychology of human mating. *Psychological bulletin*, 135(5), pp. 794–821.; Finkel, E. J., & Eastwick, P. W. (2015). Attachment and pairbonding. *Current opinion in behavioral sciences*, 3, pp. 7–11.; Hazan, C., & Diamond, L. M. (2000). The place of attachment in human mating. *Review of general psychology*, 4, pp. 186–204.

256. motivated derogation: Lydon, J., & Karremans, J. C. (2015).; Also see: Durante, K. M., Eastwick, P. W., Finkel, E. J., Gangestad, S. M., & Simpson, J. A. (2016). Pair-bonded relationships and romantic alternatives: Toward an integration of evolutionary and relationship science perspectives. *Advances in experimental social psychology*, 53, pp. 1–74.

256. wild escapades: Strauss, N. (2015). (p. 187).

257. remain faithful: Strauss, N. (2015). (pp. 167–168).

258. high expectations: McNulty, J. K. (2016). Should spouses be demanding less from marriage? A contextual perspective on the implications of interpersonal standards. *Personality and social psychology bulletin*, 42(4), pp. 444–457.

12. The Marital Buffer

261. *People want to be monogamous or promiscuous*: Strauss, N. (2015). (p. 144).

262. Neil Strauss captures this new marital zeitgeist: Strauss, N. (2015). (p. 419).; Also see: Haag, P. (2012). *Marriage confidential: Love in the*

post-romantic age. New York, NY: Harper Perennial.; Gadoua, S. P., & Larson, V. (2014).

262. not everybody seeks the identical features from marriage: Greenhalgh, S. (1988). Fertility as mobility: Sinic transitions. *Population and development review*, pp. 629–674. Quote from p. 668.; Also see: Amato, P. R. (2014). Tradition, commitment, and individualism in American marriages. *Psychological inquiry*, 25(1), pp. 42–46.

266. think in terms of specific life domains: Hofmann, W., Finkel, E. J., & Fitzsimons, G. M. (2015). Close relationships and self-regulation: How relationship satisfaction facilitates momentary goal pursuit. *Journal of personality and social psychology*, 109, pp. 434–452.

ACKNOWLEDGMENTS

I'd always heard that writing a book is like a tour through the various levels of hell, but that wasn't my experience. I had a blast, and a major reason why is that I had so many enjoyable interactions along the way.

My agent, Katinka Matson, took a risk on a first-time author. She helped me craft a proposal and, on a particularly thrilling day, helped me sign a contract with Dutton.

Stephen Morrow, my editor at Dutton, had undying faith in this book, and his enthusiasm and editorial genius were priceless from the first word to the last. Maddy Newquist, Stephen's editorial assistant, was heroic in keeping the project on track, Andrea Monagle was a ninja in the copyediting room, and Emily Brock and Elina Vaysbeyn were brilliant in publicizing and marketing the book.

Five intrepid souls—Candida Abrahamson, Stephanie Coontz, Paul Eastwick, Alison Finkel, and Gráinne Fitzsimons—read an early draft, offering feedback that corrected errors and sharpened ideas. In doing so, they helped me avert several layers of humiliation. Lydia Emery and Keith Payne offered detailed feedback on chapter 7, and Terri Conley did the same on chapter 11. Both chapters benefited immensely from their insights. Drew Gorentz, Yasemin Doğruol, Julia Kovalenko, and Daria Lenderman provided valuable research assistance.

While writing the book, and while gearing up to do so, I had helpful conversations with more people than I can list here. Some of the most enjoyable and constructive conversations were with Aziz Ansari, Dan Ariely, Karen Asbra, Roy Baumeister, Galen Bodenhausen, David Brooks, Jeni Burnette, Pam Burnette, Andy Cherlin, Amy Cuddy, Adam Doppelt, Liz Dunn, Alice Eagly, Brian Ellison, Kate Ellison, Renee Engeln, Rand Fishkin, Susan Fiske, Wendi Gardner, Dan Gilbert, Francesca Gino, Paul Green, Jonathan Haidt, Chip Heath, Matt Kaplan, Eric Klinenberg, Nour Kteily, Jon Maner, Dan McAdams, Devah Pager, Jeff Pollack, Joel Pollack, Jamie Ryerson, George Sieburg, and Heidi Stevens. I am also grateful to the following individuals, who supported the book in crucial ways: Adam Grant, Esther Perel, Dan Pink, Peter Sagal, and especially, Logan Ury.

The book is an extension of ideas I initially developed in collaboration with then-doctoral-students Katie Carswell, Elaine Cheung, Lydia Emery, Ming Hui, and Grace Larson. The ideas began to take shape when Ronnie Janoff-Bulman invited me to publish a Target Article for the scholarly journal *Psychological Inquiry*. The scholars who published the thirteen Commentaries on that Target Article challenged me to think much more deeply about the ideas.

Some of the research described in the book came from my own lab, and virtually all of our work—much of it funded by the National Science Foundation—is collaborative. Some of the collaborators who have been particularly influential in my thinking, and who have made life as a social scientist so much fun, are Roy Baumeister, Gurit Birnbaum, Jeni Burnette, Keith Campbell, Jody Davis, Nathan DeWall, Caitlin Duffy, Alice Eagly, Lydia Emery, Shelly Gable, Jeff Green, Kenny Herbst, Peggy Hannon, Will Hofmann, Ming Hui, Emily Impett, Lucy Hunt, Sarah Johnson, Madoka Kumashiro, Grace Larson, Laura Luchies, Jacob Matthews, Jim McNulty, Dan Molden, Nickola

Overall, Jeff Pollack, Francesca Righetti, Caryl Rusbult, Erica Slotter, Sue Sprecher, Michelle vanDellen, and Kathleen Vohs. I particularly want to thank my two most significant collaborators—Paul Eastwick and Gráinne Fitzsimons—who regularly stretch my intellectual skills beyond their limits.

In my career, I have been blessed with a robust stream of generous mentors. During my undergraduate years at Northwestern University, Mike Bailey, Joan Linsenmeier, and Neal Roese fueled my passion for psychology. During my grad school years at the University of North Carolina, Chet Insko and Keith Campbell taught me how to execute a program of research. Since then, I've been formally or informally mentored by wise scholars like Roy Baumeister, Galen Bodenhausen, Andy Cherlin, Margaret Clark, Susan Fiske, Dan Gilbert, Chip Heath, John Holmes, Ben Karney, Brayden King, George Loewenstein, Jennifer Richeson, Jeffry Simpson, and Harry Reis. My most important mentor was my doctoral advisor and friend, Caryl Rusbult (1952–2010), who demonstrated not only how to be a social psychologist, but also how to live with joy and die with grace.

Ideas develop in a specific place, and Northwestern University has been an intellectual mecca for me. I am particularly grateful to the university president, Morty Schapiro; the dean of the Kellogg School of Management, Sally Blount; and the erstwhile dean of the Weinberg College of Arts and Sciences, Sarah Mangelsdorf, for their resolute support. I appreciate my colleagues in the psychology and management departments for providing such a stimulating and supportive environment.

My parents and stepparents—Candida and Yaakov Abrahamson, and Sandy and Fern Finkel—not only created and raised me, but always loved and supported me, even throughout a childhood characterized by more school suspensions and expulsions than any parent should have to endure. They also endowed me with a love of learning and clear ideas about what wisdom and kindness look like. My sister, Rhona Finkel, is a lifeline for me and the very personification of bravery.

ACKNOWLEDGMENTS

My children, Norah and Ben, continually teach me new lessons about love, helping me savor the present and feel excited about the future. My parents, sister, and parents-in-law—Eve and Scott Mermel—have been an adoring family for Norah and Ben, and their dedication to the kids has blessed me with lots of quiet time alone with my wife.

Most of all, I thank Alison for making our time together—whether quiet or otherwise—such a delight.

INDEX

INDEX